A Book for Every Teacher

Teaching English Language Learners

A Book for Every Teacher

Teaching English Language Learners

By

Nan Li
Claflin University

Information Age Publishing, Inc.
Charlotte, North Carolina • www.infoagepub.com

Library of Congress Cataloging-in-Publication Data

CIP data for this book can be found on the Library of Congress website:
http://www.loc.gov/index.html

Paperback: 978-1-68123-050-4
Hardcover: 978-1-68123-051-1
eBook: 978-1-68123-052-8

CONTENTS

PART III: BASIC VOCABULARY

PREFACE

A Book for Every Teacher: Teaching English Language Learners is a unique and compressive text written for mainstream classroom teachers. The passion for writing this book comes from our working experiences with the K–12 teachers in four school districts through our ELL Center professional development program. Through this program, we provide professional training through our federally funded research and service projects. The purpose of our professional training is to prepare general education teachers to work effectively with English language learners (ELLs). While working with the teachers on a daily basis, we know the immediate needs of the teachers. This motivated us to embark this book project. In recent years, the ELL school population has the highest increase among school populations. As the National Education Association data indicates, providing ELL students with high quality services and programs is an important investment in America's future (National Education Association, 2013). This book is our investment in helping teachers to meet their challenges and provide useful information and strategies for teaching ELLs.

UNIQUENESS OF THE HANDBOOK

This handbook has a significant uniqueness. First, it provides comprehensive information. This comprehensive information is basic and useful for all K–12 teachers in meeting their immediate needs and serving ELL students in the classrooms. Second, this book is reader-friendly in comparison to a voluminous book related to teaching ELLs. For example, this book combines basic vocabulary, teaching strategies, L2 theories, and requirements into one book. It can be used as a daily reference book for

A Book for Every Teacher: Teaching English Language Learners
pp. xi–xvi

teachers or as professional training materials. Third, the book is carefully crafted with eight chapters. Each chapter has a topic that is practical, with a particular topic for teachers to work with. For example, each chapter begins with a real-case scenario to know ELLs. Relevant content, information, and strategies are provided in each chapter.

Through working with the teachers to provide them with professional training, we must cope with the training materials. Due to this need, we worked hard to find the appropriate book with the basic information for teachers. We need to examine many texts for materials used for training each year. Yet we often find it difficult to purchase the appropriate books. For example, some textbooks on teaching ELLs are too voluminous (i.e., over 300 pages) and do not meet our program needs. There are short strategy books focusing on teaching strategies, yet strategies alone are not enough. Some vocabulary books have no relevant information on L2 theories and no basic vocabulary. For this reason, we decided to work on this comprehensive book with useful information, L2 theories, basic vocabulary, and teaching strategies to meet the immediate needs of teachers in classrooms. This book fits in the published literature, but it also fills the gap created by the lack of comprehensive books for teachers and training programs. In all, this book is unique and most needed for K–12 teachers who work with ELLs. This book can help teachers work with all students effectively in classrooms.

WHO IS THE AUDIENCE FOR THIS BOOK

The book is designed with K–12 teachers in mind. It is best used by teachers who have or will have ELLs in their classrooms and who seek information and strategies to better work with and serve their ELLs to achieve academic success. With this design, teachers can use the book as a text or reference tool.

According to national data, ELL school enrollment has had a high percentage of increase in schools across the nation in the last few decades (NCES, 2013). For example, the increase in ELL school enrollment was 714% in South Carolina from 1995 to 2005, and the increase in the ELL population was 105% nationally (U.S. Department of Education, 2008). The teacher force is relatively unprepared to meet the needs of the ELL students who are one of the most heterogeneous groups with differences in cultural backgrounds, first language, socioeconomic status, prior schooling, and English language proficiency. Through our training programs, we are connected with the K–12 teachers on a daily basis and work them in four target districts. The teachers who participate in our training programs and provide field data also come to our university campus for training. Through such a work relation and connection, we established a unique tie with the teachers, knowing their needs in working with ELL students in classrooms. This experience provided a unique opportunity for us to work on this book project in order to provide useful information and strategies for the teachers.

This book can also be adopted as text materials for professional training. Teachers are the most important factor for ELLs' academic success. The ELL school population will continue to increase, and it is projected that 1 in 4 students will be ELLs in the next two decades. With this trend, preparing teachers through professional development training will be important. Thus, this comprehensive book for training programs will be in great need. As mentioned, most textbooks on market with over 300 pages are too voluminous to be adopted for training programs, which are usually on an 1-year basis. Those textbooks are not designed to meet teachers' immediate needs or designed for professional development training. From our experiences, it is difficult to find effective training materials. Through our professional training program, we work with teachers daily and know what works for training materials. In addition, this book can be used and adopted as the text in TESOL programs or teacher education programs as supplementary materials at the university level for preservice teachers and any prospective teachers who are interested in teaching ELLs.

HOW TO USE THIS HANDBOOK

This book consists of four parts and has eight chapters. Part I focuses on the ELL school population, with basic information on knowing ELLs and engaging their participation in the classroom. Part II focuses on teaching ELLs with L2 theories, teaching models, useful teaching strategies, and tips. Part III focuses on basic vocabulary, including academic words, daily words, and words on traditions and holidays. These basic words are needed for all ELLs to function in school. Part IV focuses on information related to the professional requirements, standards, and statistics for teachers.

Eight chapters are embedded within the four parts. Each chapter provides the basic information and useful strategies relevant in classrooms. For example, Chapter 2 provides the basic theories in second-language (L2) acquisition to help teachers know concepts working with ELLs. These basic L2 acquisition concepts include Basic Interpersonal Communication Skills (BICS) and Cognitive Academic Language Proficiency (CALP), as well as Comprehensive Input and Affective Filter. These basic theories explain the L2 learning stages and provide a foundation that guides teachers in classrooms to work with ELLs. Chapter 3 includes a popular lesson model, the SIOP (Sheltered Instruction Observation Protocol), an empirically validated approach for teachers, and it helps them prepare lessons all students, especially ELLs.

If teachers choose to teach a certain topic, for example, a food unit, they can refer to the chapter title and subtitle as an index to select this topic. For example, the basic daily words listed in Chapter 6 are in these categories: Directions, Greetings, Food & Cafeteria, Families & Relatives, and Weather & Sports. ELLs need to know these basic words. For instance, they need to eat lunch in the school cafeteria. It is often difficult for them to know the food words due to cultural and language difference. The food vocabulary is listed with pictures under the subtitle Food & Cafeteria in Chapter 6. Useful activities and strategies for teaching the academic and daily words are also provided for teachers. ELLs also need to learn about American traditions and holidays. The teacher can use Chapter 7: Traditions and Holidays. This chapter lists all federal and traditional holidays, with activities and strategies to teach these words. Chapter 5 provides the academic vocabulary that the ELLs need to know, such as Numbers, Shapes & Colors, and Descriptive words that are frequently used in classrooms. Activities and strategies for teaching these academic English words are provided for teachers.

CHAPTER SUMMARIES

Chapter 1 begins with a case scenario as a snapshot for teachers to know who their ELL students are. The background information on the fast growth of school enrollment in the ELL population is provided, tracing the immigration law (i.e., Johnson-Reed Act) in 1924. This chapter also discusses commonly shared characteristics of the ELLs for teachers to effectively get to know ELLs and meet the needs of this unique school population. The chapter also discusses the types of the ELL students, for example, Generation 1.5 versus. U.S.-born ELLs. Academic attainment–related issues are discussed, with an examination of common terms and myths related to ELLs. The chapter also provides sample profiles of the ELLs who are enrolled in schools and participate daily in our classrooms with their example works. The intention is to help teachers understand that the ELLs have different educational needs and cultural backgrounds. Yet it is a reality that ELL enrollment has the highest percentage of increase among all school populations. Having a better understanding of this school population helps teachers work effectively to enhance the learning outcomes of ELLs and all students.

Chapter 2 discusses the basic theories of L2 acquisition. Like the process of first-language acquisition, English language learners acquire and learn a new language through interaction and meaningful input in a contextualized and language-enriched environment. First, ELLs develop BICS and CALP at different paces. Thus, providing context-embedded support will help ELLs have access to the cognitively demanding content-area knowledge. Second, meaningful, comprehensive input at the learners' instructional level and slightly beyond is essential in helping ELLs continuously develop their English proficiency level. Finally, lowering the affective filter in the classroom will motivate ELLs to seek more input and be willing to meet the challenge.

Chapter 3 focuses on teaching ELLs. A scenario about *Martina* illustrates the frustration between the ELL and her teacher on the first day at school, not knowing what to do on both sides. The Sheltered Instruction Observation Protocol (SIOP) lesson plan model and L2 teaching methods (e.g., total physical response approach) are introduced to help teachers to prepare lessons. Useful teaching strategies that are proven to work through our experience and have been used by the teachers in the classrooms are provided. These strategies cover four areas: using visual aids, relating to existing knowledge, presenting contextual information, and integrating technology for working with ELLs. These strategies are intended to help teachers better work with ELLs and all students, and produce positive learning outcomes.

Chapter 4 discusses the importance of engaging ELLs' participation. Some useful strategies and tips are provided to help teachers get to know their ELL students. The chapter discusses different ways to encourage their participation. The chapter also discusses the importance of building a positive teacher-student relationship as well as involving ELL parents and family support. Despite the need to develop their English-language proficiency, ELL students are often quiet during classroom discussions. Therefore, it is important to improve the learning environment that makes ELLs feel welcomed to be willing to involve their participation. The information and strategies in this chapter are intended to help teachers work with ELLs in a positive way.

Chapter 5 introduces the basic academic English words in different subject areas, such as words related to numbers, shapes, colors, words used in subject contents, and words used in classrooms. Meaningful activities and strategies about how to introduce these academic words are introduced as well. Regardless of the ELLs' age group or grade level, the academic words listed in this chapter can help ELLs at beginning and early intermediate levels lay a foundation for their understanding of the academic content and increase their vocabulary related to academic content.

Chapter 6 introduces basic daily vocabulary. These daily words include those commonly used words related to greetings, asking about directions, talking about food and cafeteria, words about families and relatives, and words about weather and sports. In order to function in school and classrooms, ELLs need to know these daily words. These words also help them cope with life more easily in new environments. It is not easy for ELLs on this journey. Many ELLs have no choice but to come with their families to the United States, facing a new language and unknown environment. Therefore, these daily words with activities are helpful for them.

Chapter 7 introduces words about major American traditions and holidays. The vocabulary is a foundation that helps ELL students to read instructions and understand text. It contributes to their overall learning English and achieving academic success. There are some basic words and vocabulary that ELLs need to know to be successful in classrooms. Due to the importance of the vocabulary, teachers need to teach vocabulary through explicit instruction with some basic steps. In addition to the major traditions and holiday words, there are also other traditional words and special events that teachers need to introduce to ELLs. Some lesson ideas are provided for teachers to work with ELLs in learning American culture while teaching vocabulary.

Chapter 8 addresses the issue of whose responsibility it is to teach ELLs. Common core standards, trends in teaching ELLs, programs for ELLs, assessment and related issues, ELL population statistics, and suggestions for teacher education programs are then discussed. With the implementation of the Common Core State Standards, the role of ESOL teachers are not limited to teaching English, but also advocating for ELLs and actively collaborating with mainstream teachers to provide the academic language needed for ELLs to succeed. Different types of programs for ELLs are discussed. This chapter also discusses assessment issues and the types of assessments used to assess ELLs. As a result of school demographics, every teacher needs to have basic knowledge and skills to better serve ELLs and all students in classrooms. Thus, preparing both preservice and in-service teachers with effective instructional practices and knowledge is critical for the academic progress of ELLs and all students.

REFERENCE

National Education Association. (2013). A NEA policy brief: Professional development for general education teachers of English language learners. Retrieved from http://www.nea.org/assets/docs/PB32_ELL11.pdf

U.S. Department of Education. (2008). The survey of states' limited English proficient students and available educational programs and services and consolidated state performance reports. Washington, DC: U.S. Department of Education.

ACKNOWLEDGMENTS

I would like to express my gratitude to the many people who saw me through this book; to all those who supported me, reviewed the chapters, offered comments, allowed me to quote their cases in the scenarios, and assisted in the editing and proofreading. In all, I am thankful to all my families—my immediate family and my academic family and friends.

I would like thank to my immediate family who supported and encouraged me in spite of all the time it took me away from them on a long and difficult journey. I give my special thanks to my parents and my son Sining, who provided much emotional support.

My thanks must go to my academic family and friends: to Mr. George Johnson, my publisher, who encouraged me on this long journey; to Ms. Yvonne Mitchel, the ESOL Coordinator and a good friend, who faithfully supported me and provided much insight.

Last but not least: I give my thanks to Ms. Barbara Ragin, my hardworking assistant, who is completing her TESOL MA program, for her time, critique, and review; to all the ESOL teachers and mainstream teachers in the four school districts that I have worked with. They are my inspiration and encouragement on this long and difficult journey.

Without my families and friends, this book would never find its way to the final stage of publication. I give my sincere thanks to all of these people and even to those whose names I might fail to mention for their support and contribution.

Sincerely,
Nan Li

PART I

ELL SCHOOL POPULATION

.

CHAPTER 1

WHO ARE THE ELLS?

CASE SCENARIO

Anna was a seventh grader. She came to the United States 3 years ago with her family from China. Her father and mother were both working in a restaurant. They went to work at 10 a.m. and came home from work after 10 p.m. every day. Anna was responsible for preparing dinner for her two younger brothers. She also had to help with some household chores when her parents were away. Although she had been in the United States for 3 years, she still needed to go to the ESOL class. ESOL stands for English Speakers of Other Languages. An ESOL class is a resource classroom where the ELLs are provided additional English language support so that they can improve their English skills. The ESOL programs are required in schools because of the *Lau v. Nichols* decision made by the Supreme Court in 1974. Anna went to her ESOL classroom and worked with an ESOL teacher for an hour daily, and then she spent the rest of the day in mainstream classrooms to learn subject content. Yet she often sat quietly in the mainstream classrooms. Anna did not have many friends and went home directly after school. She spoke some broken English with her ESOL teacher. At home, she spoke Chinese. She knew that English was important. Yet she had limited opportunities to speak and interact with her English peers. She struggled with the basic English skills, such as reading and writing, and could not express herself clearly in English either. Academically, she lagged behind, although she had the intention to do well and to improve her English.

A Book for Every Teacher: Teaching English Language Learners
pp. 3–21
Copyright © 2015 by Information Age Publishing

LIFE EXPERIENCES AND CULTURES

In the above scenario, Anna is one of the 5.3 million ELLs who are attending our schools. The term ELL stands for the English Language Learners, formerly referred to as the LEP (i.e., Limited English Proficiency) students. The fast increase in ELL school enrollment is one of the major trends in our schools across the nation. The ELL school population has made and is continuing to make its way into our school system. Based on the National Center for Educational Statistics (NCES, 2012), this school population reached 5.3 million in 2010 with an increase of 29.7% since 2000. The NCES data further reveals that the general school enrollment in the United States reached 49.5 million in 2010 from 46.6 million in 2000, with the increase rate of 5.7%. According to the NCES data, the ELL population was 18% of the total school enrollment in the United States in 2010: about 21% in large cities and about 30% in some states, such as Texas, New Mexico, Nevada, and California (NCES, 2012). The data from the National Clearinghouse for English Language Acquisition also reveals that from the 1997–1998 school year to the 2008–2009 school year, the number of ELLs enrolled in public schools increased by 51% from 3.5 million to 5.3 million, the highest increase in the last three decades (NCELA, 2011). The rapid increase in the ELL school population poses a unique challenge for K–12 teachers, who strive to ensure that these language-minority students get access to the core curriculum in schools and acquire academic content knowledge as well as English-language skills.

Teachers may ask what has caused the ELL school population to grow so fast. The burgeoning increase in ELL school enrollment has its background. In 1968, Congress voted to eliminate the Johnson-Reed Act, an immigration law created in 1924 that had a quota system to discriminate against non-European immigrants. Since the elimination of this discrimination law, the immigration population has evidenced the increase in the United States with a noticeable change in country sources (i.e., the immigration population represents more diversity in its country source). National demographics affect school population. The students whose primary language is not English have thus increased fast, mainly from non-European countries (Ovando, Collier, & Combs, 2005). Data reveals that ELL school enrollment increased by 105% from 1995 to 2005, when the general school population growth was less than 10% (NCELA, 2011) and over 5 million school-aged students were ELLs (NCES, 2012; Zelasko & Antunez, 2000). With the new demographics in schools, how to educate this population effectively becomes a challenging issue for K–12 teachers in classrooms.

So who are the ELLs? Typically, an English language learner is a student whose first language (L1) is not English, who is in the process of learning English, not yet able to profit fully from English-only instruction, and who needs instructional support in order to access academic content in school (Bardack, 2010; Li, Howard, & Mitchell, 2011; Singhal, 2006). ELLs are the fastest growing segment of the school population, and they are also a most heterogeneous group of students. ELLs come with different life experiences and cultures. ELLs also have diverse gifts, educational needs and goals, as well as different family backgrounds and languages. Some ELLs may live in their own cultural enclaves while other ELLs may live in a non-ELL family community; some ELL families may have lived in the United States for over a generation while others may be newcomers; some ELLs can be high achievers in schools while others can be struggling readers. Thus, it is hard to adequately describe all ELL students with one definition, or it is not accurate to use one single profile to represent the needs of all ELLs. Yet ELL students do share some characteristics that teachers can use to get to know them and to accommodate their learning needs based on these following factors:

- Length of residence in the United States
- Literacy skills in the primary language(s)
- Previous schooling
- Education background of parents
- Socioeconomic status and resources available at home
- Personal life experiences
- Cultural norms

Each of these factors has an effect on ELLs in acquiring English language skills and content knowledge as they enter new schools in the United States.

The *length of residency* in the United States is an important factor that affects ELLs' English proficiency and acculturation. The term *Generation 1.5* is often used to describe some ELLs. This term refers to ELLs who immigrated to the United States in elementary or high school years, who are U.S. educated but do not have English as a home language, and who may be orally proficient in English but do not have adequate academic English proficiency (Mikesell, 2008; Roberge, 2002; Short & Fitzsimons, 2007). These ELLs can have diverse educational experiences and a wide range of language proficiency and literacy skills. In a sense, these ELLs are caught by generations, that is, they belong to neither the first nor the second generation of immigrants. That is why they are classified by the term Generation 1.5 ELLs. In comparison to U.S.-born ELLs, they bring with them characteristics from their home country but continue assimilation and socialization in the new country. Thus, Generation 1.5 students are often identified as having a combination of new and old cultural traditions. Depending on the age at immigration, the community into which they settle, and the extent of education in their native country, along with some other factors, Generation 1.5 ELLs identify with their countries of origin to varying degrees (Mikesell, 2008; Oudenhoven, 2006). Yet this identification is also affected by their experiences growing up in the new country. These ELLs are usually bilingual and are more easily assimilated into the local culture and society than people who are adult immigrants such as their parents.

Although some ELLs are immigrants coming with their families to the United States, many ELL students are born in the United States. According to data, a growing number of ELLs are, in fact, U.S. born (Flannery, 2009; Li et al., 2011; NCES 2012). These U.S.-born ELLs may have lived in the United States for many years in households where family members or caretakers speak a language other than English. Thus, although English may be the dominant language for these ELLs, they may not have developed the academic English skills and vocabulary needed to function successfully at their grade level in the English-speaking environments. They are also likely to suffer the same achievement gaps as other ELL students because of the fact that they are from a home where no English language support is available. Yet, as the second generation of the immigrants, these U.S.-born ELLs do have some advantages in overcoming academic challenges because they emerge in the English-speaking context from an early stage as they start schooling. With the proper support from teachers, educators, and policymakers to implement the high quality early educational support programs, such as appropriate dual-language or ESOL programs, and with good assessments, these ELLs have the potential to do better in school than other ELL students.

Literacy skills in the primary language and *previous schooling* can affect ELLs' learning English and academic content knowledge, especially for those ELLs immigrating to the United States with their families. Even if the ELL students are U.S. born, they still face such a challenge. For example, some young ELLs in the primary grades of U.S. schools must acquire initial literacy concepts and skills through the medium of English, a language that they have not mastered orally before their schooling because they often lack the emergent literacy support at home due to non-English speaking home environments. Some ELLs may have developed literacy and academic skills in their home language(s). For these ELLs, the major challenge is that they must learn to read in English. Once they know how to read in English, they can transfer their L1 skills to the L2. Yet some ELLs may have not experienced consistent previous schooling or appropriate instruction in the primary language(s). This compounds the difficulties because they must learn to read and write in English when they have the challenge to learn academic content at the same time. Some ELLs may already know some English when they arrive in the United States and also have strong literacy skills in their home language and adequate previous schooling. These students usually grasp the concepts more easily in the L2 context than other ELLs, and they are likely to become high achievers in school.

Further, as to the literacy skills in the primary language, some ELLs may have an L1 that is totally different from English in terms of language structure, word order, sound system, or word formation patterns (Freeman & Freeman, 2003; Jalongo & Li, 2010). For example, some ELLs' L1 may greatly differ from English in a nonalphabetic writing system (e.g., Chinese), in alphabets (e.g., Russian), or in directionalities (e.g., Hebrew). Other ELLs' home language may be similar to English in these respects. For example, Spanish, French, and Portuguese have more in common with English than do Swahili or Vietnamese. Some ELLs may have an L1 that shares some commonalties with English in terms of the usage of the Roman alphabet or grammar (e.g., Italian and Polish). Other ELLs may have an L1 that shares even cognate words with English. For example, many words in English and Spanish are cognates, such as *observe/observar, anniversary/aniversario, stomach/estómago*. Similarities between ELLs' home languages and English tend to make learning English easier, while differences tend to make the process more difficult (Callahan, Wilkinson, & Muller, 2010; Meltzer & Hamann, 2005).

Other factors, such as *education of parents, socioeconomic status (SES)*, and *resources available at home* also affect ELLs' acquiring L2 skills and academic content knowledge. The education of ELL parents has an impact on ELLs' learning L2 skills and literacy. Research has documented that parents' education has a long-term effect on children's learning and academic success and that the parent's education, especially the mother's level of education, is one of the important factors influencing children's reading levels and school achievements (NCFL, 2003; Roeser & Peck, 2009; Sticht & McDonald, 2009). Other studies find that parent education is one of the indicators in predicting the quality of family interactions and child behavior and thus further shape, by late adolescence, educational achievement and aspirations for future educational and occupational success of their children (Davis-Kean, 2005; Eccles, Templeton, & Barber, 2005; Guerra & Huesmann, 2004). These studies believe that it is possible that, in addition to lower parental educational levels, lower socioeconomic status also affects positive family interaction patterns. It may result in child behavioral problems, such as aggression, as measured by these studies. In turn, it causes lowered achievement-oriented attitudes and thus affects academic outcomes.

Although many variables may affect student academic success, the SES often predicts resources available at home and is among the factors associated with student school attainment. For example, the SES of a family determines resources available at home. Many ELLs are likely to live in low-SES conditions, thus requiring needed learning resources and family literacy support, and this can affect ELLs' performance in school (Abedi, Leon, & Mirocha, 2005; Batalova & McHugh, 2010). Research also shows that some ELL parents with a lower-educational level may face barriers to supporting children's schooling. These barriers include an inability to understand English, unfamiliarity with the school system, and differences in cultural norms and cultural capital (Abedi et al., 2005; Arias & Morillo-Campbell, 2008; Callahan, 2005). Some ELL parents may have significant communication challenges that impact their lives and that of their children. When teachers try to involve the parents in their children's learning, these factors can limit the parents' school participation.

However, research indicates that the ELL parents do have the desire to participate in and support for their children's education (Mikesell, 2008; Roberge, 2002). Research also supports the importance of parental involvement for improved student achievement, better school attendance, and reduced dropout rate (Arias & Morillo-Campbell, 2008; Batalova & McHugh, 2010; Callahan, 2005). Parental involvement in education can play a crucial role in children's learning. It is thus important to ensure appropriate communication between the school and parents to involve ELL parents who can be an inspiration for their children to meet their educational needs. It is also important that teachers establish a climate that encourages growth in cultural responsiveness, sensitivity, and appreciation in order to involve ELL parents in important school functions such as parent conferences and meetings.

Educators therefore must find ways to communicate with ELL parents and encourage their school participation. To effectively involve parents, good communication skills are required (Genesee, Lindholm-Leary, Saunders, & Christian, 2005; Saunders & O'Brien, 2006). The following are some communication techniques when involving ELL parents:

- Have an interpreter involved for the school meetings with parents so that immediate communication is available to reduce misunderstanding.
- Translate frequently used school documents for the ELL parents such as an invitation letter or other school documents for parents.
- Provide ELL parents with choices, such as using nonverbal feedback, to make communication easier in order to improve their participation.
- Use telephone conferencing with an interpreter available in the conference meetings with ELL parents if they are unable to come due to transportation concerns.

- Use technology-based media, for example, website and Internet techniques, to encourage ELL parents' participation with a reliable design and easy access so that ELL parents can participate in and support their children's schooling.

- Encourage ELL parents' participation by giving them more opportunities, such as involving them in working with their children on some class projects.

Finally, the *life experiences* and *cultural norms* of ELLs also affect how they learn English and literacy skills. For example, Generation 1.5 students, especially those who are Latino, may come from family backgrounds that place a premium on family values. ELLs may be expected to place priority on the family instead of school. As a result, some ELLs may have to drop out of school to help their parents and support their family in times of financial need. In one case scenario, Anna was sacrificing her time for school work to take care of her younger siblings and help her parents with family responsibilities when she needed that time for her academic work. In her own words, it was her responsibility to help her parents and support the family because they would have no way to survive if the parents did not work. ELLs bring with them not only different life experiences but also cultural norms that may have shaped their notions of appropriate teacher-student relationships. For example, ELLs from some cultures may have learned to show respect for adults by listening quietly instead of asking questions or displaying knowledge by volunteering answers. Some ELL students may have the desire for closeness with their teachers through physical proximity and hugs, while others may expect a more formal or distant relationship with their teachers.

Some ELL students may even come from a refugee background. According to the Geneva Convention definition, a refugee is a person who, due to fear of persecution or due to war, violence, or natural disaster, is forced outside the country of his or her nationality and seeks refuge or asylum (Kanno & Varghese, 2010; U.S. Citizenship and Immigration Services, 2013). Since 1980, when formal U.S. refugee resettlement began, 1.8 million refugees have been invited to live in the United States, with annual refugee arrival typically between 40,000 and 75,000 (BCME, 2009; U.S. Citizenship and Immigration Services, 2013). Refugee ELLs not only have limited English proficiency but also constraints unique to this population. For example, they may have limited financial resources, a tendency to self-eliminate, or they may be suffering from grief, anxiety, depression, guilt or symptoms of posttraumatic stress disorder (Kanno & Varghese, 2010). Compared to other ELLs, refugee ELLs are more likely to have difficulties with schoolwork or adjustment issues related to these facts:

- Their education may be interrupted or postponed due to war in their home country or a waiting period of settlement in a refugee camp.
- They are faced with a sudden, unexpected transition to a new culture and new country, which may create confusion, difficulty, or uncertainty for them; it is thus difficult for them to adjust to school codes of conduct.
- These ELLs may have a sense of loss and trauma that could be profound for them; for instance, the loss may include family members or personal property, which can have psychological and emotional impacts.
- The family business in the home country may be left unsettled after leaving in a hurry; thus, basic needs and requirements, such as food, housing, and immediate medical and dental care may be an urgent issue.
- They may even be without parents or family guardians, experience some dramatic emotional and physical difficulties, thus, returning home is not an option for them.

Educators need to be sensitive to the needs of the ELLs and all students and strive to help them succeed academically and socially. Due to the difference in life experiences and cultural norms of the ELLs who come to school with different backgrounds, it is up to teachers to get to know their students and make necessary adjustments in instructional aspects and learning environments to accommodate the needs of all students so that they can succeed.

Academic-Related Issues

As a fast-growing segment of the school population, ELL students' academic attainments and related issues concern many educators. Achievement data suggest that ELL students generally lag behind their English-speaking peers, and the performance gap between English language learners and their English-speaking peers (non-ELLs) is persistent. For example, the National Center for Educational Statistics on student achievement reveals that the students of the nation's second largest ethnic group, that is, Hispanic students, are underperforming their Caucasian peers (NCES, 2012). This NCES data, released in June 2012 by the U.S. Department of Education, shows that scores have gone up for both groups. For instance, at the 4th-grade level, the average mathematics scores in 2011 for Caucasian students increased by 249 points and Hispanic students by 229 points, which were higher for both groups than their respective scores in 1990. However, Hispanic students still lagged behind their Caucasian peers by the same points as they did in 1990. This means that the achievement gap between Hispanic and Caucasian students has been unchanged for the past two decades while 80% of the ELL population are Hispanic speaking (Batalova & McHugh, 2010; Flannery, 2009). Generally, 4th-grade ELL students are about 3 years behind 4th-grade Caucasian students in reading and 8th-grade ELLs are about 4 years behind (Fry, 2007; NCTE, 2008; Ortiz & Pagan, 2009).

Furthermore, between 1990 and 2010, the percentage of public school students who were White decreased from 67% to 54%, and the percentage of those who were Hispanic increased from 12% or 5.1 million students to 23% or 12.1 million students (NCES, 2012). The NCES data shows that Hispanic students are also less likely to complete high school than their Caucasian peers, with the high school graduation rate for White students to be 75% and 53.2% for the Hispanic students. Nationally, only 12% of students with limited English proficiency (LEP) scored "at or above proficient" in mathematics in the fourth grade on the 2009 National Assessment of Educational Progress, compared with 42% of students who were not classified as English-language learners (Ortiz & Pagan, 2009; Slavin, Madden, Calderon, Chamberlain, & Hennessy, 2010). Therefore, it is crucial that teachers build capacity for learning success and seek strategies to support ELLs so that the academic attainment of this school population can be achieved. In this respect, it is imperative that K–12 teachers know the basics in L2 acquisition and teaching strategies in order to work with this unique student body.

To begin with, teachers need to understand the basic terminology related to ELLs and the programs within the school system. These terms are provided in Table 1.1, with the purpose of helping teachers know the basic information and resources in schools to better work with ELLs and help them in learning success.

In the process of working with ELLs and understanding their needs, teachers need to distinguish truth from some misconceptions about ELL students that can affect the teachers' attitude in serving ELLs. In Table 1.2, seven common myths are provided. The purpose is to help teachers have a better understanding of ELLs in order to help them achieve success.

ELL Profiles and Work Samples

Julio Gonzales Profile

Julio, a kindergartener and U.S.-born ELL, is energetic and enjoys active learning. He looks forward to the sessions with his English tutor, who works with him twice a week for supplementary L2 support. Julio has

Table 1.1.   Common Terms Related to ELLs and Programs

	Acronym	*Definition*	*Context*
Terminology related to ELLs	EL	English Learners: *This term is interchangeable with the term ELLs*	U.S. Department of Education has started to use this term to substitute the previous term *LEP.*
	ELL	English Language Learner: *A student who is in the process of acquiring English; whose primary language is not English*	This term has been used more frequently in recent years to substitute other terms such as LEP or ESL students.
	LEP	Limited English Proficiency: *A student who has limited English proficiency*	Educators believe that this term has a connotation focusing on limitation. It is substituted with other terms such as ELs or ELLs in recent years.
	Generation 1.5	Generation 1.5 students: *U.S. educated ELLs but who belong to neither Generation 1 nor Generation 2 of immigrants*	They may have limited skills in L1 but strong oral skills in L2; yet they are less proficient in academic language related to school achievement.
ELL-related programs	EFL	English as a Foreign Language: *English is taught by teachers whose native language is not English.*	A program for students who learn English as a foreign language in a country where English is not the L1.
	ESL	English as a Second Language: *English is taught by teachers whose native language is English.*	The ESL student is now a less common term than ELL and more often refers to an educational approach to support ELLs in learning English.
	ESOL	English for Speakers of Other Languages: *English is taught by teachers whose native language is English.*	It is also referred to as ENL, *English as a New Language*; the program offered in public schools often pulls ELLs out of regular classes to learn English.
	TESOL	Teaching English to Speakers of Other Languages: *Teaching English to non-English speakers*	It is an international association with the mission to advance professional expertise in English language teaching and learning for students of languages other than English.

Note: This table is modified based on information from Bardack (2010).

made an improvement on recognizing a majority of the letters in the alphabet. Flash cards are used as a great tool in working with him. On a Monday morning, Julio and his tutor were working on the alphabet. They used flash cards to identify the different letters and sounds. Each alphabet circle had diverse letters and pictures of items for each letter. Julio and

Table 1.2.   Seven Common Myths With Truth Related to ELLs

Myth	Truth	Rationale
Myth #1: ELLs can learn English easily simply by being exposed to L2 contexts.	Exposure to L2 contexts alone is insufficient. An ELL may appear proficient in basic communication skills, but he or she may not have developed the academic language proficiency to function in school (Ovando et al., 2005).	Good lesson planning and teaching strategies apply to all students, including ELLs.
Myth #2: The ability to speak fluently in English indicates that an ELL should do well in the classroom.	Proficiency in social language cannot be used to judge an ELL's academic proficiency. Spoken English may be acquired in 2 or 3 years, yet cognitive academic language proficiency takes about 5 to 7 years to be developed (Cummins, 2000).	Oral English has different rhetoric, structure, vocabulary, and requirements from that of academic L2.
Myth #3: All ELLs learn English in the same way and thus can be taught in the same manner.	ELLs are a heterogeneous group and different in many ways, such as previous schooling, family background, L1 knowledge, and immigration status. All these factors can affect how ELLs learn an L2, and they learn in varied paces and ways (McCarthey, Garcia, Lopez-Velasquez, & Guo, 2004).	No one strategy can fit all ELLs; teachers must use multiple ways to assess and meet the ELL students' needs.
Myth #4: ELLs have disabilities, which is why they are often overrepresented in special education.	Inappropriate placement of ELLs in special education classes can limit the growth of ELLs when they have no disabilities; they can perform better if placed accordingly; quality instruction and inclusive environments are more effective for ELLs (Callahan, 2005; Artiles & Ortiz, 2002).	Overrepresentation reflects the assessment system problem that does not differentiate disabilities from the ELLs' L2 needs.
Myth #5: Teaching ELLs focuses on teaching them vocabulary.	Learning an L2 is a recursive process and integrating listening, speaking, reading, and writing skills into instruction from the start helps ELLs who need to learn not only the forms and structures of academic language but also understand the relationship between forms and meanings, and need the opportunities to express complex meanings in written English (Callahan, 2005; Schleppegrell & Go, 2007).	Curricula organized around authentic reading and writing experiences provides textual choices and meaningful content for ELL students.
Myth #6: Providing accommodations for ELLs benefits these students only.	Making mainstream classrooms more responsive to ELLs will also help other underserved students in general because many cognitive aspects of teaching ELLs are common to the native English speakers, although teachers should pay additional attention to background knowledge, interaction, and word use with ELLs (Meltzer &. Hamann, 2005).	ELLs tend to perform much better when teaching responds to their needs and the environment is supportive to learning.
Myth #7: ELL students should concentrate on English and stop speaking their L1.	Proficiency in the L1 facilitates L2 development; academic achievement is significantly enhanced when ELL students are able to use their L1 knowledge to learn academic content in the L2 context (Cummins, 2000; García, 2000).	Denying the native language of an individual is to deny his or her existence.

Note: Common myths are modified from Espinosa's (2008) *Challenging Common Myths about Young English Language Learners*, with truths and rationales added for better understanding ELLs.

Figure 1.1.   Julio focused on recognizing the letters in the above session. He was given many opportunities to practice in a meaningful way by reading, writing, listening, and playing the game. The drawing is his sample work after learning the Letter "A".

the tutor also played the "Name that Letter" game. This game allowed Julio to shuffle the flash cards, close his eyes, and then select one card. After selecting the card, he excitingly announced that it was the letter "A." Julio informed the tutor that "A" was the first letter in the alphabet and made the "ah" sound. Next, they used the *Oxford Picture Dictionary* to identify some items that begin with the letter "A." Julio pointed to a red apple, an ant, and a green alligator, and he drew a picture (see Figure 1.1). He truly enjoyed this session. They also read *Silly Monsters ABC* by Gearld Hawksley. Julio was ecstatic and excited when he saw the different monsters. His favorite monster, the "J" monster, played jump rope, ate a jellybean, and juggled balls. Julio recognized that the monster participated in activities that began with the letter "J." He identified most of the letters in the book! Reading with Julio was an adventure. The joy in his eyes showed that he was happy and enjoyed learning.

Edwin Perez Profile

Edwin, a first grader and also U.S. born, enjoys learning but can become distracted. Edwin works better with one-on-one guidance. He is

Figure 1.2.   This is Edwin's sample work. After reading the story *The Fence* by Debra Blenus, Edwin drew a picture of the different animals in the story. He also described what happened in the story with a brief summary. As a first grader, he was enjoying learning, although there appeared to be the need for him to improve his writing skills.

focused when there is less distraction such as in the ESOL resource room. It was at the beginning of the school year and Edwin was working with his tutor, who assisted Edwin with learning sessions twice a week as supplementary support. This was an afternoon session inside the mainstream classroom reviewing the new vocabulary words before his one-on-one session. Students were doing independent work while the teacher prepared for the next lesson. Edwin seemed to be unable to concentrate on his work. The assignment was for all the students to review 10 vocabulary words. After the students completed this review assignment, Edwin and the tutor worked in a quiet location so that Edwin would feel comfortable and not be distracted. They reviewed the vocabulary words again. Edwin knew some of the words, yet did not comprehend others. He was guided to create sentences for each word and drew pictures for some words. He was able to enunciate some words with ease while needing more assistance with the others. Edwin also needed to improve his writing skills. Practice was key in helping Edwin with word development. Edwin enjoyed the session with the tutor and appeared eager to learn.

Ann Sanchez Profile

Ann is a 5th-grade ELL who has recently immigrated to the United States with her parents and a younger brother. Although she was a good student in her home country, it is not easy for Ann to keep pace with the academic work in her new school. In all, Ann is experiencing some difficulty in getting good grades due to an inability to understand the content covered by her teachers in English. This is also the unfortunate situation for many other ELLs because they cannot comprehend the content due to the English language barrier. Although many teachers want to help, they

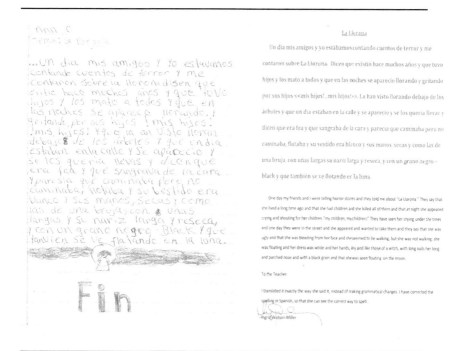

Figure 1.3.   This is Ann's sample work. On the left is a story that Ann wrote in Spanish as an assignment on her first day in school. The teacher allows her to express in the language she understands. Under the story is the picture Ann drew, which depicted a ghost floating in the night sky because it was around Halloween. The word "Fin" at the bottom represents "The End" in Spanish. The translated version of the story is provided on the right with the help of another Spanish teacher. This is an example of the teacher going out of her way to help her student.

seem to feel a limitation for what they can do in terms of helping Ann because Ann could not speak or understand English. However, Mrs. Daniels (pseudonym), Ann's 5th-grade teacher, went out of her way and provided Ann with additional assistance whenever she could, such as translating versions of assignments and assessments and giving Ann more time so that Ann could have an opportunity to complete her assignments. This required the teacher to go beyond her normal work. Yet Ann improved her academic work once the language barrier was overcome.

These ELL profiles provide further information on ELLs who have different learning needs, which were accommodated accordingly. As a diverse, fast-growing student body, the ELL school population offers both challenges and opportunities to American education (Nieto, 2000). They bring diversity and rich cultures with them to our school and classrooms. It is important for teachers to recognize that the ELLs' L1 and home cultures should be positioned as resources so that teachers can help ELLs see that their L1 ability and their cultures are valued and contribute to education rather than something to be overcome. Involving ELL students in activities, such as writing about home and school, helps them develop abilities in text comprehension, collaboration with peers, and the construction of a writer identity (Nieto, 2000; Yi, 2007). Teachers can use different strategies to reduce the distance between home and school while helping ELLs become more invested in school learning.

Continuing engaging teachers in professional development to ensure that all teachers are adequately prepared to work with ELLs is important in the next few years. Teachers need to know basic knowledge and strategies to work with ELLs. Research indicates that a low percentage of teachers received professional development on teaching ELLs despite the growing numbers of ELLs; and fewer states have policies that have requirements for K–12 teachers to obtain certain expertise in teaching ELLs (Freeman & Freeman, 2003; Karabenick & Noda, 2004). As a result, many ELLs find themselves in mainstream classrooms taught by teachers with no formal preparation in working with these linguistically diverse students. Thus, it is imperative that teachers of ELLs gain knowledge and skills through various efforts so that they can produce positive effects. In this process, getting to ELLs and their educational needs is the initial step for teachers in devising strategies and working with them.

SUMMARY

This chapter begins with a case scenario as a snapshot to help teachers understand who ELLs are. The background for the fast growth of ELL school enrollment is introduced, tracing information on the immigration law (i.e., Johnson-Reed Act) in 1924. The chapter also discusses common characteristics of ELLs in helping teachers know ELLs and meet the special needs of this school population. The chapter discusses the types of the ELL students, for example, Generation 1.5 versus U.S.-born ELL students. Academic attainment–related issues are addressed with an examination of common terms and myths related to the ELLs. The chapter also provides sample profiles of ELLs with their sample works. The intention is to help teachers understand that ELLs have different educational needs and learning styles. It is reality that teachers need to be engaged in professional development so that all teachers are prepared to meet the special needs of ELLs as this school population continues to increase. Having a better understanding of this school population is an initial step in helping teachers work effectively with ELLs and enhancing the learning outcomes of ELLs and all students.

REFERENCES

Abedi, J., Leon, S., & Mirocha, J. (2005). Examining ELL and non-ELL student performance differences and their relationship to background factors: Continued analysis of extant data. *The Validity of Administering Large-Scale Content Assessments to English Language Learners*, 1–43. Los Angeles, CA: NCRESST.

Arias, B., & Morillo-Campbell, M. (2008, January). Promoting ELL parental involvement: Challenges in contested times. *EPIC/EPRU*. Retrieved December 12, 2012, from http://epsl.asu.edu/epru/documents/EPSL-0801-250-EPRU.pdf

Artiles, A. J., & Ortiz, A. A. (2002). *English language learners with special education needs*. McHenry, IL: Center for Applied Linguistics and Delta Systems.

Bardack, S. (2010, April). Common ELL terms and definitions. *English Language Learner Center: American Institute for Research*. Washington, DC: AIR. Retrieved December 29, 2012, from http://www.air.org/sites/default/files/downloads/report/NEW_-_Common_ELL_TERMS_AND_DEFINITIONS_6_22_10_0.pdf

Batalova, J., & McHugh, M. (2010). Top languages spoken by English language learners nationally and by state. National Center on Immigrant Integration Policy. *Immigration Policy Institute: ELL Information Center Fact Series*, 3(1), 1–5.

British Columbia Ministry of Education (BCME). (2009, October). *Students from refugee backgrounds: A guide for teachers and schools*. Retrieved from http://www.bced.gov.bc.ca/ell//refugees_teachers_guide.pdf

Callahan, R. M. (2005). Tracking and high school English learners: Limiting opportunities to learn. *American Educational Research Journal, 42*(2), 305–328.

Callahan, R. M.,Wilkinson, L., & Muller, C. (2010). Academic achievement and course taking among language minority youth in U.S. schools: Effects of ESL placement. *Educational Evaluation and Policy Analysis, 32*(1), 84–117.

Cummins, J. (2000): *Language, power, and pedagogy. Bilingual children in the crossfire*. Clevedon, UK: Multilingual Matters.

Davis-Kean, P. E. (2005). The influence of parent education and family income on child achievement: The indirect role of parental expectations and the home environment. *Journal of Family Psychology, 19*(2), 294–304.

Eccles, J., Templeton, J., & Barber, B. (2005). Adolescence and emerging adulthood: The critical passage ways to adulthood. In M. Bornstein, L. Davidson, C. L. M. Keyes, K. A. Moore, & The Center for Child Well-Being (Eds). *Well-being: Positive development across the life course* (pp. 383–406). Hillsdale, NJ: Erlbaum.

Espinosa, L. M. (2008). Challenging common myths about young English language learners. *PCD Policy Brief-Advancing PK–3*. New York, NY: Foundation for Child Development.

Flannery, M. E. (2009). A new look at America's English language learners. *NEA Today*. Washington, DC: NEA.

Freeman, D. E., & Freeman, Y. S. (2003). *Essential linguistics: What you need to know to teach reading, ESL, spelling, phonics, grammar*. Portsmouth, NH: Heinemann.

Fry, R. (2007, June 6). How far behind in math and reading are English language learners? *Pew Hispanic Center*. Retrieved from http://www.pewhispanic.org/2007/06/06/how-far-behind-in-math-and-reading-are-english-language-learners/

García, E. (2010). *Education and achievement: A focus on Latino "immigrant" children*. Washington, DC: The Urban Institute.

Genesee, F., Lindholm-Leary, K., Saunders, W., & Christian, D. (2005). English language learners in U.S. schools: An overview of research findings. *Journal of Education for Students Placed at Risk, 10*(4), 363–385.

Guerra, N. G., & Huesmann, L. R. (2004). A cognitive-ecological model of aggression. *International Review of Social Psychology, 17*(3),177–203.

Jalongo, M., & Li, N. (2010). Young English language learners as listeners: Theoretical perspectives, research stands, and implications for instruction. In B. Spodek & O. Saracho (Eds.), *Contemporary perspectives on language and cultural diversity in childhood education* (pp. 95–115). Greenwich, CT: Information Age.

Kanno, Y., & Varghese, M. M. (2010). Immigrant and refugee ESL students' challenge to assess four year college education: Language policy and educational policy. *Journal of Language, 9*(5), 310–328.

Karabenick, A. S., & Noda, P. A. (2004). Professional development implications of teachers beliefs and attitudes toward English language learners. *Bilingual Research Journal, 28*(1), 55–75.

Li, N., Howard, C., & Mitchell, Y. (2011). What a case study reveals: Facing the new challenge and learning the basics in L2 acquisition. *The National Teacher Education Journal, 3*(2), 57–69.

McCarthey, S. J., Garcia, G. E., Lopez-Velasquez, A. M., & Guo, S. H. (2004). Understanding contexts for English language learners. *Research in Teaching of English, 38*(4), 351–394.

Meltzer, J., &. Hamann, E. T. (2005). *Meeting the literacy development needs of adolescent English language learners through content-area learning*. Providence, RI: Education Alliance at Brown University.

Mikesell, L. (2008). Generation 1.5 and ESL learners' use of past participles: A corpus-based comparison. *Proceedings of the CATESOL State Conference, 2006.* Retrieved December 30, 2012, from http://www.catesol.org/06Mikesell.pdf

National Center for Educational Statistics (NCES). (2012). *The Condition of Education 2012* (NCES 2012-045). Washington, DC: U.S. Department of Education, National Center for Education Statistics, Institute of Education Sciences.

National Center for Family Literacy (NCFL). (2003). *Dissemination process submission to the Program Effectiveness Panel of the U.S. Department of Education.* Louisville, KY: NCFL.

National Clearinghouse for English Language Acquisition (NCELA). (2011). The growing numbers of English learner students, 1998/99–2008/09, Washington DC: NCELA.

National Council of Teachers of English (NCTE). (2008). *English language learners: A policy research brief, National Council of Teachers of English*, Urbana, IL: NCTE.

Nieto, S. (2000). Linguistic diversity in multicultural classrooms. In *Affirming diversity: Creating multicultural communities* (pp. 189–217). New York, NY: Addison Wesley Longman.

Ortiz, T., & Pagan, M. (2009). *Closing the ELL achievement gap: A leader's guide to making schools effective for culturally and linguistically diverse students.* Rexford, NY: International Center for Leadership in Education.

Oudenhoven, E. D. (2006). Caught in the middle: Generation 1.5 Latino students and English language learning at a community college (Doctoral dissertation, Loyola University Chicago). *Digital Dissertations,* AAT 3212980.

Ovando, C. J., Collier, V. P., & Combs, M. C. (2005). *Bilingual and ESL classrooms: Teaching in multicultural contexts.* New York, NY: McGraw-Hill.

Roberge, M. M. (2002). California's generation 1.5 immigrants: What experiences, characteristics, and needs do they bring to our English classes? *The CATESOL Journal, 14*(1), 107–129.

Roeser, R. W., & Peck, S. C. (2009). Education in awareness: Self-motivation and self-regulated learning in contemplative perspective. *Educational Psychologist, 44*(2), 119–136.

Saunders, W. J., & O'Brien, G. (2006). Oral language. In F. Genesee, K. Lindholm-Leary, W. M. Saunders, & D. Christian (Eds.), *Educating English language learners: A synthesis of research evidence* (pp. 2–63). New York, NY: Cambridge University Press.

Schleppegrell, M. J., & Go, A. L. (2007). Analyzing the writing of English learners: A functional approach. *Language Arts, 84*(6), 529–538.

Short, P. J., & Fitzsimmons, S. (2007). *Double the work: Challenges and solutions to acquiring language and academic literacy for adolescent English language learners—Report to Carnegie Corporation.* New York, NY: Alliance for Excellence Education.

Singhal, M. (2006). Academic writing and Generation 1.5: Pedagogical goals and instructional issues in the college composition classrooms. *The Reading Matrix, 4*(3), 3–15.

Slavin, R. E., Madden, N., Calderon, M., Chamberlain, A., & Hennessy, M. (2010). *Reading and language outcomes of a five-year randomized evaluation of transitional bilingual education*. Baltimore, MD: Johns Hopkins University, Center for Data-Driven Reform in Education.

Sticht, T. G., & McDonald, B. A. (2009). *Teach the mother and reach the child: Literacy across generations*. Geneva, Switzerland: International Bureau of Education.

U.S. Citizenship and Immigration Services. (2013). The refugees and refugee process. Retrieved from http://www.uscis.gov/humanitarian/refugees-asylum/refugees

Yi, Y. (2007). Engaging literacy: A biliterate student's composing practices beyond school. *Journal of Second Language Writing, 16*(1), 23–39.

Zelasko, N., & Antunez, B. (2000). *If your child learns in two languages*. Washington, DC: George Washington University and National Clearinghouse for English Language Acquisition.

PART II

TEACHING ELLS

CHAPTER 2

THEORETICAL PERSPECTIVES IN L2 ACQUISITION

CASE SCENARIO

Samantha Ortiz came to the United States from Honduras with her parents when she was 6 years old. Samantha started school in the first grade. Because she didn't speak English, she required ESOL service daily. Samantha was shy and quiet in the classroom, but she was encouraged to do her best. Her father spoke some English and worked at a sod farm; her mother did not speak any English and stayed home to take care of children. Yet the mother checked Samantha and all children's schoolwork to make sure that Samantha and the children did their schoolwork and completed homework assignments. By the end of the second grade, Samantha was able to speak English. In fact, her oral English became very good. She could tell stories in English. During her third grade, Samantha continued to improve in English and was mainstreamed. However, at the beginning of the fourth grade, her teacher noticed that Samantha struggled with lesson content in certain subject areas, such as in social studies, math, and science. She could not understand the lesson content in these subject areas. Her teacher was confused about why she could speak English but could not understand the lessons explained in English. Samantha struggled most in understanding math problems. This made the teacher think that Samantha might have a learning disability issue. According to the teacher, if Samantha had oral English fluency, she should understand lessons. The teacher knew that Samantha had been in America for 4 years

A Book for Every Teacher: Teaching English Language Learners
pp. 25–38

and thus began to think that Samantha should have a diagnosis to find out about her learning disability problem.

As the above scenario shows, many teachers may find their ELLs in a similar situation in classrooms. They have fluent oral English skills but they struggle to understand lessons in subject content areas. This chapter will discuss the reason from an L2 theoretical perspective. Based on L2 acquisition theories, oral English is different from academic English. Social or oral English skills can be acquired in a relatively shorter period, from 6 months to 2 years. Yet academic English proficiency takes much longer time. To understand subject contents, for example, to grasp a math concept, academic English proficiency is needed. This explains why Samantha had oral English fluency while she could not understand lesson contents. This indicates to educators that we should not expect that a mainstreamed ELL can meet full academic challenges in classrooms solely based on their oral English fluency. As the above scenario indicates, it might lead teachers to believe that ELLs have learning disability issues or they do not work hard enough. Without getting appropriate instructional support, these ELLs are likely to continue struggling in classrooms. Teachers have the obligation to help all students succeed and make yearly academic progress in our classrooms. Knowing the theoretical perspectives in L2 acquisition and basic concepts can help teachers achieve this goal.

BICS and CALP

According to L2 acquisition theories, there are two types of the second language proficiencies: Basic Interpersonal Communicative Skills (BICS) and Cognitive Academic Language Proficiency (CALP). BICS refers to those oral, social language skills or "surface" L2 skills of listening and speaking that are typically acquired quickly by many ELL students; particularly by those from language backgrounds similar to English who spend a lot of their school time interacting with native speakers. CALP refers to Cognitive Academic Language Proficiency; as the name suggests, it is the basis for an ELL's ability to cope with the academic demands in school placed upon her or him in the various subjects. Cummins (1984) developed this L2 acquisition theory. According to him, the language used in school has a broad range of competences and thus Cummins distinguishes these two types of English language proficiency. In other words, he makes a distinction between conversational English language skills and cognitive academic English language competency, that is, BICS and CALP. According to Cummins, in an English-speaking environment, it takes from 6 months to 2 years for an ELL to develop Basic Interpersonal Communicative Skills (BICS); yet it takes from 5 to 7 years for an ELL to develop Cognitive Academic Language Proficiency (CALP), which is crucial for academic success (Collier, 1987; Cummins, 1984).

Cummins (1984) further explains that people can reach the autonomous stage called a plateau, where they feel no more progress made in learning the language. Many reasons cause plateaus; yet a major cause is believed to be sticking to the same habits, whether it's writing, typing, learning a language, or programming, and it often results in failing to progress, despite investing a lot of time (Ericsson, 2006). In a nutshell, people feel OK with how good they are, turn on autopilot or stop improving their work, allowing their evident flaws, and lose conscious control over what they are doing. However, what separates experts from other people is that they tend to engage in a directed, highly focused routine, something called deliberate practice. Experts and top achievers in various fields tend to follow the same general pattern of development. They develop strategies for consciously keeping out of the autonomous stage. Three things common for them are focusing on their technique, staying goal oriented, and getting constant and immediate feedback on their performance. As applied to L2 learning, it means ELLs can reach near-native-like oral skills. Yet academic language proficiency needs deliberate practice and takes much longer for ELLs to reach in order to cope with demanding schoolwork on the same level as a native speaker.

Understanding of the basic concepts in BICS and CALP answers the question in the scenario on why it is challenging for Samantha to understand lesson contents even if she appeared to be fluent in her oral English skills and can speak English very well. This is because it takes longer for an ELL to develop the cognitive academic language proficiency (CALP), even if they have gained basic interpersonal communication skills (BICS). For example, without any context clue, an ELL could associate the word table with a chair in a lesson, while a native speaker might already know the multiple meanings of this word and can relate this word to a math concept in a math lesson (see Figure 2.1).

Basic Interpersonal Communicative Skills (BICS)

As mentioned, two types of language proficiencies in learning an L2 are BICS and CALP. Basic Interpersonal Communication Skills (BICS) refers to the social language skills of everyday English, or it is the oral English skills used in daily conversational contexts. BICS is gained through communication and interaction. This second-language theory is consistent with educational theories and both believe that language is a social concept developed through social interactions. Lev Vygotsky (1978), a 20th century Soviet psychologist, believed that language acquisition involves not only a

Figure 2.1.   Multiple meanings of an English word, such as "table."

child's exposure to words but also an interdependent process of growth between thought and language. According to Vygotsky, children develop first-language skills through social interaction. By interacting with others in environment, a child develops the ability for inner speech. Through the development of inner speech, children straddle the divide between thought and language, eventually being able to express their thoughts coherently to others. Consistent with Vygotsky's theory, L2 acquisition theories believe that ELLs acquire English language skills through interaction with others (Donato, 1994; Echevarria, Vogt, & Short, 2010; Lantolf, 2000). Like learning L1, ELLs learn English through interacting with their teachers and peers in an English-speaking environment, such as classrooms, the playground, the school cafeteria, or libraries, as well as from videos, television shows, movies, sports, games, computers games, magazines, or electronic devices such iPods, iPads, and iPhones.

In all, ELLs need to be exposed to the enriched English language environment and learn how to retell stories, orally describe activities, share their personal experiences, tell their preference and opinions, and talk about events and their experiences. Theoretically, in such a language-immersed situation, it takes from 6 months to 2 years for ELLs to develop their oral English or basic interpersonal communication skills. Yet, as mentioned, BICS is also referred to as the surface language skills of listening and speaking, which are typically acquired quickly by many ELL students and particularly by those from language backgrounds similar to English who spend a lot of their school time interacting with native speakers. This explains why it is easy for an ELL to acquire fluent oral English skills. In other words, ELLs may speak English fluently within 6 months to 2 years. However, this does not mean that they have acquired the academic English language proficiency that is crucial for them to fully function in academic activities in schools; for example, to understand words and concepts related to academic subject content, such as understanding math or science concepts and terminology. They need time to develop their cognitive academic English proficiency.

Cognitive Academic Language Proficiency (CALP)

According to L2 acquisition theories, Cognitive Academic Language Proficiency (CALP) is the academic English language needed to understand subject content. This is cognitively demanding language skills and takes 5 to 7 years to develop. Schools usually measure ELLs' L2 proficiency based on four language skills: listening, speaking, reading, and writing. ELLs can be competent in having a face-to-face conversation, but they may still lack the academic language proficiency to comprehend the concepts that are cognitively demanding and at the same time require a significant amount of background knowledge and vocabulary specifically related to the content area. Thus, it is important that classroom teachers do not assume that ELLs who have attained a certain degree of fluency in everyday spoken English have the corresponding academic language proficiency (Collier, 1987; Cummins, 1984). Understanding the concept of CALP can also help teachers avoid labeling ELLs who exhibit this disparity as having special educational needs when what ELLs actually need is more time. In other words, although ELLs may have exited from the ESOL program, they may still be in the process of acquiring their academic language proficiency.

This L2 theory concurs with educational theories. Bloom's Taxonomy was first created in 1956 under the leadership of educational psychologist Dr. Benjamin Bloom in order to promote higher levels of thinking skills in classrooms, such as analyzing and evaluating concepts instead of simply remembering facts or rote learning (Bloom, 1956a). Based on Bloom's Taxonomy, academic activities that acquire students to accomplish at each level are different from those in the social context (see examples in Table 2.1). For handling academically demanding tasks, cognitive competence is needed at these six levels: (a) knowledge to remember previously learned information (e.g., define, describe, identify, state, select, label, list, outline, reproduce); (b) comprehension to demonstrate understanding (e.g., classify, describe, discuss, explain, identify, paraphrase, predict, recognize, summarize, select, rewrite, review); (c) application to apply knowledge in the actual situation (e.g., apply, choose, demonstrate, illustrate, interpret, predict, produce, show, solve, use, write); (d) analysis to break down ideas in order to find evidence (e.g., analyze, categorize, compare, distinguish, examine, identify, infer, model); (e) synthesis to compile ideas into a new whole (e.g., arrange, assemble, categorize, col-

Table 2.1.   Examples of Social and Academic Language Based on Bloom's Taxonomy (1956)

Social Language	*Academic Language*
• Everyday conversation: 　○ *Hello!* 　○ *It is cold today.* 　○ *Tom likes to play football.*	• Knowledge: define, describe, identify, state, select, label, list, outline, etc. 　○ *Please name three natural disasters based on our reading yesterday.*
• Culturally related: 　○ *They are invited to a cocktail party to celebrate their class reunion.* 　○ *We had a birthday party for my younger brother last week and she turned 7.* 　○ *Please bring your brown bag for the planning meeting tomorrow.*	• Comprehension: classify, describe, discuss, explain, identify, paraphrase, predict, recognize, summarize, review, etc. 　○ *Please summarize the author's main ideas in one or two paragraphs.*
• Instructionally related: 　○ *Please raise your hand if you have any questions before we move on.* 　○ *Let's turn to page 12 and read the first paragraph of this book.* 　○ *Please remember to use double space and the font size 12 for this research paper.*	• Application: apply, choose, demonstrate, illustrate, interpret, predict, produce, show, solve, use, write, etc. 　○ *Please predict what happens next in the story by writing it down a sentence.*
	• Analysis: analyze, categorize, compare, distinguish, examine, identify, infer, model 　○ *Please compare the differences between amphibians and reptiles based on your reading.*
	• Synthesis: arrange, assemble, categorize, collect, combine, construct, develop, generate, rearrange, reconstruct, rewrite, summarize, synthesize, etc. 　○ *Please provide three categories of food discussed in the text.*
	• Evaluation: appraise, assess, judge, evaluate, justify, rate, summarize, support, etc. 　○ *Please summarize the main ideas of the author with one sentence.*

Note: Please also see those action words in the revised Bloom's Taxonomy in Chapter 3 in Bloom (1956b).

lect, combine, construct, develop, generate, rearrange, reconstruct, rewrite, summarize, synthesize); and (f) evaluation to make a judgment (e.g., appraise, assess, choose, evaluate, judge, justify, rate, support). In order to accomplish academic assignments, students need to have these higher-order-thinking skills in order for ELL students to apply different forms of language.

Cummins (1984) contributed to the concepts of BICS and CALP and also created a graphic (see Figure 2.2) to aid in understanding what makes language easier or harder for English language learners in the learning process. Difficulty is based on the relationship between the two factors:

	Context-Embedded	Context-Reduced
Understanding	I Cognitively Understanding + Context-Embedded	II Cognitively Understanding + Context-Reduced
Demanding	III Cognitively Demanding + Context-Embedded	IV Cognitively Demanding + Context-Reduced

Figure 2.2. This is the modified format of Cummin's quadrants. Teachers can help their ELLs understand the information by providing contextual support. The chart is created based on Cummins's (1984) framework to evaluate language demand in content activities.

the cognitive demand of the task and the amount of available contextual support. In Figure 2.2, BICS and CALP are further illustrated. The first factor, the degree of cognitive challenge, is represented in Cummins's framework as basically easy or hard. The two quadrants (I and II) on the top of Cummins's chart represent oral or written tasks that are cognitively undemanding, as in the blue section, that is, they can be either socially or academically easy tasks, such as read with picture cues, get lunch from the lunch line, play on the playground, talk on the phone, or shop for school supplies. The two lower quadrants (III and IV) of the chart represent tasks that are cognitively demanding, as in the red section. These tasks are academically difficult, requiring higher levels of thought processing and language skills.

The second factor in Cummins's (1984) framework evaluates the amount of contextual support inherent in the task. Contextual supports offer clues to the meaning of words. The more spoken and written words are embedded in context, the easier they are to understand. Spoken language can be given contextual support through facial expressions, gestures, body language, demonstrations, visual cues, and physical environment. Written language can offer contextual support through pictures, graphs, charts, tables, and textbook aids. Oral and written tasks with these kinds of supports are called context-embedded. The two quadrants (I and III) on the left side of the chart represent tasks that are contextually embedded, as in the green section. Tasks in which students have only spoken or written words alone to work with are termed context-reduced, as in Quadrants II and IV, as in the yellow section. Combining the two elements of cognitive challenge and contextual support, the quadrants move in difficulty from I to IV. ELLs will find Quadrant I tasks easy because they are low in cognitive demand and high in contextual support. Quadrant IV tasks will be most difficult because they are academically demanding and lack contextual support. Standardized assessment falls into this category (Gottlieb, Katz, & Ernst-Slavit, 2009). Therefore, providing contextual support and scaffolding strategies, such as visual aids, hands-on activities, and working with peers, can help ELLs understand better.

The following are some examples of activities that illustrate Cummins' (1984) quadrants. Teachers can help their ELLs understand the information by providing contextual support.

Quadrant I: Cognitively undemanding and context embedded

  (a) Engaging in face-to-face social conversation with peers
  (b) Ordering lunch from a picture menu in a fast food restaurant
  (c) Listening to a presentation about pet animals with pictures and videos
  (d) Participating in physical education classes
  (e) Participating in shows and games
  (f) Learning to play baseball with a coaching demonstration

Quadrant II: Cognitively undemanding and context reduced

  (a) Engaging in social conversation on the telephone
  (b) Getting travel direction via the telephone
  (c) Ordering dinner from a menu in a formal restaurant with no picture clues
  (d) Listening to a presentation about caring for pets without visual aids
  (e) Reading a list of required school supplies
  (f) talking with friends about shows and games

Quadrant III: Cognitively demanding and context embedded

  (a) Solving math word problems with manipulatives and/or pictures
  (b) Solving simple math computation problems
  (c) Doing a science experiment by following a demonstration
  (d) Understanding written text through pictures, graphics, and small-group discussion

(e) Reading the illustrated (comic book) version of Shakespeare's Romeo and Juliet

(f) Listening to a lecture with visual aids; e.g., gesture and PowerPoint

(g) Writing a report paper with a detailed explanation and ample examples

Quadrants IV: Cognitively demanding and context reduced

(a) Solving math word problems without manipulatives and/or pictures

(b) Doing a science experiment by reading directions from a textbook

(c) Writing research reports on assigned topics in social studies

(d) Listening to a lecture on an unfamiliar topic

(e) Reading Shakespeare's Romeo and Juliet in its original format

(f) Taking a standard test, such SAT, ACT, and TOFEL

Source: Adapted from Paul Gardner (2012).

To summarize the chart in Figure 2.2, it is clear that a context-embedded task is one in which an ELL has access to additional visual and oral cues. For example, an ELL can look at illustrations of what is being talked about to confirm understanding. A context-reduced task is one such as listening to a lecture or reading a difficult text where there are no other sources of support or help other than the language itself. Therefore, providing contextual clues is very important in helping ELLs develop CALP. Cummins' (1984) contribution to the distinction between BICS and CALP is influential. However, his framework of BICS and CALP also received some criticism. Some critics believe that language is always "contextualized" as opposed to Cummins' definition that CALP is "decontextualized" language (Bartolomè, 1998; Gee, 1990). Others argue that Cummins' framework does not provide enough specific information to help teachers meet the diverse needs of ELLs, and the framework of BICS and CLAP emphasizes the weaknesses of the low cognitive skills of ELLs rather than the fund of knowledge that students can bring to the classroom (Edelsky, 2006; McSwan & Rolstad, 2003; Scarcella, 2003). Yet BICS and CLAP contribute greatly in helping teachers understand the differences between social and academic languages and the process of the ELLs' academic growth in content areas.

Comprehensible Input and Affective Filter

Comprehensible input refers to the language input that can be understood by ELLs despite them not understanding all the words and structures in it. It is described as one level above that of the learners, if it can only just be understood. Krashen (1982), an American linguist and educational researcher, proposed his theory of the L2 acquisition. In this chapter, his hypotheses of the Comprehensible Input and Affective Filter are introduced as the basic concepts of L2 acquisition needed for helping ELLs in classrooms.

Comprehensible Input Hypothesis

According to Krashen (1982), providing ELLs with comprehensive input helps ELLs acquire language naturally rather than learning it consciously. For example, the teacher can select a reading text for upper intermediate-level ELLs that is from a lower advanced-level coursebook. Based on what the teacher knows about the learners, the teacher believes that this will give them comprehensible input to help them acquire more language. In the classroom, it is important that teachers understand that language slightly above their level encourages ELLs to use natural learning strategies, such as guessing words from context and inferring meaning. As the example suggests, a teacher needs to know the level of the learners very well in order to select comprehensible input, and in a large class of mixed ability, different learners will need different texts. Krashen proposes this Comprehensible Input Hypothesis and states that language acquisition requires meaningful interaction in the target language through natural communication. By natural communication, he means that speakers should not be concerned with the form of their utterances but with the messages they are conveying and understanding. He believes that the best way to learn a second language is to supply comprehensible input in low-anxiety situations. In other words, the input conveyed to ELLs must be comprehensible. This further indicates that ELLs should not be forced into early production in learning the second language but produce when they are ready. This requires teachers to understand that ELLs' learning progress largely comes from supplying communicative and comprehensible input and not from forcing and correcting production.

Krashen (1982) further explains that languages are learned in context through the learner's knowledge of the world. Knowing the structure of a language will not help an ELL to develop communication competence. His Comprehensive Input Hypothesis proposes that ELLs acquire L2 through understanding the meaning before they learn the structure. He also presents an idea using the formula $i + 1$, in which i stands for input, the meaningful and comprehensible communication in a context that is understood by ELLs immediately; and +1 refers to the level that is slightly beyond the current level of the learners, but challenging enough for the learners to advance their language proficiency. In other words, if the lesson content is at the level of $i + 0$ or $i+2$, it will either lack challenge or be too difficult. In classrooms, teachers can enhance ELLs and all students' comprehension by using the $i+1$ formula through incorporating strategies, such as scaffolding; embedding rich context; linking to the learner's prior knowledge; using graphic organizers; providing modeling, visual aids, and ample examples; preteaching the content; and collaborating with the ESOL teachers.

Affective Filter Hypothesis

An effective language teacher is someone who can provide input and help make it comprehensible in a low-anxiety situation. Krashen (1982) also proposes the Affective Filter Hypothesis, an L2 theory that can help teachers better understand and assist their ELLs. According to this theory, emotional factors can encourage ELLs to learn L2 skills. Comprehensible input is not enough to ensure language acquisition, so an ELL must be receptive to that input. In the human brain, there is a language acquisition device (LAD), which functions to process the L2. However, if ELLs are nervous, unmotivated, bored, frustrated, or stressed, they may not be receptive to language input; in other words, they may filter the input to reach LAD. This filter is called the affective filter. It includes several variables, such as motivation, self-esteem, confidence, and anxiety. Krashen believes that when learners have high motivation, self-esteem, confidence, a good self-image, and low anxiety, they are more receptive to learning content and thus better equipped for success in L2 acquisition. On the other hand, low motivation, low self-esteem, and debilitating anxiety can cause learners to increase the affective filter and form a mental block that prevents comprehensible input from being used for acquisition. In other words, when the affective filter is high, it impedes language acquisition.

Applying this hypothesis in classrooms suggests that ELLs learn better in an environment that makes them feel motivated and that builds their self-esteem and confidence while lowering their anxiety. When learners are nervous, unmotivated, frustrated, bored, or stressed, they are unlikely to be productive in learning a second language. This L2 acquisition theory has a practical implication for all K–12 mainstream teachers in terms of creating a supportive classroom atmosphere for ELLs and all students and in designing lessons that motivate ELLs and all students to learn while lowering affective filters, that is, reducing anxiety for students. Understanding this L2 theory, teachers know that lowering anxiety is important in the process of language acquisition. If a learner's affective filter is high, he or she is less likely to take risk or be willing to participate; therefore, he or she will take less input. Those students who have lower anxiety in learning a new language are more likely to take risk and be willing to seek more input. The Affective Filter Hypothesis chart is illustrated in Figure 2.3.

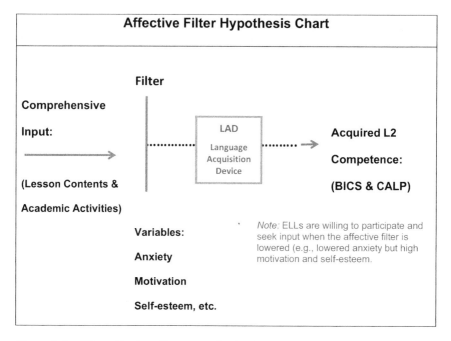

Figure 2.3.   The Affective Filter Hypothesis Chart, based on Krashen (1982).

What can classroom teachers do to lower ELLs' anxiety and motivate them to learn? The initial interaction between ELLs and the classroom teacher and peers plays an important role in helping them get adjusted to the new learning environment. Whether or not they feel being accepted as valued members of the learning community is significantly important to either increase their anxiety or motivate them to participate in class activities. Some of the things that the teachers can do to welcome new ELLs may include touring ELLs around the campus, introducing them to the school personnel, assigning them a buddy, or embracing their cultures by inviting them to share about their cultures and languages. These are some recommended practices to help lower ELLs' affective filter after they first arrive.

SUMMARY

This chapter discusses the theoretical perspectives in L2 acquisition theories, such as BICS, CALP, Affective Filter, and Comprehensive Input. Like the process of learning the first language or acquiring the native language, ELL students develop their English language proficiency through interaction and meaningful input in a contextualized linguistic environment. ELLs develop BICS and CALP at different paces. It takes 6 months to 2 years to develop BICS but 3 to 5 years to develop CALP. Providing context-embedded support helps ELLs have access to the cognitively demanding content areas. Meaningful, comprehensive input at the learners' instructional level and slightly beyond is essential to helping ELLs continuously develop their English proficiency level. Lowering the affective filter in the classroom motivates ELL students to seek more input and to be more willing to meet the challenge.

REFERENCES

Bartolomè, L. I. (1998). *The misteaching of academic discourses.* Boulder, CO: Westview.

Bloom, B. (1956a). *Bloom's taxonomy.* Retrieved from http://www.bloomstaxonomy.org/Blooms%20Taxonomy%20questions.pdf

Bloom, B. S. (1956b). *Taxonomy of educational objectives, Handbook I: The cognitive domain.* New York, NY: McKay.

Collier, V. P. (1987). Age and rate of acquisition of second language for academic purposes. *TESOL Quarterly, 21*(4), 617–641.

Cummins, J. (1984). *Bilingualism and special education: Issues in assessment pedagogy.* San Francisco, CA: College-Hill Press.

Donato, R. (1994). Collective scaffolding in second language learning. In J. Lantolf & G. Apple (Eds.), *Vygotskyan approaches to second language research* (pp. 33–56). Norwood, NJ: Ablex.

Echevarria, J., Vogt, M., & Short, D. J. (2010). *Making content comprehensible for secondary English learners: The SIOP model.* Boston, MA: Allyn & Bacon.

Edelsky, C. (2006). *With literacy and justice for all: Rethinking the social in language and education* (3rd ed.). London, UK: Falmer.

Ericsson, K. A. (2006). The influence of experience and deliberate practice on the development of superior expert performance. In K. A. Ericsson, N. Charness, P. Feltovich, & R. R. Hoffman (Eds.), *Cambridge handbook of expertise and expert performance* (pp. 685–706). Cambridge, UK: Cambridge University Press.

Gardner, P. (2012). *Teaching and learning in multicultural classrooms.* New York, NY: Routledge.

Gee, J. P. (1990). *Sociolinguistics and illiteracies: Idealogy in discourses.* London, UK: Falmer.

Gottlieb, M., Katz, A., & Ernst-Slavit, G. (2009). *Paper to practice: Using the TESOL English language proficiency standards in PreK–12 classrooms.* Alexandria, VA: Teachers of English to Speakers of Other Languages.

Krashen, S. (1982). *Principles and practice in second language acquisition.* London, UK: Prentice Hall.

Lantolf, J. P. (2000). *Socialcultural theory and second language learning.* Oxford, UK: Oxford University Press.

MacSwan, J., & Rolstad, K. (2003). Linguistic diversity, schooling, and social class: Rethinking our conception of language proficiency in language minority education. In C. B. Paulston & R. Tucker (Eds.), *Sociolinguistics: The essential readings* (pp. 329–340). Oxford, UK: Blackwell.

Scarcella, R. (2003). *Accelerating academic English: A focus on English language learners.* Oakland, CA: Regents of the University of California.

Vygotsky, L. S. (1978). *Mind in society: Development of higher psychological processes.* Cambridge, MA: Harvard University Press.

CHAPTER 3

TEACHING ELLS IN CLASSROOMS

CASE SCENARIO

Martina arrived in America a week after she celebrated her 14th birthday. Although she was nervous about going to a new country where she did not speak the language, she was excited to see her father, who had left Mexico 5 years before and was working on a small chicken farm. Martina boarded the bus to Arizona and left her mother, grandmother, a cousin, and her friends. The bus trip took 2 days before she finally arrived. Her father enrolled her in a public school, where the Guidance Counselor asked her father to complete a Home Language Survey in Spanish. The survey asked many questions. Martina could understand these questions. Yet, as to what the people in school were saying, she had no clue. Her father spoke a little English and was able to explain to Martina that she would be in the ninth grade. She completed the eighth grade and was a good student in Mexico. Here on her first day at school, she was paralyzed, and everything was in English. However, she was greeted by a smiling teacher, who told Martina that she was her ESOL teacher. The ESOL teacher told Martina that she was going to take a test to see how much she understood English. Of course, Martina did not know what the teacher was saying, but she understood the gesture of asking her to follow. When she looked at the test, everything was in English. Martina started crying and knew that school would be difficult. Soon she was attending an English class where the teacher was as nervous as Martina because she had never had a non-

A Book for Every Teacher: Teaching English Language Learners
pp. 39–80
Copyright © 2015 by Information Age Publishing
All rights of reproduction in any form reserved.

English-speaking student before. The lesson was on Macbeth. The teacher wondered how she was going to teach this ELL who did not speak, read, write, or comprehend a word of English.

The above scenario occurs daily in schools, from big cities to small towns of every state across the country. Schools in the United States are facing the ever-present challenge of providing effective instruction for a growing population of immigrant students, most of which are ELLs (Egbert & Ernst-Slavit, 2010; OELA, 2010; Zacarian & Haynes, 2012). From the school year 1997–1998 to 2008–2009, the number of English-language learners enrolled in U.S. public schools increased from 3.5 million to 5.3 million, an increase of 51%, according to a 2012 Report from the National Clearinghouse for English Language Acquisition (NCELA, 2012). During the same period, the general population of students grew by only 7.2% (OELA, 2010). As the number of immigrants from many countries continues to grow, teachers are faced with the challenge of how to best help children who come to school with little or no English.

In the above case scenario, we can see that the frustration is on both sides on the first day at school between the teacher and the ELL. The teacher is frustrated not knowing what to do. She knew that she could not just watch Martina sit quietly in the corner of her classroom without taking any action. Yet should she give this ELL the same materials but speak a little slower so that the ELL could understand? What will happen when the ELL needs to take the standardized test in the spring? To help teachers deal with this challenge as described in the scenario and faced by many teachers daily, this chapter provides specific lesson plan models and useful instructional strategies to help the them prepare lessons. Most of these teaching strategies, such as using visual aids, relating previous knowledge, and presenting contextual information, have been proven to work in classrooms.

Planning to Teach

Due to the challenge that confronts teachers daily on how to work with ELLs, researchers have been in search for answers. Data reveals that teachers' lack of preparation has made the situation worse in meeting the needs of the English language learners. The official report from the Office of English Language Acquisition in the U.S. Department of Education indicates that the national ratio of ESL-certified teachers to ELL students is 1 to 44, with many states with even higher numbers (OELA, 2010). The OELA data also indicates that professional development needs attention because a growing number of teachers who have English learners in their classrooms have little or no preparation. The National Center for Education Statistics survey data also reveals that 42% of teachers reported having ELLs in their classrooms; yet only 12.5% had received more than 8 hours of training geared toward educating ELLs (Jong & Harper, 2005). However, since the Supreme Court ruling in the *Lau v. Nichols* case in 1974 (U.S. Department of Education, n.d.), teachers and schools have to ensure that the students whose first language is not English receive equal services when it comes to the delivery of instruction. For instance, here is an excerpt from this ruling as the guidelines for teachers:

> The failure of the San Francisco school system to provide English language instruction to approximately 1,800 students of Chinese ancestry who do not speak English, or to provide them with other adequate instructional procedures, denies them a meaningful opportunity to participate in the public educational program and thus violates § 601 of the Civil Rights Act of 1964.... Where inability to speak and understand the English language excludes national origin-minority group children from effective participation in the educational program offered by a school district, the district must take affirmative steps to rectify the language deficiency in order to open its instructional program to these students ... designed to meet such language skill needs as soon as possible and must not operate as an educational dead end or permanent track.

With this ruling, school districts and educational experts have sought various ways to deliver adequate educational services to ELL students. Many approaches and philosophies on teaching English language learners have been created and implemented. Among them, the SIOP model is among the most successful and widely accepted models.

SIOP Lesson Model

The term SIOP stands for *Sheltered Instruction Observation Protocol*. It is considered as an empirically tested approach that helps teachers prepare all students, especially English language learners, to become college and career ready (Person, 2013). The SIOP model was developed by Dr. Jana Echevarria, Dr. Mary Ellen Vogt, and Dr. Deborah Short as a framework for mainstream teachers to effectively teach ELLs and give the students like Martina access to content areas. This model of teaching has been tested among mainstream teachers across the country, and now many schools with growing number of English language learners are implementing this teaching model with much success.

Teachers should know that, for school-age ELL students, academic language is crucially important for the students' school success (Francis, Rivera, Lesaux, Kieffer, & Rivera, 2006). The SIOP model helps ELL students like Martina, who would be graduating from school in a few years, to meet their linguistic and academic needs simultaneously. Teachers can also provide ELLs with access to content areas for a beginner English learner if they implement the SIOP model. In addition, research shows that English learners acquire English best when language forms are explicitly taught and when the students have many opportunities to practice the language in meaningful contexts (Goldenberg, 2008). In this chapter, the SIOP model will be introduced and explained in detail, with activities for implementation. Specifically, the SIOP model consists of these eight interrelated components:

- Lesson preparation
- Building background
- Comprehensible input
- Strategies
- Interaction
- Practice/Application
- Lesson delivery
- Review/Assessment

Component #1: Lesson Preparation

The SIOP model requires teachers to incorporate these components when planning and preparing a lesson: clearly define *content* and *language objectives* (i.e., write on the board and as well as state these objectives orally); choose age-appropriate *content concepts* (i.e., appropriate for the educational background of students); use *supplementary materials* to make lessons clear and meaningful; adapt content to all levels of student *proficiency* (i.e., using graphic organizers, study guides, taped texts, jigsaw reading); provide meaningful and authentic *activities* that integrate lesson concepts with language practice and opportunities (i.e., surveys, letter writing, making models, plays, games).

To clearly define the *content* and *language objectives* means that teachers need both to write and state these objectives and review them with students at the beginning and the end of the lesson to see whether the objectives have been met. *Content objectives* need to state the content that the students need to know. When writing the content objectives, teachers should make language student-friendly while not simplifying the content. *Language objectives* should specify the type of language that students need to learn in order to accomplish the lesson content objectives. Quality language objectives should complement the content knowledge and skills identified in content area standards and address the aspects of academic language that will be developed or reinforced during the teaching of

Table 3.1.   Writing Content and Language Objectives

7th Grade Social Studies on Colonial Communities		
Content Area Standard	*Content Objective*	*Language Objective*
State Standard: Students will use a variety of intellectual skills to demonstrate their understanding of the geography of the interdependent world in which we live.	Students will be able to show how geographic features have affected colonial life by creating a map.	Students will be able to summarize in writing how geography impacted colonial life.

Note: For resources on the SIOP Lesson Plan Model tools, teachers can go to this website: http://siop.pearson.com/books-resources/index.html. The SIOP Lesson Plan Model template can be downloaded at http://www.gcu.edu/Documents/Education/Clinical-Practice-SIOP-Lesson-Plan-Template.pdf. There are also other modified SIOP lesson templates that can be downloaded for teaching with this website as an example: http://www.wl.k12.ia.us/Page/94.

grade-level content concepts. The language objectives should also cover the four aspects of the language skills (i.e., speaking, listening, reading, and writing), but they can also include the language functions related to the topic of the lesson (e.g., justify, hypothesize); vocabulary essential to a student being able to fully participate in the lesson (e.g., axis, locate, graph); and language-learning strategies to aid in comprehension (Echevarria, Vogt, & Short, 2010; Thrower, 2009). Table 3.1 is an example of how to write content and language objectives.

The SIOP lesson model requires teachers also to choose *content concepts* that are appropriate for the age and educational background of students. For example, teachers need to consider the ELL students' L1 literacy, L2 proficiency, and the reading level of the materials. It is also important that mainstream teachers collaborate with ESOL teachers and discuss ELL student information in order to plan well for instruction. In preparing a lesson, teachers must also select *supplementary materials* to be used to promote comprehension. These include charts, graphs, pictures, illustrations, realia, math manipulatives, multimedia, and demonstrations by teacher and other students. Teachers also need to adapt content to all levels of student *proficiency* by using appropriate graphic organizers, study guides, taped texts, and jigsaw reading. The use of these materials can promote higher critical thinking and engage students in interacting with various resources instead of listening to lectures that could be boring to children. Finally, teachers must also prepare to engage students in *meaningful activities* that integrate lesson concepts with language and also provide opportunities to practice listening, speaking, reading, and writing across content areas in the learning process.

Component #2: Building Background

Building background requires that teachers link concepts to students' backgrounds and experiences. These backgrounds and experiences can be personal, cultural, or academic. A reader's schema knowledge of the world provides a basis for understanding, learning, and remembering facts and ideas found in texts. Teachers must know that ELLs from culturally diverse backgrounds may struggle to comprehend texts and concepts due to a mismatch in schema. It is important for teachers to know their students' background, not assuming that the students understand the context of the lesson. For example, if the lesson is related to winter activities like sledding or skiing, many students from the Hispanic background may not have even seen a photo of a sled. If they have, they may not know how it is used unless a teacher can bring a real sample of a sled or show a video of people sledding. Now, they may have something similar that they use in their country for a race through the sand or in the desert. Most reading material, such as content area texts, relies on an assumption of common prior knowledge and experience.

In building background knowledge, it is also important to recognize the value of vocabulary development or vocabulary proficiency. Knowledge of vocabulary correlates strongly with academic achievement and reading comprehension. Students' limited vocabulary can hinder them in comprehending content texts, following instructions correctly, in directions for completing assignments, or overall academic achievement. In math, there are many words that students need to be taught explicitly, such as *addition, subtraction, continent, sentence, classify, summarize, identify, beaker, compare, paragraph.* Key vocabulary words must be emphasized (e.g., introduced, written, repeated, and highlighted for students to see). Do not just say it but show it; write it; give illustrations; give examples and be more powerful; discuss and ask students what they know. A great teacher must also explicitly link past learning to new concepts. After all, students are not just blank slates, even if they may have limited knowledge of English. By linking past knowledge to the lesson, a teacher is making learning relevant. One great way is to link student background knowledge is to use the graphic organizer, such as the K-W-L chart. Ask the students *what* they already know about the topic, what they *want* to know, and after the lesson has been completed, students should write or state what they have *learned*. This chart is a great way to activate students' background knowledge.

Component #3: Comprehensible Input

The SIOP model requires that teachers use speech that is appropriate for students' language proficiency level so that it is comprehensible to them. For example, students who are at the beginning levels of English proficiency benefit from teachers who slow down their rate of speech, use pauses, and enunciate clearly while speaking. As students become more comfortable with the language and acquire higher levels of proficiency, a slower rate becomes unnecessary. In fact, for advanced and transitional students, teachers should use a rate of speech that is normal for a regular classroom. Effective teachers adjust their rate of speech and enunciation to their students' levels of English proficiency. Students will respond according to their proficiency level. The following is an example of using appropriate speech for different levels of ELL students who have different English proficiency when asking them to describe the setting in a story related to the cold day:

- Level 1: (No response, not sure what setting is yet or in silent period)
- Level 2: "Cold day."
- Level 3: "The day is cold and there is snow."
- Level 4: "The day is very cold and heavy snow is falling."
- Level 5: "It is a cold, winter day, and it is snowing more heavily than usual."
- Level 6: "The unusually heavy snow on the day the story takes place causes a number of problems for the characters."

Paraphrasing and repetition enhance understanding for ELLs and all students. Brain research tells us that repetition strengthens connections in the brain (Jensen, 2005). ELLs benefit from repeated exposures to a word in order to hear it accurately because they often lack the auditory acuity to decipher sounds of English words. Teachers should also explain academic tasks clearly and use a variety of techniques to make content concepts clear; for example, modeling, visuals, hands-on activities, demonstrations, gestures, body language (Thrower, 2009). An example of a clear explanation of tasks is to write on the board for a reading selection which contains lots of words about people, places, and things in the community as follows:

- Read the story together.
- Read word cards with your partner.
- Place each card in a column: people, places, things.
- Tell your partner why the card goes in that column.
- The teacher goes over each step showing visuals with each step.

Use of a variety of techniques helps make content concepts clear. These techniques could include modeling, hands-on materials, visuals, demos, gestures, film or video clips. Yet teachers need to focus attention selectively on the most important information, introduce new learning in context, and help students learn strategies such as predicting, summarizing.

Component #4: Strategies

   Teachers must provide many opportunities for students to use strategies such as problem solving, predicting, organizing, summarizing, categorizing, evaluating, and self-monitoring. These learning strategies should be taught through explicit instruction to help students develop independence for self-monitoring. Scaffolding techniques should be used consistently throughout the lesson with the right amount of support to move students from one level of understanding to a higher level. When introducing a new concept, teachers should use scaffolding but gradually decrease support as time goes on. The following are several strategies teachers can use to help students build strategies to learn productively:

- Use visual cues, such as pictures, objects, gestures, demonstrations, graphic organizers, and hands-on learning. These visuals increase comprehension by equating words with the objects and ideas they represent. Refraining from using idioms, speaking slowly and clearly, and finding ways to repeat the words, phrases, or sentences are useful strategies in increasing lesson comprehension (Allen & Franklin, 2002).

- Preparing thematic units that reuse or recycle vocabulary is a good strategy to help reinforce important concepts for ELLs and all students. For example, teachers can encourage the students to reuse vocabulary connected to the topic by putting pictures around the walls of the classroom and ask the students to walk around to look at the pictures/photos and stop next to one that they want to talk about.

- Utilize multicultural/bilingual texts that reflect the backgrounds of the students to help students respond better to texts (Drucker, 2003). These types of text capture their interest and encourage them to work harder to understand the content. Teachers can even further enhance the reading comprehension skills of ELLs by providing audiotapes corresponding to the text they are reading. This can be recorded by the teacher or another student. This gives ELLs more opportunities to hear the spoken word and equate it with its graphic representation on the page (Drucker, 2003).

- Building collaborative learning communities enhances ELLs' learning experiences. Teachers can pair ELLs with an English-speaking "buddy" to read text together, encouraging reading and pronunciation development. Students often feel less intimidated working in a one-on-one situation with no fear of being laughed at by the entire class. Teachers may also use the *Language Experience Approach* within the paired students. The ELL can orally describe a personal experience and the buddy can write the response and repeat it back to the ELL. This tactic helps ELLs learn how language is encoded and builds sight-word knowledge and fluency (Reed & Railsback, 2003).

• Making appropriate accommodations for ELL students is another important way, especially during state assessments. Teachers should offer ELLs extra time, bilingual dictionaries or glossaries, and clarify the meaning of words on tests when they do not relate to the test content (Echevarria et al., 2010). Teachers may also read the directions or even simplify the questions on the test without altering the difficulty of the content so that ELLs can understand the content being tested.

Component #5: Interaction

Teachers should provide opportunities for interaction and discussion between teacher and student and among students, and encourage elaborated responses. To fully connect with the content concepts and develop a deeper understanding of the content-specific vocabulary, ELLs must have opportunities to use the language in authentic situations. Opportunities to interact with others also create an environment for students to develop oral literacy. Thus, when designing a lesson, teachers must plan activities that give students opportunities to talk with their peers about the key concepts by using the key vocabulary terms. Corporative learning is a great way for ELLs to interact with peers, and teachers can use activities such as clock buddies, pair-shares, and cooperative groups.

Sometimes, ELLs may struggle to respond appropriately to teachers' prompts and questions because questions are not clearly understood. Teachers should provide clarity and give enough waiting time to promote higher-order thinking. ELLs may also come from cultures that do not expect students to ask or answer questions during class time. These students often perceive the teacher to have elevated status and think that, as students, they should respectfully listen rather than talk in the company of their teachers. In this case, teachers should be patient and encouraging. Technology can help engage students in the interactive world. Teachers can use technology resources to involve students in an active, dynamic, and interactive learning process instead of being a passive bystander. In all, benefits of interaction are many, such as increased comprehension, personalized input, feedback on output, opportunities for hypothesis testing, and identifying gaps in knowledge. To be proficient and productive learners, ELLs must have many opportunities to interact with peers and teachers.

Component #6: Practice and Application

Teachers should provide hands-on materials and manipulatives for students to have opportunities to practice when learning new knowledge. Teachers also need to provide activities for students to apply content and language knowledge in the classroom. These activities need to integrate all four language skills: reading, writing, listening, and speaking (Echevarria et al., 2010). Students have a greater chance of mastering content concepts and skills when they are given multiple opportunities to practice in relevant, meaningful ways. Reading, writing, listening, and speaking are complex, cognitive language processes that are interrelated and integrated. These four language processes are also mutually supportive. Although the relationships among these language processes are complex, practice in any one domain promotes the development in the others.

As mentioned, the purpose of practice is to increase the chances for students to remember what they have learned and transfer that learning to new situations. When planning hands-on activities to practice, teachers may want to know how long the practice should be. Hunter (1982) suggests that teachers keep these questions and answers in mind when practicing:

Questions	Answers
How much material should be practiced at one time?	It should be a short meaningful amount and always use meaning to divide content into parts.
2. How long should a practice period be?	It should be a short time so the student exerts intense effort and has intent to learn.
3. How often should students practice?	For new learning, practice should be massive; for older learning, practice should be distributed.
4. How should teachers give feedback?	It should be frequent, early, positive feedback that supports students' beliefs they can do well.

For ELL students acquiring a new language, the need to apply new information is critically important because discussing or *doing* makes abstract concepts concrete. Application can occur in a number of ways, such as clustering, using graphic organizers, solving problems in cooperative learning groups, writing a journal, engaging in discussion circles, or a variety of other meaningful activities (Peregoy & Boyle, 2005).

Component #7: Lesson Delivery

The SIOP lesson model requires teachers to effectively deliver each lesson by supporting the content and language objectives. To support content objectives in the lesson delivery, teachers should write these objectives in a student-friendly format, focusing on the lesson content, providing a structure for classroom procedures, allowing students to know the direction of the lesson, and helping students on task. To support lesson delivery, language objectives may be related to an ESL strand. For example, students will write to communicate with different audiences for different reasons. Language objectives may also be related to the teachers' scope and sequence of language skills that their own students need to develop. For example, students will make text-self and text-world connections. In addition, language objectives must be addressed explicitly during the lesson and reviewed at the end. Teachers should also pace the lesson appropriately to the students' ability level.

Generally, teachers should engage students approximately from 90% to 100% of the class period for lesson delivery. This means that students should take part in tasks throughout the lesson. This also requires that teachers be sure that students are able to follow the lesson, respond to teacher directions, and perform activities as expected. Teachers must also balance time by allocating class time appropriately and by engaging students in appropriate time. Effective teachers balance teacher presentation time and the time for students to practice and apply the information in meaningful ways. Students need to have time for active participation. The more actively students participate in the instructional process, the more they achieve (Hunter, 1982). Thus, it is important to create interesting and fun activities relevant to the lesson objectives and pace the lesson to students' ability so as to reduce boredom, inattention, or off-task behaviors in order to deliver each lesson that maximizes student engagement.

Component #8: Review and Assessment

The process of review and assessment is to gather and synthesize information concerning students' learning. In gathering this information about what students understand or do not understand, teachers can adjust their instructional plan accordingly. Basic features of review and assessment should include these components: comprehensive review of key vocabulary, comprehensive review of key content concepts, regular feedback provided to students on their output, assessment of student comprehension, and learning of all lesson objectives throughout the lesson.

Comprehensive review of *key vocabulary* and *key concepts* means that teachers take the time to review and summarize key vocabulary and concepts throughout the lesson and wrap up at the end of the lesson. There are several ways to review vocabulary words. For example, teachers can help students review words in nonprint ways, such as using the pictures in a picture dictionary or using games, for example, flyswatter and Jeopardy. An example of comprehensive review of key concepts in a lesson can be demonstrated by reviewing Egyptian mummification. Teachers might say something like, "Up to this point, we learned that little was known about Mummy No. 1770 until it was donated to the museum. After the scientists completed the autopsy, they discovered three important things. Who remembers what they were?"

It is important to link the review to content objectives so that the students stay focused on the basic content concepts. Students' responses to review should guide the decisions on what to do next, such as summative evaluation or additional reteaching if needed. A favorite wrap-up technique for many teachers is the use of outcome sentences. A teacher can post sentence starters on the board or on a transparency to review and wrap up the lesson:

- I have learned …
- I wonder …
- I still want to know …
- I still have a question about …
- I still don't know …
- I discovered …

It is also important to provide regular feedback. Periodic review of language, vocabulary, and content enables teachers to provide specific academic feedback that clarifies and corrects misconceptions and misunderstandings. Such feedback helps students' proficiency in English when it is supportive and validating. Teachers should also provide assessment of student comprehension and learning of all lesson objectives throughout the lesson. Such assessment, as evidenced in lesson plans and in periodic review, should be used to determine if students understand and are able to apply content concepts. The format of assessment should be multidimensional, with multiple indicators that reflect student learning. For example, portfolio assessment is an authentic way to gather information on student learning over the period.

Total Physical Response

Another popular approach in teaching ELLs is the Total Physical Response (TPR) method. This method was developed by James Asher in the 1960s and it is based on the theory that the memory is enhanced through association with physical movement (Byram, 2000). Thus, TPR incorporates physical movement to react on verbal input. It allows students to react to language without thinking too much and therefore reduces stress, lowers affective filter, and facilitates long-term retention. Asher developed this method based on his observation of interactions between parents and children: (a) language is learned primarily by listening, (b) language learning must engage the right hemisphere of the brain, and (c) learning language should not involve stress. TPR often used alongside other methods is popular with beginner ELLs and with other young learners, although it can be used with students of all levels.

The TPR approach is supported by theories. It is believed that the left brain is for logical function when analyzing, talking, or discussing is involved. Most classroom activities are aimed at the left brain. The right brain is used when moving, acting, using metaphor, drawing, pointing, and such. It is targeted by sports and extracurricular activities. When language is taught by lecturing or explaining, the left brain is targeted and the information is kept in the short-term memory. It will be soon forgotten if it never becomes *real* to the student. When language is taught actively through movement, the right brain retains the information, in the same way that skills such as swimming or riding a bicycle are remembered in the long term.

Teachers using TPR usually give commands to students in the target language, and students respond with whole-body actions. For example, teachers can use TPR to teach action words, such as words related to body movements. An example is to teach the movement of *stand up* and *sit down*. Teacher and students can sit in a circle. The teacher makes the movement by standing up while saying the words, "Stand up" and using a gesture to command all students to stand up. Then, the teacher can sit down while saying the words, "Sit down" and using the gesture to tell students to sit up. The teacher can repeat the movement a few times until the students understand these words through command and action. Similarly, the teacher can teach other action words, such as *touching shoulder*, *walking*, *stopping*, and *turning around*. TPR can also help introduce speaking. For example, the teacher can play a ball game by throwing a soft ball to one student when saying clearly, "Tom, catch the ball." Then ask the student, "Tom, throw the ball back to me" with a gesture and clue. Then repeat this action with the second and third students and among students and ask students to speak in action. The teacher can then ask, "Who has the ball?" TPR can be used along with other teaching strategies to enhance the ELLs' understanding and learning success. Other teaching strategies will be introduced in the following sections with the purpose of helping teachers to engage ELLs and learn productively.

Teaching Strategies

Teaching strategies refers to the combined instructional methods, learning activities, and materials that are used to help actively engage students and that reflect learning goals to improve student learning outcomes. An effective teacher chooses a strategy to fit a particular situation. It's important to consider what students already know and the learning goals for the specific situation. In this section, different teaching strategies are introduced to help teachers better work with the ELLs and all students. These strategies discussed in these categories are *using visual aids*, *relating to existing knowledge*, *presenting contextualized information*, *other teaching tips*, and *integrating technology*. Many of these strategies have been used by teachers and proven to help improve student learning outcomes and achieve their academic goals. Mainstream classroom teachers should be able to implement these teaching strategies easily and use them help their ELLs with access to the academic contents.

Using Visual Aids

Visual aids refers to a device (e.g., a picture, image, chart, map, gesture, or model) that students can look at and that is used to make learning easier to understand. Using visual aids can help students visualize information and convey an idea in a vivid way for ELLs and all students, especially for those ELLs who have language barriers to understanding the concepts. When using visual aids in classrooms, teachers not only provide supplementary information to students, but the visual aids show visual images that allow students to connect a topic to what it looks like and increase students' interest. There are many types of visual aids teachers can use and adapt creatively to make learning motivational and comprehensible.

Using Pictures and Images

Using pictures and images is a powerful way to build student engagement and interest. This is because pictures and images can help ELLs make the connection between what is presented to them and what it means in a visualized context. Teachers can use pictures, images, or even real objects to help ELLs understand the concepts. Technology also provides easy access to downloading many forms of pictures and images. For example, teachers can download any images easily by using the Google search engine to find pictures and images to help ELLs learn the concept.

Earthquake is an abstract concept. Without an image, it is difficult to explain to ELLs. Yet, if the teacher types the words, "earthquake images" in the Google search, tons of images and pictures on earthquakes can help ELL students make an instinctive connection to the concept. Many cartoon pictures and images can also be found by a Google search to make learning more interesting.

Using Graphic Organizers

A graphic organizer is a communication tool through visual symbols to express knowledge, concepts, thoughts, ideas, and relationships. A graphic organizer is also seen as a knowledge map, concept map, cognitive organizer, advance organizer, or concept diagram. Graphic organizers make concepts and information more accessible to ELLs and all students and make complex information manageable because they help organize information in a meaningful way. There are many different graphic organizers, such as a K-W-L chart, sematic map, Venn Diagram, flow chart, and story map. Using the story map as an example, it helps students organize the story, that is, the main character, place and time, order of events, and the ending. A story map sample is provided in Table 3.2, and teachers can use it to help ELLs organize the story for better understanding. For more graphic organizers for ELLs, teachers can visit Judy Haynes' everythingESL.net, which provides many free graphic organizers for teaching ELLs: http://www.everythingesl.net/inservices/graphic_organizers.php.

Semantic Mapping

Semantic mapping is a visual strategy that graphically represents concepts and portrays schematic relations that compose the concept. Semantic mapping is introduced because this visual aid can help ELLs expand vocabulary. Based on prior knowledge, it helps display word categories and how they are related to one another. A unique feature of semantic mapping is that it recognizes important components and shows the relationships among the concepts. For example, when discussing food, teachers can create a semantic map to help students expand their vocabulary based on categories (see Figure 3.1). With modeling, the teacher can ask students to provide food categories they know and use the semantic map to confirm familiar words and learn new vocabulary. Teacher can encourage ELLs to also share food items that they consume in their cultures. This strategy can even be used for previewing and assessing how much knowledge students have about the concepts.

Table 3.2.   Story Map

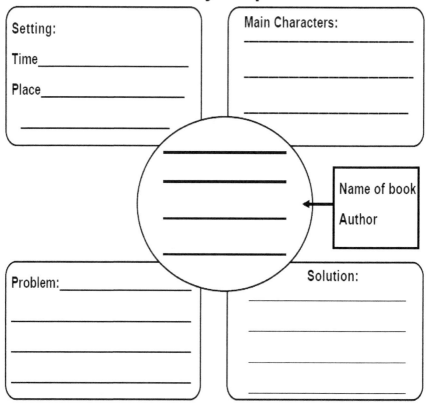

Source: http://www.everythingesl.net/downloads/story_map.pdf

K-W-L Chart Strategy

The K-W-L chart is an instructional strategy that helps students better understand through reading a text. The teacher can guide students by start with brainstorming about things they *know* about a topic and having an initial discussion with the students to ask what already know about this topic in the text. This information is recorded in the *K* column of a K-W-L chart. The teacher can then ask students what they *want* to know and generate a list of questions about what they want to know about the topic. This information is listed in the *W* column of the chart. After reading, students answer the questions that are in the W column. Ask the students to

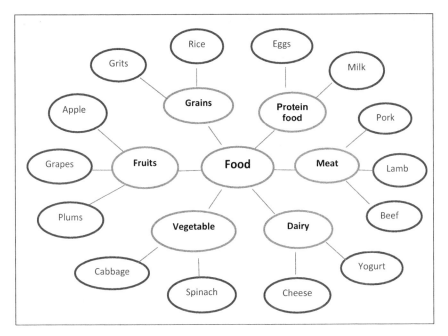

Figure 3.1.　Example of the semantic map to teach food concepts. The orange color in the center is the main concept and green is for categories and blue is for specific food items.

write down what they have learned from the reading. This information that they have *learned* is recorded in the *L* column of the K-W-L chart. To use a K-W-L strategy, the teacher can create a chart easily on the smart-board or on an overhead transparency. In addition, students should have their own chart on which to record information. See the example of a K-W-L chart in Figure 3.2.

Many other visual aids, such as the Venn diagram, flow chats, flash-cards, videos, or artworks, can be used making learning easier. When a graphic organizer is designed, teachers can expand its use or adapt it to teach other learning concepts. The following websites provide graphic organizer information in subject areas with interactive activities. Teachers can find and download a graphic organizer and print it out for learning.

1. Venn Diagram: a graphic organizer with a set of diagrams that shows all possible logical relations between concepts. Venn diagrams were created around 1880 by John Venn, an English logician and philosopher. Here is a useful link on Venn Diagrams: http://www.readingquest.org/strat/venn.html

K	W	L

Figure 3.3.   Example of a K-W-L chart to help students.

2. K-W-L-S Chart: this is an extension of the KWL strategy and K-W-L-S stands for what I already *know*, what I *want* to know, what I have *learned*, and what I *still want* to know. Here is a link for the K-W-L-S chart: http://www.readwritethink.org/files/resources/lesson_images/lesson398/kwls2.pdf

3. More useful graphic organizers that teachers can download from these links:
    http://edhelper.com/teachers/graphic_organizers.htm
    http://www.eduplace.com/graphicorganizer/
    https://www.teachervision.com/graphic-organizers/printable/6293.html

Relating to Existing Knowledge

Prior knowledge affects how students perceive new information, and relating existing knowledge can help make learning easier. This is because students cannot be perceived as blank slates to passively inscribe. Even ELLs bring their interpretation associated with their existing knowledge and cultural background. Therefore, learning new information is often conditioned by what they already know about a concept, and it is closely related to their particular background knowledge or cultural information. When teachers link new information to their existing knowledge, it activates the students' interest and curiosity. Schema theory also indicates that personal previous experiences, knowledge, emotions, and understandings affect what and how people learn new information (Harvey & Goudvis, 2000).

Providing Background Information

Providing background information helps students make connection. Here is a scenario explaining why it is important. An ESOL teacher was decorating the classroom with ELLs for Easter. Colorful eggs and an Easter bunny were created. A new ELL suddenly pointed to the bunny and said that this was wrong. To this ELL growing up in a farm country, chickens should be associated with eggs instead of a bunny. The ELL student could not make the connection because of the lack of background information. Therefore, helping ELLs build background and make the connection is important. Egbert and Ernst-Slavit (2010) believe that language is vital to content access and thus to academic achievement. In their book, *Access to Academics: Planning Instruction for K-12 Classrooms with ELLs*, the authors suggest using three types of connection to improve student learning: personal, academic content, and instructional connection.

1. *Personal connection.* Teachers need to help students connect learning to their personal experiences. Making personal connections can make learning accessible by connecting students' personal experiences. For example, teachers can use students' familiar experiences such as exercises to make connections. ELLs may have some types of exercises that American students do not have, yet they may never have a chance to, for instance, learn to ski. Graphic organizers, for example, the chart of text-self and text-world connection, can be a useful tool to help students make personal connection (see Table 3.3).

2. *Academic content connection.* Making academic connection means to connect learning content in a meaningful way and make it connected and accessible. For example, teachers can connect current learning to past learning by reviewing previous lessons or making connections across content areas. In a math lesson, the teacher can make language connections by asking students, "Sophia had five peaches. She gave Tom two. How many peaches are *left* in her basket?" The purpose of this math problem is to teach the concept of subtraction. Yet the teacher can also teach the language. After using the word, "left," the teacher can introduce new phrases and alternatives, such as *"What is the difference now in Sophia's basket?"* or *"How many peaches are still there in her basket?"* In doing so, teachers are making academic connections.

3. *Instructional connection.* Instructional connection means that teachers provide instructional support to help students make connec-

tions by using instructional strategies to make learning productive. For example, teachers can invite guest speakers to talk about experiences relevant to the lesson content and help students make connections; teachers can also assign students to work on a project through research to make connections related to students' needs, interests, learning styles, and cultural and linguistic backgrounds for instructional connections. In all, it is important that teachers build background by making connections through a variety of means and strategies.

Preteaching

Preteaching is a strategy of teaching students before an activity. For example, ELLs are going to hear a discussion on the topic of environmental issues. Before listening, the teacher can help the students match key environment words to definitions. Or teachers can also give students a list of words and look up any of the words on the list that they don't know. Then discuss the words and ask students to guess what the text will be about. Such preteaching helps ELLs develop confidence in mainstream classrooms. Preteaching also helps the teacher find out what the students already know and what might cause problems. Thus, teachers

Table 3.3. Text-Self Chart to Make Personal Connections

Text-to-Self Connections	
Student Name: _____ Date: _____	
Title of the Story: _____	
Author: _____	
Choose a book you have read. Think about parts of the book that are similar to your own life and write or draw about them in the boxes below.	
In the Story	*In My Life*

Note: This text-self chart can be adapted to the text-world chart to help ELLs make connections.

should take time to preteach and identify problem areas. It is also a better idea to work in a small group to avoid overwhelming ELLs when pre-teaching concepts.

Making Vocabulary Connections

Teachers can help ELLs make vocabulary connections by exploring new meanings from familiar words. This strategy helps ELLs expand their vocabulary based on existing words. For example, when teaching vocabulary, teachers can guide students to explore new meanings in the context of familiar words, such as finding *synonyms*, *antonyms*, *homophones*, or *homonyms* to expend their vocabulary. In this way, teachers are helping students enlarge their vocabulary words and make connections from familiar words to new meanings. Instead of presenting the students with those new words, teachers can encourage ELLs to be active learners and find new meanings by doing. Helping ELLs create a chart and listing the familiar words to compare with new meanings can be a helpful tool (see Table 3.4).

Preview Survey

The purpose of preview survey is to find out what students know and don't know. Although the K-W-L chart strategy is helpful, ELLs may struggle with writing down what they know or don't know. This is because they may have developed basic oral English skills but not cognitive academic language proficiency. Thus, they may not be able to write down the ideas or what they have known about the topic. Yet creating a brief survey that *connects to the students' existing scheme* can help ELLs overcome this barrier. For example, a "True" or "False" preview survey can help find out ELLs' knowledge level. The survey can be also used as the pre-assessment tool. The following is an example of such preview survey:

Table 3.4. Making Vocabulary Connections: Connect Familiar Words With New Meanings

Familiar words	*New meanings*
I saw these words in the text:	I know the synonyms (or antonyms) are:

According to what you have known about hurricanes, please put either "T" for true or "F" for false in the blank.

- _____ Hurricanes are large storms with rotating winds.
- _____ Hurricanes usually happen in the summer.
- _____ A hurricane forms over oceans in tropical climate regions.
- _____ A hurricane has another name for tornados.
- _____ A hurricane can cause more damage than a tornado.
- _____ The wind speed of a hurricane is always over 100 kilometers per hour.
- _____ The eye of a hurricane can be up to 20 miles wide.
- _____ Hurricanes can cause severe flooding.

Presenting Contextual Information

Contextual information is relevant information that helps in understanding the text. Presenting contextual information requires the teacher to provide relevant contextual information about learning content. This strategy helps students understand the important concepts in the relevant context and helps with students' comprehension. For example, an arithmetic problem may be difficult to explain to students, but teachers can connect to the relevant real-life situation to *contextualize* the math problem and make it understandable for students. An example is that a teacher uses simple cooking ingredients that the students are familiar with to explain a math calculation concept, for example, a measuring cup with familiar ingredients.

Using Context and Modeling

Context refers to the circumstances that form the setting and environment for an event, statement, idea, or the background information that helps in understanding and accessing information. When providing the contextual information related to new content and providing modeling, the teacher helps students understand the meaning of a word more easily. For example, teachers can guide students to search for hints and clues. Modeling is an instructional strategy in which the teacher demonstrates a new concept or approach to learning, and students learn by observing. Theory of modeling as an instructional strategy indicates that it helps students' to better understand the content through modeling. Therefore, when teachers provide contextual information and also modeling, it helps unlock the meaning of an unfamiliar word by providing the context in which a new word appears. To provide modeling, the teacher can use a variety of contextual modalities, such as visual, auditory, or kinetics to help ELLs see, hear, and interact with the teacher and peers in the process for a better understanding of the new information and the concepts to be taught.

Using Idiomatic Expressions Related to Cultural Context

Teachers can find familiar idiomatic expressions that have similar meanings related to concepts and students' cultures. For example, the following sayings in English may be found in other cultures: "*Hit the nail on the head*," "*Bite off more than you can chew*," or "*Between a rock and a hard place.*" However, these idioms, proverbs, or expressions may have cultural connotations, so teachers need to explain them to ELLs. For example, a sent-home flyer with the invitation for an event may not be understood by ELLs and parents: "Come to join our tailgating party at 6:00 before the game starts." Tailgating is one American event that ELLs may not be familiar with. Therefore, teachers need to explain the words and their cultural connotation.

Writing down idiomatic words on the board is helpful. Encourage ELLs to see if they have similar sayings in their languages. Teachers can also help ELLs create an *Idiom & Expression Dictionary* (see Table 3.5) that connects English idioms and expressions with ones in the ELLs' culture, and encourage them to add a new expression each time when they learn a new idiomatic expression. The teacher should allow students to write idioms in their native languages. This strategy also offers the students an opportunity to share their own cultures and develop an ownership in learning. Teachers can also involve parents.

Table 3.5.   English Idiom and Expression Dictionary

English Idioms/Expressions	*Similar Idioms in My Culture*
Costs an arm and a leg. Meaning: Something very costly	In my language:
Hit the nail on the head. Meaning: Do something preciously right	In my language:
Between a rock and a hard place. Meaning: In a very difficult position	In my language:
Let the cat out of the bag. Meaning: Disclose a secret	In my language:
Bite off more than you can chew Meaning: Take more than one can handle	In my language:
Rob Peter to pay Paul. Meaning: Solving a problem that makes another problem worse	In my language:

Other Useful Tips and Integrating Technology

Thinking Aloud

Thinking aloud is a reading strategy that allows the teacher to model how a good reader thinks about text while reading. This strategy can be taught through explicit modeling, and it benefits ELLs and all students as they strive for deeper understanding of what they read. The teacher can model this strategy by reading an appropriate selection, stopping period-ically to make predictions, clarify meaning, decode words, make personal connections, question the author, and summarize what has been read. This strategy also helps students learn to monitor their thinking while reading the passage. It is relatively easy for teachers to use in the class-room. Teachers can discuss this strategy with students and show students how good readers often read, reread, read ahead to look for context clues and to make sense. Teachers can guide students to (a) connect what they are reading to their own life experience, (b) predict what is going to hap-pen next, (c) agree or disagree with what the author talks about, and (d) give their own opinion about a statement. The teacher can model this strategy by reading any appropriate text. For example, when teaching the poem by Langston Hughes (1926) entitled, "Dream Variations," which was published in his first collection entitled, *The Weary Blues*, teachers can read the poem and pause to demonstrate thinking aloud by talking about thoughts as follows:

> To fling my arms wide
> In some place of the sun,
> To whirl and to dance
> Till the white day is done.
> Then rest at cool evening
> Beneath a tall tree
> While night comes on gently,
> Dark like me—
> That is my dream!

The teacher may stop several times during reading to say things like, *"I'm picturing a young girl with bare feet who is twirling with her arms out-stretched." "I can see a large willow tree where she's sitting underneath when eve-ning comes." "The girl seems to have many dreams."* After modeling, the teacher can put students into groups of three or four and distribute cop-ies of a poem or reading text that is unfamiliar to each group, then direct students to read and use the think-aloud strategy. Each group should record the responses that were used.

The following are resourceful websites to further use the think-aloud strategy:

- Think Aloud Video: http://int.cysd.k12.pa.us/strategies/Reading/thinkaloud.htm
- Think Aloud Lesson Plan: http://www.readwritethink.org/lessons/lesson_view.asp?id=139
- Thinking Aloud and Reading Comprehension: http://www.readingrockets.org/strategies/think_alouds
- Teaching students think aloud: https://www.teachervision.com/skill-builder/problem-solving/48546.html

Thumb Up and Thumb Down

This strategy, commonly known as TUTD, is helpful for the ELLs, especially when they cannot express orally. It is also a fun way to test the student's knowledge. The teacher can ask ELLs to use their thumbs to *agree* or *disagree*. For example, the teacher can read a statement and ask students to put their thumbs up if they agree or thumbs down if they disagree with the statement. This technique can be used in a small group or a large group with a follow-up discussion on why they have their thumbs up or down. The teacher can use alternatives for TUTD. For instance, the teacher can ask students to clap their hands: once for *yes* and twice for *no*. Or the teacher can ask students to keep their heads up for *yes* and heads down for *no*. Teachers can also create a *yes* or *no* sign. If they agree with the answer, the students show the *yes* side; if they disagree, they turn to the *no* side. If students need movement, the teacher can ask them to stand up and move to one side if they agree and another side if they disagree after reading the statement. The movement can increase the students' participation and avoids routine boredom.

Teaching Transitional Words and Phrases

Transitional words or phrases can be compared to the *bridges* that carry a reader from section to section in reading. They function as road signs to help a reader understand the direction of thoughts and provide coherence in writing. Transitional words can indicate the relationship, such as cause and effect, compare and contrast, and time sequence. Transitional words and phrases are used between sentences and paragraphs. The teacher can teach ELLs transitions by highlighting, circling, or underlining transitional words in reading. Encouraging students to use different alternative transitional words to restate the sentence is a good strategy. Learning transitional words and phrases also helps ELLs tell the main idea from supporting details and improve their writing. Teachers can help ELLs learn transitional words through a variety of exercises. For example, the teacher can give a list of transitional words and ask students to choose appropriate transitional words they know and give examples of how to use them. The website from McGraw-Hill provides the most common transitional words and phrases: http://www.mhhe.com/mayfieldpub/tsw/tran-cwp.htm

Using comic strips is another helpful way to practice transitions. Teachers can ask students to describe a comic story by using transitional words. This also helps develop ELLs' oral and written English skills. Teachers can find appropriate comic strips online, from newspapers, or books and use them in several ways. One way is to ask students to describe the comic stories orally by using transitional words and connect the ideas between the pictures. Teachers can cut out comics pictures and paste them on index cards and shuffle them, and then show the written scripts of the comics on one side and ask the students put the comics in order. The following website provides many printable comic strips that teachers can use for teaching transitional words: http://www.pinterest.com/pinningteacher/comic-strip-stories/

Teaching Pronouns and Antecedents

ELLs often struggle with identifying pronouns and antecedents in complex sentences. Teachers can provide help on how to identify and use these pronouns and antecedents. This also helps with ELLs' comprehension of text. Teachers should explain to students that when a pronoun is used, an antecedent must be present. Here is an example of reading text and how to teach pronouns with scaffolding:

> The children appeared to have a real fondness for *their* new teacher and *they* were often taking leave of *their* playmates just to spend more time with *her*. *This* was very surprising to the parents who did not expect *she* would become so popular.

> "*their*" refers to _____.
> "*they*" refers to _____.
> "*her*" refers to _____.
> "*This*" refers to _____.
> "*she*" refers to _____.

After reading the paragraph, the teacher can ask students to highlight all the pronouns in the reading and their corresponding antecedents, then provide the worksheet and enough time for the exercise. Explicit instruction may be helpful, and teachers can also incorporate meaningful exercises on grammatical structures when practicing the pronouns. This website provides commonly used pronouns: http://www.esldesk.com/vocabulary/pronouns

Teaching Words Ending With -ed and -ing

Words that end with *–ed* or *–ing* are called participles. A participle forms from a verb that can be used as an adjective. The participle ending with *–ing* is call a present participle and a past participle ends with *–e* or sometimes with *-en,-n,* or *-t.* The challenge for ELLs is when to use present participles and when to use past participles to describe in a sentence. Providing examples and modeling can help students understand. When a new participle is learned, try to make a connection to what has been taught. The teacher can provide a list of example sentences and ask students to compare the differences by discussing the subjects, as in the example below, with some commonly used participles.

Amazing and amazed; annoying and annoyed; bored and boring; confusing and confused; disturbing and disturbed; exciting and excited; exhausting and exhausted; fascinating and fascinated; frightening and & frightened; interesting and interested; satisfying and satisfied; surprising and surprised;

We were *amazed* by the show.	The **show** is *amazing* to us.
The **driver** was *confused* by the road.	The **road** is *confusing* to the driver.
People are *disturbed* by the news.	The **news** is *disturbing* to people.
They were *exhausted* by the trip.	The **trip** is *exhausting* for them.
He was *frightened* by the dog.	The **dog** is *frightening* to him.
Fans are *interested* in the song.	The **song** is *interesting to fans*.
Children are *amazed* by the story.	The **story** is *amazing* to children.

The teacher can also ask students to fill in the blanks of the paired sentences with given present and past participles by taking the particles out of the sentences as an alternative exercise, such as, I am _____ by the show; the show is _____ to me (e.g., *bored* or *boring*).

Learning Prefixes and Suffixes

In English, new words can be formed by adding prefixes and suffixes to root words. A prefix or suffix is a grammatical/lingual component attached to a word stem to form a new word, such as *agree* by adding *dis-* to form *disagree*. Prefixes are placed before and suffixes are placed after a base word to add to new meaning. Teaching prefixes and suffixes helps ELLs increase their vocabulary, and it also adds to their word knowledge. Generally, adding prefixes changes the meaning of the word and adding suffix changes the parts of speech. Teacher can introduce suffixes and prefixes in meaningful contexts and help students understand word structure and also learn words effectively. Many useful websites list common prefixes and suffixes. This following website provides the most common prefixes and suffixes: http://teacher.scholastic.com/reading/bestpractices/vocabulary/pdf/prefixes_suffixes.pdf. Based on ELLs' English proficiency, teachers can teach appropriate prefixes and suffixes and help students expand their vocabulary and increase word knowledge. For example,

1. At the beginning level, the teacher can introduce basic words with suffixes such as *-er, -or,* or *-ress*, which indicates the person who performs the job.

   act (v); *bank* (v/n); *drive* (v); *run* (v); *teach* (v); *work* (v); *wait* (v); *actor* (n); *banker* (n); *diver* (n); *runner* (n); *teacher* (n); *worker* (n); *waiter* (n); *actress* (n); *waitress* (n)

   Prefixes with *un-* or *re-*: *un + do = undo*; *re + cover = recover*; *un + lock = unlock*

2. At the intermediate level, the teacher can introduce more complicated words with suffixes such as *-tion* or *-ment* and add *-er,* and *-or* if they are from the same word stem.

   assess (v); *entertain* (v); *facilitate* (v); *move* (v); *translate* (v); *assessor* (n); *entertainer* (n); *facilitator* (n); *mover* (n); *translator* (n); *assessment* (n); *entertainment* (n); *facilitation* (n); *movement* (n); *translation* (n)

   Prefixes like *did-* or *mis-*: *dis + agree = disagree*; *mis + plac e= misplace*

3. At the advanced level, the teacher can teach those advanced words with suffixes such as *-ion, -ship, -ist* and add the related ending, for example, *-ant or -sive* in words such as

   act (v); *consult* (v); *lead* (v); *produce* (v); *submit* (v); *activist* (n); *consultant* (n); *leader* (n); *producer* (n); *submitter* (n); *activity* (n); *consultation* (n); *leadership* (n); *production* (n); *submission* (n); *active* (adj); *consultative* (n); *leading* (adj); *productive* (adj); *submissive* (adj)

   Prefixes with *il-, in-, ir-*: *il + legal = illegal*; *in + complete = incomplete*; *ir + regular = irregular*

This following link provides the most commonly used root words, suffixes, and prefixes for more practice: http://www.readingrockets.org/article/root-words-roots-and-affixes

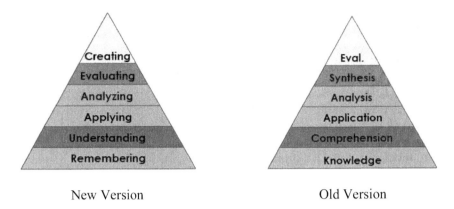

New Version   Old Version

Figure 3.3. Compare the revised version of Bloom's Taxonomy to the old version. Information can be found at http://ww2.odu.edu/educ/roverbau/Bloom/blooms_taxonomy.htm

Teaching Bloom's Action Words

Benjamin Samuel Bloom was an American educational psychologist. In 1956, Bloom edited the first volume of *Taxonomy of Educational Objectives: The Classification of Educational Goals*, which outlined a classification of learning objectives known as Bloom's Taxonomy. Bloom's Taxonomy remains to be foundational to guide teaching and learning in classrooms. However, in the 1990s, a group of educational psychologists revised his old version. See Figure 3.3 for the old and revised versions of Bloom Taxonomy. The new version is more current, and teachers can incorporate the action words by asking questions and checking understanding. It is especially helpful when teachers use Bloom's action words to set learning goals and help students develop critical thinking skills. Of three domains, six levels of the revised critical thinking skills in the cognitive domain are *remembering, understanding, applying, analyzing, evaluating,* and *creating.*

Remembering is basic thinking skills. At this level, a learner is required to recall or retrieve previous learned information. An example is to recite a text. The action words at this level include define, describe, identify, know, label, list, match, name, outline, recall, recognize, reproduce, select, and state. The teacher can use these action words and ask questions (i.e., *who, where, when, what,* and *how).* Answers can be directly located from the text at this level.

Understanding is to comprehend the meaning and interpret instructions and problems. An example is to ask students to explain in their own words the steps for performing a complex task. The action words at this level include comprehend, convert, defend, distinguish, estimate, explain, extend, generalize, give an example, infer, interpret, paraphrase, predict, rewrite, summarize, and translate. Teachers can ask questions such as, "*When the author says ..., what does this mean?*" or "*Why*" questions at this level.

Applying is to use a concept in a new situation. An example is to apply what was learned in the classroom to situations in the workplace. The action words include apply, change, compute, construct, demonstrate, discover, manipulate, modify, operate, predict, prepare, produce, relate, show, solve, and use. The teacher can ask students to provide examples of a natural disaster and explain how it affects people's life.

Analyzing is to separate concepts into component parts so that their organizational structure may be understood. Students are required to distinguish between facts and inferences. Action words include analyze, break down, compare, contrast, diagram, deconstruct, differentiate, discriminate, distinguish, identify, illustrate, infer, outline, relate, select, separate. An example is to ask students to compare the differences between two sets of information.

Evaluating is to make judgments about the value of ideas or materials. An example is to select the most effective solution for a problem. Action words include appraise, compare, conclude, contrast, criticize, critique, defend, describe, discriminate, evaluate, explain, interpret, justify, relate, summarize, support. For example, teachers can ask students to predict what happens in a given situation and evaluate the consequences.

Creating is to build a structure or pattern from diverse elements. Putting parts together to form a new whole, new meaning, or structure is an example. Action words include categorize, combine, compile, compose, create, devise, design, explain, generate, modify, organize, plan, rearrange, reconstruct, relate, reorganize, revise, rewrite, summarize, tell, and write. Asking student to design a class newsletter belongs to this category.

ELLs need to develop skills at all six levels, especially the last three levels, which are considered the higher-order thinking skills. Teachers can use Bloom's action words meaningfully and ask those critical-thinking questions to promote students' academic growth. The following website provides a comprehensive list of these action words that teachers can use as a resource: http://www.highperformancetrainingworks.com/EPSS/TechNotes/Bloom.htm

Visualizing the Characters in Reading

Visualizing is a technique that is essential for building reading comprehension. When students have a mental picture, they comprehend easily. Teachers can help ELLs visualize the character in a story reading. Teachers can encourage students to think and visualize how the characters would think and write down their thoughts. When teaching ELLs to visualize, it is also important to choose the right text. There are many incredible books on the art of creating pictures in a reader's mind. Cynthia Rylant's (1998) *Scarecrow* is a good book for teaching students how to visualize the character. For example, the teacher can instruct students to practice visualizing in these steps:

- Please listen carefully as I read the story.
- Write about what you see as you hear the story.
- Use illustrations, words, phrases, sentences, or combinations.
- Draw and write what you see it in your mind; no right or wrong answers but just fill up the paper as you visualize the story characters.

Mei Mei is another character in a Blue Ribbon award-winning book entitled *I Hate English* by Ellen Levine (1995). This story tells about a young girl named Mei Mei, who moves from Hong Kong to New York City. The strangest thing about her new school is that people speak English instead of her Chinese language. The teacher can engage students in using the *visualizing* strategy and do an activity called "Picture the Characters in My Mind" with these steps:

- Using a piece of paper, preferably 8 1/2 × 11 inches, make a hamburger fold and cut it in the shape of the human head.
- Draw a facial picture of Mei Mei on the front side and color it with crayon.
- Write any words or sentences inside on how Mei Mei feels, using the first person "I."
- Punch a hole along the folded edge and tie each student's work with a piece of string to display the work in the classroom with the student's name on the back side.

Making a Flip Book

A flip book is one of the earliest forms of interactive media. It usually involves a series of pictures that vary gradually from one page to the next, and the pictures appear to be animated by simulating motion. Children like to write when writing is interesting. Students also like to see the final products that demonstrates their learning. Making a flip book can arouse children's interest, and it also connects writing with reading to motivate students to write. In the process of organizing ideas and writing down their ideas, the students are creating a book. Depending on the levels of the student proficiency, the teacher can guide students to create a flip

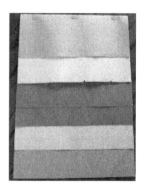

Figure 3.4.   Example of making a flip book.

book, write sentences or paragraphs, or draw pictures to illustrate their ideas on each page. These steps to make a flip book are as follows:

1. Provide each student with three pieces (or more) of colored paper (8 1/2 × 11 inches) or construction paper, which works even better, although regular copy paper works as well and can be written on clearly. Different colors make a flip book look interesting.

2. Ask the students to line up the colored papers so that they overlap about 1 or 2 inches with a small "tab" left for each color (see Figure 3.4) so that on each page students can write a paragraph or illustrate ideas with pictures about reading.

3. Guide the students to fold the paper over so that you get six tabs in all, and staple the top to make it into a flip book (see Figure 3.4). In addition to writing paragraphs or illustrating ideas, teachers can encourage students using the flip book for taking notes while reading, making picture books, collecting facts, or creating question and answer booklets.

Writer's Workshop

A writer's workshop, also known as a writing workshop, is a method of teaching writing (Calkins, 2006). It focuses on fostering lifelong writers with four basic principles: (a) students will write about their own lives, (b) they will be engaged in a consistent writing process, (c) they will write in authentic ways, and (d) it will foster their independence. The teacher can use the writer's workshop strategy to develop students' interest in writing. The teacher can guide students with four basic steps in the writing process:

(a) Prewriting: brainstorm, with a minilesson to help students with ideas
(b) Writing: writing and editing the first and second drafts
(c) Conferring: meeting with individuals to discuss their writing progress
(d) Publishing: sharing a clean final copy

In all, the writer's workshop is intended to help students understand the writing process and be good writers. Connecting writing to reading is helpful when using a writer's workshop because reading and writing are reciprocal processes. For more information on the writer's workshop, teachers can find different resources online and this following link is a helpful one: http://www.busyteacherscafe.com/literacy/writing_workshop .html

Interactive Writing

Interactive writing is a method of teaching writing, in which students and the teacher are actively involved in a cooperative way (Swartz, Klein, & Shook, 2001). Dr. Stanley Swartz, a professor of education at California State University, San Bernadino, wrote a book with his colleagues called *Interactive Writing and Interactive Editing*. They believe that the teacher and students should take active roles and negotiate what they want to write. They can literally share the pen to construct joint sentences or writing passages. This method is helpful for ELLs at the beginning level who find writing terrifying. The interactive writing method also helps children learn to view literacy in a more meaningful way through teacher-student interaction. Basic goals to be accomplished through interactive writing usually include

- Learning upper- and lowercase letters
- Becoming more aware of the nature of words
- Increasing vocabulary
- How to organize narrative text
- The nature of correspondence
- How to target writing to an audience

In the interactive writing process, the teacher can use these methods to guide students: writing letters to each other, keeping dialogue journals, and using a message board. Students should be able to choose their own topics. Here is an example of how the interactive writing method works. After reading a passage about hobbies, the teacher can ask students, "*Who wants to talk about your hobbies? Does anyone like to play football?*" Some students may raise their hands and the teacher can ask one student, *"Carlos, do you like football?"* He may nod his head. Then the teacher can say, *"Let's write down a sentence about Carlos's hobby. Where should we start? Can we start in this way—Carlos likes ..."* Then, the teacher can invite students to join in the process of constructing the sentence. Together: *"Carlos likes to play football."* The teacher can begin to model writing by writing *"Carlos"* on the board, then invite students to finish the sentence. For more references about interactive writing, please visit Swartz's website about interactive writing at http://www.stanswartz.com/IAW%20excerpt.pdf

Creating Word Walls

Teaching vocabulary is one of the most important activities teachers must do with ELLs and all students. Creating *word walls* provides not only a literacy-rich classroom but also a rich resource for learning vocabulary. A word wall is an organized collection of words prominently displayed in a classroom. This display can be used as an interactive tool for teaching reading and spelling to children. There are different types of word walls, including high frequency words, word families, and names. Some walls can be creative, such as *portable walls, words on poster frames*, or *ceiling tiles* (i.e., words on the ceiling to save space). Integrated into instruction, the word-wall strategy can help expend students' word knowledge and learning vocabulary. The basic steps of creating word walls are as follows:

- *Select words for the word walls.* Words should be selected from content units for high frequency words or "must-know" words for the walls. Print the words in a large, simple font so that students can *use* and *refer to* the words from across the classroom. For ELLs, teachers may include daily words.

- *Create word walls with students.* Pasting words on color-coded construction paper to make word walls that provide literacy visual support for children. Words can be categorized by parts of speech or grouped in alphabetical order. For ELLs at the beginning level, grouping words by parts of speech is helpful.

- *Display the walls.* Every time a new word is learned, invite students to add the new word to the wall. Word walls can be displayed in different shapes and sizes. For example, *portable word walls* can be used for categorizing or grouping words, cupboard doors can be used to display words to save space, poster frames can be used to display words within the frame, and tall file cabinet can be used to display words of all types by sticking a small magnet on the back of each word.

- *Practice words on the walls.* Teachers should model how to use the words from the word walls and help students construct meaningful sentences. For example, teachers help students

- select words and use them in a sentence, find rhyming words, use flashcards, and play word bingo or tic-tac-toe in small groups. For more activity ideas on using word words, this link is helpful: http://www.teachingfirst.net/wordwallact.htm

Integrating Technology With ELLs

ELL students are a fast growing segment of the school population. At the same time, technology has become more and more widely used in classrooms today. To combine these two trends, integrating technology in working with ELLs becomes important. Technology-based projects allow ELL students to draw on their cultural strengths and background experiences through integrating technology in classrooms to make learning assessable, fun, engaging, and interactive. Projects that incorporate visual and aural media address a variety of learning styles and modalities. Teachers can incorporate the advantages of technology into their teaching practices, such as using online resources, new technological techniques, and software programs. Several strategies are introduced here to help teachers work more effectively with ELLs through integrating technology.

- *Digital Storytelling*: Digital storytelling is the method of using computer-based tools to tell stories. Teachers can use this technology-related strategy to make learning interesting and engaging. Much like traditional storytelling, digital stories focus on a specific topic. Yet digital stories usually have a mixture of computer-based images, video clips, text, recorded audio narration, and music. Topics can range from personal tales to historical events or from student life experiences to life of other universe. Literally, digital storytelling can cover unlimited topics. Teachers can guide students to appropriately use digital stories, and digital storytelling in classrooms can be used in countless ways. For example, creating personal stories helps students learn important literacy skills of voice in a narrative form and first-person perspective. Since modern communication involves writing with pictures and music, having students create digital stories helps them build media-creation skills. Digital storytelling can also be used to address curriculum areas beyond language arts and media literacy. For example, students can retell an event from the life of a famous person to help themselves and their

Table 3.6.   Basic Steps of Creating a Digital Story

		Procedures
Step I: Collect Data	1.	Select a topic for a digital story and create a folder on the desktop to store the materials found for the story.
	2.	Search for image resources for the story, for example, pictures, drawings, photographs, maps, and charts; save these resources in the folder.
	3.	Locate audio resources such as music, speeches, interviews, and sound effects; save these resources in the folder.
	4.	Locate informational content, which might come from websites, word processed documents, or PowerPoint slides; save these resources in the folder.
	5.	Decide the purpose of the story, that is, to inform, convince, provoke, question.
Step II: Create the story	1.	Select the images to be used for your digital story.
	2.	Select the audio to be used for your digital story.
	3.	Select the content and text to be used for your digital story.
	4.	Import images into Photo Story (Note: Photo Story is free software available for download from Microsoft).
	5.	Import audio into Photo Story.
	6.	Modify images and image order as needed.
	7.	Use a computer microphone and record the narration of the script and import the narration into Photo Story.
	8.	Finalize the digital story and save it as a Windows Media Video file.

audience better understand why this person acted the way he/she did. Students can discuss habitat, food, predation, and other life-cycle issues. Public service announcements can be used as both a persuasive writing exercise and a way to address science topics like health and conservation. Telling a digital story successfully depends largely on how teachers can guide students to create their digital stories. Step-by-step procedures on how to create a digital story are provided in Table 3.6.

- *Exploring the basics of using an iPad:* Teachers need to take time and explore the basic use of an iPad so that they can become comfortable and effectively help their students. The more time spent with the iPad, the more comfortable the teacher will be using it. To practice accessing all of the apps to be used, teachers can write down a list of any questions for the things that are important. Spend time to learn and to answer those questions. It is critical to note that introducing an iPad into a classroom requires a lot of time and a great deal of patience. Yet the more teachers use them, the easier it will be for them and their students. Grouping the apps into areas of interest or types of application is important. Stage the use of apps and pair students for use. This will help students explore the app with others. If an iPad Cart is available, try to use a sign-out sheet with the students for the class session. Or create specific iPad "rules" and a sign-out sheet. Provide basic iPad training for the students.

There are many different ways to use an iPad. First, teachers can use the iPad as a document camera and annotate anything to be observed under the camera. Second, teachers can create multimedia eBooks with iPad. In fact, the iPad can be used for digital storytelling apps, and they can produce much better results with Book Creator for iPad. Over 3 million multimedia eBooks have been created with just this app. You can add text, images, video, audio and more. Choose from over 50 fonts, draw illustrations, and send the finished product to iBooks, Dropbox, or share by email. Third, teachers can collaborate with other classrooms using video conferencing and Subtext. We should never let our students think that their classroom is just the four walls around them. It is essential that students know that the world is their classroom, and the iPad is a great way for students to connect and collaborate with students anywhere in the world. Whether students video conference with FaceTime or Skype (both free) to discuss a book that they read together in Subtext (a social reading app), or to do a Mystery Skype, the iPad opens doors to collaborative learning experiences for students of all ages. Fourth, teachers can review almost any academic topics using the Quizlet app. Quizlet is a completely free resource that allows teachers to create flashcards for their students. Interactive games can also be done on the Web. Students can also practice individually at home for review for upcoming tests. Teachers do not necessarily need the app, as it is a Web-based service and it runs straight from the browser.

- *Learning about using apps*: *App* is an abbreviated form of the word *application*. An *application* is a software program designed to perform a specific function for the user. When an application is opened, it runs inside the operating system until it is closed. Most of the time, more than one application is open at the same time and this is known as multitasking. Applications for desktop and laptop computers are called *desktop applications* and for mobile devices are called *mobile apps*. Types of desktop applications can include word processors. A word processor allows users to write a letter, design a flyer, and create many other kinds of documents. The most well-known word processor is Microsoft Word. Personal finance software, such as Quicken, allows users to keep track of expenses, create a budget, and more. A Web browser is the tool that allows users to access the Web. Most computers come with a Web browser preinstalled. Examples of browsers can include Internet Explorer, Firefox, Google Chrome, and Safari. Many different games allow users to play games on computer. Media players allow users to listen to MP3s or watch downloaded movies. Windows Media Player and iTunes are popular media players. Gadgets are simple applications that are placed on desktop, such as calendars, calculators, maps, and news headlines.

Mobile apps are devices like smartphones and tablet computers. Other examples of mobile apps include RedLaser, which can be used to compare prices while shopping. Users can simply scan an item's barcode using the phone's built-in camera, and the app searches the Web for the best price. Word Lens is a language translator app. Like RedLaser, it uses your phone's camera to take a picture of a sign, menu, or other text you want to translate, and it displays the translation for you. Compared with traditional applications, mobile apps are relatively cheap. Many of them cost as little as $0.99 and many others are free. If the mobile device has an Internet connection, teachers can download apps directly onto the mobile device. Otherwise, you can download them to your computer and then transfer them over. The following apps are great to have and work with ELL students: Dropbox, Show Me, Google Earth, Idea Sketch (mind mapping tool), InkFlow, Visual Notebook, or TeacherKit. More information on apps and ideas can be found at AppsGoneFree. For example, Google Earth is a free Internet tool that introduces the Earth's geographic features. It allows students to view anywhere on Earth with satellite maps, terrain, 3-D images from galaxies in outer space to the canyons of the ocean, and it provides geographical information. It maps the Earth by the superimposition of images obtained from satellite imagery, aerial photography, and geographic information system (GIS) 3-D globe. Teachers can use it to teach content lessons. For example, it can take ELL students to a new place to learn about the geographic features of this place for teaching social studies and geography classes.

Educational apps and technology tools can help teachers to connect with other teachers or organize files. The following resources provide more information for teaching ELLs:

- *Uen.org* is a website that provides resources related to teaching ELLs as well as many useful links on the topics of teaching ELLs. Some of these websites include WIDA ELP Standards, Everything ESL, Lanternfish, Colorín Colorado, Dave's ESL Café, USOE's English Language Learners Web Page, One Stop English, Learning the Language. The website can be assessed at http://www.uen.org/k12educator/ell/.

- *Dave's ESL café* is an Internet meeting place for ESL teachers and students around the world. It provides a resource for students of all ages learning English and teachers to teach English as a foreign language. Features include grammar lessons, idioms, phrasal verbs, pronunciation, quizzes, slang, student forum, a Job Center, and discussion groups for students and teachers. The website link is www.eslcafe.com

- *Everythingesl.net* is a useful website that provides teaching tips, lesson plans, and resources to teach ELLs. Judie Haynes left her teaching job in June 2008 and became an educational consultant. She created this website with resources and strategies for ESL teaching and learning community, such as lesson plans and teaching tips. Teachers can also ask questions. The website link is http://www.everythingesl.net/

- *Lantern Fish* provides worksheets, flashcards, lesson plans, jobs, and a forum for ESL and TEFL teachers. It also includes many activities such as crosswords, phonics skills, alphabet, e-books, proverb communication, word skill games, and lesson plans. The website can be accessed at http://bogglesworldesl.com/worksheets.htm

- Onestopenglish is packed with resources for English language teachers, with information on ESOL, grammar, exams, skills, games, and teaching support. There are free resources or teachers can pay for a subscription to get access to even more. The website link is http://www.onestopenglish.com/

- *Emdodo* is an educational website that takes the ideas of a social network and makes it appropriate for a classroom. The users of Edmodo can post assignments, create polls for student responses, embed video clips, create learning groups, post quizzes for students to take, and create a calendar for events and assignments. Students can also turn in assignments or upload assignments for their teachers to view and grade. The website link for *Emdodo* is https://www.edmodo.com/

- *Colorín Colorado* is a bilingual website with many resources for educators, administers, and families of English language learners. For example, it provides topics on common cores and ELLs, ELL topics from A to Z, and ELL research, reports, and toolkits. The website link can be accessed at http://www.colorincolorado.org

- *Activities for ESL Students* is a website that offers activities in classrooms, for example, quizzes, tests, exercises, and puzzles to help ELL students learn English as a second language. This project of

The Internet TESL Journal (iteslj.org) has thousands of contributions by many teachers. The website link is http://a4esl.org/

- *ESL Kids Lab* is a website that provides English (ESL, EFL, ELT, ESOL) learning and teaching materials for young learners, pre-schoolers, beginners, elementary and pre-intermediate. The materials are designed to appeal to all learning styles, with resources on handouts, lessons, flashcards, phonics activities, and even shop related to help ELLs. The website link is http://www.eslkidslab.com/

- *ESL Partyland* is a webpage designed to provide teachers with the resources and connections they need to become better ESL teachers with great activities. The Teacher Page is where information and resources related to teaching ELLs from K-12 grads are provided. Teachers and students can have fun while learning English as a second language. The website link is http://www.eslpartyland.com/

- *About.com ESL Guide* provides resources and information related to English as the second language (ESL). Resources provided range from food, health, home to quizzes and tests for different levels. The website link is http://esl.about.com/

- *ESLAmerica.US* is a resourceful website where everything has sound, and it provides resources to practice conversation, vocabulary, grammar, reading, writing, holidays. Because everything has sound, it allows ELLs to listen to pronunciation and even to their own voice. The website link is http://www.eslamerica.us/

- *English Page* offers free English lessons and ESL resources with English grammar and vocabulary exercises online. Hundreds of English lessons help ELLs learn English and practice four domains of language skills (i.e., speaking, listening, reading and writing). Some resourceful topics include weekly lessons, vocabulary, grammar, verb, articles, reading, and listening. The site is at http://www.englishpage.com

- *TESOL International Association* is Teachers of English to Speakers of Other Languages. The TESOL association has a mission to ensure excellence in the English language. The TESOL website provides many professional resources related to teaching ELLs. The official website for TESOL is http://www.tesol.org/

Technology opens a new door for teaching and learning. Integrating technology to work with ELLs adds a new dimension to traditional teaching and learning in classrooms. Teachers should avail themselves of the advantages that technology offers and also take time to avidly explore and become comfortable with technology to make teaching and learning more connected and productive.

SUMMARY

This chapter discusses planning to teach with the SIOP model, TPR, teaching strategies, and tips to work with ELLs and all students. The SIOP model, *Sheltered Instruction Observation Protocol,* is an empirically tested approach that helps teachers prepare ELLs and all students to become college and career ready. TPR stands for the *Total Physical Response*, a method that incorporates physical movement to facilitate student learning. Strategies cover four areas: using visual aids, relating to existing knowledge, presenting contextual information, and integrating technology for working with ELLs. These strategies are intended to help teachers better work with ELLs and all students and produce positive learning outcomes.

REFERENCES

Allen, R., & Franklin, J. (2002). *Acquiring English: Schools seek ways to strengthen language learning.* Alexandria, VA: Association for Supervision and Curriculum Development. (ERIC Document Reproduction Service No. ED 471 636)

Bloom, B. (1956). *Taxonomy of educational objectives, handbook I: Cognitive domain.* White Plains, NY: Addison Wesley.

Byram, M. (2000). *Total physical response. Routledge encyclopedia of language teaching and learning.* London, UK: Routledge.

Calkins, L. (2006). *A guide to the writing workshop, grades 3–5.* Portsmouth, NH: First Hand.

Drucker, M. J. (2003). What reading teachers should know about ESL learners. *International Reading Association.* Retrieved from http://read4343.pbworks.com/f/Drucker.pdf

Echevarria, J., Vogt, M. E., & Short, D. (2010). *Making content comprehensible for English language learners: The SIOP model.* Boston, MA: Allyn & Bacon.

Egbert, J. L. & Ernst-Slavit, G. (2010). *Access to academic: Planning instruction for K–12 classrooms with ELLs.* Boston: MA: Allyn & Bacon.

Francis, D., Rivera, M., Lesaux, N., Kieffer, M., & Rivera, H. (2006). *Practical guidelines for the education of English language learners: Research-based recommendations for instruction and academic interventions.* Portsmouth, NH: RMC Research Corporation, Center on Instruction.

Goldenberg, C. (2008). Teaching English language learner: What the research does- and does not- say. *American Educator,* 8–44.

Harvey, S., & Goudvis, A. (2000). *Strategies that work: Teaching comprehension to enhance understanding.* Portland, ME: Stenhouse.

Hughes, L. (1926). *Dream variations. Langston Hughes collection: The Billops-Hatch Archives.* Atlanta, GA: Emory University Manuscript, Archives, and Rare Book Library.

Hunter, M. (1982). *Mastery teaching.* El Segundo, CA: TIP.

Jensen, E. (2005). *Teaching with the brain in mind* (2nd ed.). Alexandria, VA: Association for Supervision and Curriculum Development.

Jong, E., & Harper, C. (2005). Preparing mainstream teachers for English language learners: Is being a good teacher good enough? *Teacher Education Quarterly, 32*(2), 101–124.

Levine, E. (1995). *I hate English!* New York, NY: Scholastic.

National Clearinghouse for English Language Acquisition. (2012). *The growing number of English Language Learners: 1995-2005.* Washington, DC. U.S. Department of Education Office of English Language Acquisition.

OELA Report. (2010). *The Biennial Evaluation Report to Congress on the Implementation of the Title III State Formula Grant Program for School Years 2008–2010.* Washington, DC: Office of English Language Acquisition.

Pearson. (2013). The SIOP Model: Sheltered Instruction Observation Protocol. Retrieved from http://siop.pearson.com

Peregoy, S. F., & Boyle, O. F. (2005). *Reading, writing, & learning in ESL: A resource book for K–12 teachers.* White Plains, NY: Longman.

Reed, B., & Railsback, J. (2003). *Strategies and resources for mainstream teachers of English language learners.* Portland, OR: Northwest Regional Education Laboratory. (ERIC Document Reproduction Service No. ED 478 291)

Rylant, C. (1998). *Scarecrow.* San Diego, CA: Harcourt Brace.

Swartz, S., Klein, A. F., & Shook, R. E. (2001). *Interactive editing and interactive writing.* Parsippany, NJ: Pearson Learning/Dominie.

Thrower, I. M. (2009, August). *What is SIOP: SIOP is good teaching PLUS+ purposeful teaching of the language necessary for ELLs to understand content.* Retrieved from http://www.houstoncte.org/SIOP/SIOPOverviewHandouts.pdf

U.S. Department of Eduction. (n.d.). *Developing programs for English language learners: Law v. Nichols.* Retrieved from http://www2.ed.gov/about/offices/list/ocr/ell/lau.html

Zacarian, D., & Haynes, J. (2012). Educating newcomer ELLs with limited schooling: An overview. *¡Colorín colorado!* Retrieved from http://www.colorincolorado.org/article/55784/

CHAPTER 4

WAYS TO INVOLVE ELL PARTICIPATION

CASE SCENARIO

Ben was a ninth grader. He came to the United States 6 months ago with his mother and sister to join his father who came to the United States 4 years ago when Ben was in elementary school in China. According to his teachers in his new school, Ben was polite and always had good manners but was shy and quiet in the classrooms. He did not speak much English or communicate with his peers. Academically, Ben was challenged. Due to his limited English proficiency, Ben was placed in the lower-track classes in all subject areas. For example, he was in pilot English, which was the lowest-tracked English class in the ninth grade. Ben could not comprehend the content knowledge in most subject areas. Yet he did not ask questions due to the language barrier. However, Ben still expressed that he liked his new American school. According to Ben, this was because there was not much homework in comparison to his school in China. The teachers were more easygoing here in terms of disciplines. Yet Ben did mention that his biggest problem was no friends or opportunities to speak and practice English. In his own words, "I have no problem with listening and it is easy to practice because I listen all the time at school. I can watch TV in English at home, but there is seldom a chance to speak in English" [translated from Chinese]. When it was suggested that he find some American peers after school to be friends with and to speak and practice English with, Ben said it was very difficult. Isolation with limited

A Book for Every Teacher: Teaching English Language Learners
pp. 81–101
Copyright © 2015 by Information Age Publishing
All rights of reproduction in any form reserved.

opportunities to interact, speak, and communicate with others in English added to his academic challenge.

GETTING TO KNOW ELLS

The above scenario reflects some serious challenges that are faced by many ELLs. In order to be proficient and productive students in their American schools, ELL students need opportunities to interact in social and academic situations. Yet most ELLs have limited resources at home and do not have the opportunity to communicate with native English speakers outside of school. Schools are only the place for most ELLs to socialize with peers and speak English. Effective teachers encourage ELL students' participation in classroom discussions, welcome their contributions, and motivate them by such practices (Cazden, 2001; Saracho & Spodek, 2010; Stipek, 2002). However, many teachers lack the strategies to involve ELLs, and sometimes they allow these students with limited L2 proficiency to remain silent or to participate less than their English-speaking peers (Alford & Nino, 2011; Li, Mitchell, & Howard, 2012; Yoon & Kim, 2012). Engaging ELL students can make them feel welcomed and also gives them the confidence to overcome many difficulties on the journey from their home-language and culture to the English-speaking-dominated language and culture and become socially proficient and academically successful. Therefore, teachers need to find ways to engage ELLs.

Getting to know the ELLs is the first step. A little knowledge about ELL students can help educators go a long way. The things needed to know about ELLs can start with some basic information, such as when the students arrived in the United States, what countries they came from, and how much schooling they had in their home countries. This information can help teachers to not only get to know ELLs and make them feel welcomed but it is also directly related to their academic learning. If possible, determine the ELL student's level of literacy in his or her native language. Research shows that higher levels of literacy in a native language tend to provide greater chances for ELLs to succeed in English and subject content areas in schools (Jalongo & Li, 2010; Yoon & Kim, 2012).

Schools with larger ELL enrollment usually have relevant support programs, such as ESOL or a bilingual program. ESOL stands for English to Speakers of the Other Languages and ESOL teachers are good resources for working daily with ELL students. They are also experts in getting basic information about ELLs' academic information, such as English proficiency or other learning-related data. Taking time to be in touch with ESOL teachers and communicate with them often about your ELLs' learning is a good strategy to help your ELLs succeed in your classrooms. ELL students are usually required to take a placement test to determine the level of their English proficiency, for example, beginning, intermediate, or advanced level tests. Teachers can get this information to determine the levels of instruction for ELLs and prepare lessons accordingly.

In addition to ESOL, teachers can have many ways to get to know ELLs. For example, on the first day of school, teachers can create an information sheet to find out basic information about ELLs. See the sample information sheet in Table 4.1 on creating such an information sheet. It is an easy way to get to know your ELLs. If ELLs cannot write in English yet, teachers can help them write down the information or find a translator if needed. Although you do not want to invade their privacy, the more information you have about your ELLs, for example, where they come from and what their home environment is like, the better you will know the strengths or weakness in order to assist their needs.

Table 4.1.   Get to Know ELLs:
Information Sheet on the First Day of School

The First Day of School - Information Sheet	
I. ELL's Basic Information	
Name:	Age:
Date of birth:	Place of birth:
Phone number:	Email address:
II. ELL's Home Information	
Parents' or guardian's names:	
Siblings' names:	
Who else lives with you in your household:	
What language do you speak at home:	
Do your parents speak English?:	
III. ELL's Literacy and Interests	
Where did you go to school before?:	
Did you like that school?:	Why?:
Do you like your new school?:	Why?:
How do you get to school?:	How long does it take?:
What do you do after school?:	
What other interests you have?:	
Other notes:	

Ways to Encourage ELLs' Participation

ELLs may feel shy and embarrassed about their inability to speak English fluently and therefore are reluctant to talk or participate. As a teacher, you need to know the reason and provide lessons and a learning environment that encourages their participation. Teachers may ask these questions if ELLs do not talk:

- Are ELLs afraid of making mistakes or being embarrassed? If so, do I need to single them out to speak? Or do I have other ways to encourage them?
- Are my assignments at the right level for ELL students? Do I emphasize too much on correcting their speaking errors to hinder building fluency?
- Do I explain my instruction clearly with examples for the assignment?
- Are students bored because I give the same topic and practicing pattern? Do I need to redesign my lesson to make it more interesting in order to motivate their interest?

Once clear about these questions, teachers can incorporate different methods to encourage and engage ELLs' participation. As teachers plan lessons to involve ELLs in activities, they should pay attention to these areas:

Focus on Building Fluency

Although it is important for ELLs to be correct in grammar, especially when they are learning a new language, too much emphasis on accuracy at the beginning can hinder their speaking fluency. It is necessary to encourage ELLs to speak more and not be afraid of mistakes. The more they practice, the better they speak; the better they speak, the more confident they will be. This helps build a positive cycle. Also, teachers can use choral responses when the ELLs are not fluent yet so that they can recite some responses, for example, a word, phrase, sentence, or dialogue. This is also effective in building vocabulary skills that contribute to comprehension. Again, it is important to build fluency by practicing more.

Meet ELLs' Individual Needs

Teachers should have pre-assessment information of ELLs so as to design instruction that meets ELLs' individual needs. Choose those skills that are appropriate for the ELLs in order to improve their English. For example, some ELL students may be struggling with the alphabet or even initial sounds, while other ELLs may be struggling at a lower grade level of reading comprehension even if they are in the higher grade level due to no English literacy in previous schooling. As educators, we must believe that all learners can learn if we offer them the right tools and know how to teach them with appropriate instructional strategies to meet their needs. It is also important to maximize their unique skills so they can learn with confidence and achieve their highest potential.

Encourage, Praise, and Be Positive

Imagine you are in a foreign country and do not speak that country's language. Many ELLs experience the same situation. It is thus important to encourage ELLs with positive comments and provide specific praise that shows a genuine appreciation when they make a contribution to classroom discussions and activities. Creating a friendly environment is essential to making ELLs feel welcome in your classrooms, so be sure to respond appropriately to issues that may cause discomfort such as seating arrangements or bullying behaviors that might occasionally occur. Being a good role model presenting a positive atmosphere, and not tolerating bias in classrooms are good for all learners. Sometimes when students respond incorrectly or insufficiently to teacher questions, the teacher may feel disappointed because the teaching-learning process does not seem to be proceeding as efficiently as expected. However, teachers must avoid the temptation to blame ELLs for not listening or processing questions well. Instead, the teacher should find appropriate responses as a means of ongoing assessment to determine students' needs and misunderstandings.

Make Learning Exciting to Motivate Interest

In planning lessons, teachers need to be aware that learning is a meaning-making process and needs to be interesting and engaging instead of passive. Teachers can create an exciting lesson with activities that incorporate movement or gestures to engage students' attention and increase their understanding. Younger ELLs need even more movement from time to time to maintain their attention. If your ELLs appear uninterested, sometimes just having students stand up and switch partners or seats can get their attention. To make lessons exciting and inviting, teachers can use a variety of materials and techniques, such as pictures, photos, real objects, visual simulations, role-plays, games, flashcards, magazines and newspaper articles, authentic projects, computer-based learning, field trips, guest speakers, or question-and-answer sessions. Teachers can give ELLs a choice and ask for their input for topics in order to engage them in active learning.

Provide Modeling With Clear Instruction and Allow Time

For some difficult assignments, teachers need to provide modeling with clear instruction and examples on how to respond. Teachers can demonstrate a response and have ELLs repeat it. When modeling, remember to speak clearly and not use long wording. Teachers can also use visual aids to help ELLs understand instructions. Be careful to phrase the wording of the instruction to the level that ELLs can understand. Also, make sure that you have allowed enough time for them to think before they respond. When ELLs appear to struggle with a certain skill or understanding, help them clarify. It is also necessary that teachers find the balance between providing modeling and allowing time for ELLs to practice. The main purpose is to enhance the students' speaking skills. Thus, it is important for them to have time and develop the speaking skills through practice so that teachers can avoid talking too much.

Use Choral Responses, Switch Groups, and Choose the Right Topics

For beginner ELLs who are not yet comfortable speaking on their own, it is helpful to use choral responses in classrooms. This technique incorporates the whole class speaking together, usually repeating after the teacher on a sentence or dialogue they have read. This is an easy way for lower-level students to practice speaking, especially with a large class size. From time to time, ELLs also need chances to interact with peers. Make sure to pair ELL students with different group partners and change often so they have the opportunity to hear and speak with more peers and classmates. Also, make sure to combine some learning tasks so that ELLs can speak in pairs, in groups, as a whole class, or directly with teachers. Choosing the right speaking topics that are relevant to your ELLs is also important. Teachers can conduct a quick needs-assessment survey at the beginning of the class with a short questionnaire to find the right topics for students, which also gives them a choice of topics to talk about.

These are the areas that teachers need to pay attention to when making efforts to involve ELLs and increase their participation. There are many ways that teachers can use to encourage and involve ELLs' participation. Some websites provide good suggestions. For example, a resourceful website for teaching ELLs is www.everythingesl.net. This website provides teachers with a variety of resourceful activities to involve ELLs' participation.

Useful Tips to Engage Your ELLs

Tip 1: Create a Language Learning Center for Newcomers

Your ELLs probably do not talk or speak when they first come to your classroom. The Language Learning Center (LLC) is a strategy to welcome ELLs on the first day when they do not speak English by organizing a space in the classroom with learning materials for their needs, pairing ELLs with buddies, and making ELLs feel comfortable in learning while having their own space. More details on how to create a Language Learning Center is provided in the following section. The key is that ELLs should feel comfortable in learning with help from buddies while they can have their own space in the new classroom environment.

Prepare for a Language Learning Center. Teachers can select a quiet space in the classroom. Prepare a small table with several comfortable chairs. If available, also try to furnish this center with a shelf, closet, and one or two large boxes to keep equipment and materials organized and convenient for your ELLs and their buddies, tutors, and volunteers to use (Haynes, 2007). Label everything so that they can easily find the materials when needed. The LLC is helpful for the lower-grade ELLs who can work in this area or carry materials back to their desk as long as they return them.

A workable schedule should be established, posted, and updated that guides the ELLs and their buddies and tutors to work in an orderly way on a daily or weekly basis. Draw pictures or write page numbers on the schedule to show what specific work they need to do with the lower-grade ELLs, for example, second and third graders. Be organized. ELLs feel more comfortable if they have their own space, a clear purpose, and know what is expected with the activity guide. ELLs should also have the freedom to go to this language learning area to work on the assignments and tasks, especially when they need more time than the regular time required for the rest of the class. This gives ELLs a choice to work at their own pace and space, and it is especially helpful for beginners when they are new to school.

Gather Materials and Supplies for the LLC. Teachers need to prepare all possible materials and supplies for the Language Learning Center that help ELLs and their peer tutors to learn in this area. Although you cannot prepare everything, items that are basic for learning activities may include in Table 4.2.

Collect a Literacy Package. Teachers can collect a literacy package or binder for each individual ELL and their needs. Reading and learning materials for entry-level ELLs is important for them to sometimes work

Table 4.2.   Materials and Supplies for the LLC

• Materials & Supplies	• Purpose
• Beginning phonics books with tapes	• Learning phonics and listening
• Crayons, scissors, pencils, eraser, paper	• Different activities
• Flash cards with alphabet, vocabulary, or picture cards	• Learning ABC
• Games	• Fun learning, for example, word searches, sequencing activities, jigsaw puzzles, concentration games, and dot-to-dot activities
• Home-language magazines with pictures	• Keeping ELLs interested
• Home-language stories and literature books	• Reading at the appropriate level
• Index cards	• Making flash cards or concentration games
• Labels	• Labeling objects and places
• Object boxes	• Storing small manipulative objects for beginning vocabulary or phonics learning
• Old magazines with illustrations	• Cutting pictures
• Photo copies of activities	• Recording activities in a binder or a folder
• Picture books or nonfiction books	• For beginners to read with tapes or learning content in science, health, and social studies
• Picture dictionary with bilingual	• For ELLs to look up
• Picture file of class-made or commercial	• Interesting class activities
• Tape recorder and earphones	• For ELLs to listen to and practice
• Taped bilingual music	• Motivating ELL interest
• Textbooks in content areas with controlled vocabulary	• Learning content

Note: See more resources at www.everythingesl.net

independently. To prepare this package, teachers should think of an ELL's individual needs and also prepare based on their language proficiency level:

- Select the appropriate ESOL reading materials for beginners.
- Organize these learning materials and keep them in a large, clearly marked folder so that students can keep them neatly in their own binders.
- Add any additional materials that you find interesting for the beginner ELLs. Omit sections or pages that are not appropriate to your students' needs.
- Require that ELLs read the pack through and work independently.

Establish a Regular Routine.   At first, things can be chaotic when your ELLs begin to work in the LLC area. Give them help in organizing time, space, and materials. Make a schedule to give your students a sense of structure. Tape this schedule to their desks, or have them keep it in the front of their ESL notebooks. Send a copy home so that parents can help their children feel more connected to the classroom. It is important to remember that the ELLs need to be a part of your class. Be sensitive to this when assigning work. Don't isolate ELLs from their peers with separate work all day long. When necessary, a buddy or volunteer can work with your ELLs.

Tip 2: Pair Your Newcomers With Buddies

Assign a buddy or a higher-grade tutor to your English language learner and watch them work together and both grow in academic and social skills. Your ELLs will gain English and literacy learning with the buddies, who will gain self-esteem for tutoring. This is an opportunity also for ELLs to socialize. A buddy or higher-grade tutor who speaks the ELL's language is a wonderful asset at the beginning of the school year. Ideally, buddies should be classmates and higher-grade tutors who are in the same school and older than the ELLs. The best-case scenario is to pair an older bilingual student with the same-language ELL. During the adjustment phase, the buddy can explain about the school routines and what is going on in school. This is a good self-esteem builder for the buddies and an opportunity for ELLs to make new friends. Teachers may rotate buddies depending on needs so that ELLs do not become too dependent on one person and the buddies will not miss too much schoolwork either.

Teachers can also use English-speaking buddies. For many ELLs, the English-speaking buddies are more helpful in terms of learning social language. The language used in the classroom is often academic language. ELLs often lack the ability to interact socially with English-speaking peers and have great difficulty learning the social language. Therefore, the English-speaking buddies can help the ELLs not only academically but socially. Teachers need to help these buddies learn how to work with non-English speakers and to reward those who take their job seriously. Teach buddies the importance of being patient, repeating, and not overloading. Help them understand that some newcomers might not want to speak for several months after arriving. However, this doesn't mean they should give up talking to them. Ask buddies to brainstorm on the things that they can do to help newcomers and make them feel welcome, such as how they can have fun together and learn from each other. For example, buddies may learn some basic greetings from ELLs in their language. However, it is important to make sure that buddies and ELLs can get their schoolwork done together.

In addition to schoolwork, buddies can help ELLs and get adjusted to new schools. For example, teachers can encourage the buddies to do these things with new ELLs:

- Help them learn classroom/school norms.
- Learn how to communicate with them using gestures and short phrases.
- Teach them the ABCs, numbers, and beginning vocabulary.
- Play student-made vocabulary games with them.
- Listen to taped books with them.
- Take them to ESOL class and back again.
- Sit with them in the lunchroom.
- Include them in games on the playground.
- Walk home with them or sit with them on the bus.
- Learn a few words of the newcomer's language.

Set up some regular hours for the ELLs to work with their buddies. For example, allow the ELLs to spend time each day during the first few weeks speaking and talking with the buddies of the same native language. ELLs need to know about school routines and find out "What's going on in the new school?" Sometimes there are no students in the newcomer's class who speak the ELLs' language. Keep a list of the people in your building or within your reach who speak the languages of your ELLs. Sometimes you may need someone to translate important messages. This list can include other teachers, same-language students in other classes, or bilingual parent volunteers. Make sure that the main office and the school nurse have a copy of this list so that it can be available when needed.

Tip 3: Getting Started With Newcomers

When English language learners first enter the classroom, it can be overwhelming for teachers who are responsible for their learning. It is sometimes difficult to find where to start and how to work with them when they cannot communicate with you. The following are things teachers can do to get a good start with newcomers:

- Think of a few beginning activities and prepare materials to work with your ELLs with the purpose of building basic vocabulary. For instance, you can prepare a packet that includes materials used to introduce colors, numbers, shapes, number words, body parts, and survival vocabulary. Once your students know their basic vocabulary, you can work with them on a variety of activities.

- Find out whether your ELL students know the Roman alphabet. If not, you need to be patient and allow time for them to have a plenty of practice. Those students who know the Roman alphabet may not know how to read in cursive. Some cultures require different ways of writing.

- Find a bilingual volunteer available during the beginning weeks. Involve this volunteer for assistance when your ELLs are adjusting to the new environment, such as translating school normal and classroom routines. Some bilingual parents of the buddies can play this role and fill the gap by serving as a translator between you and your new students during the first few weeks to make them feel comfortable.

- Work with your ELLs together to prepare a picture dictionary. Staple sheets of construction paper together and have students cut out pictures from magazines. Use categories that complement your curriculum (e.g., a Healthy Foods section to go with your health unit on nutrition). Encourage ELLs to add to their dictionary whenever they learn new words. This is an excellent cooperative learning activity in which teachers can involve the input of the mainstream students.

- Make a vocabulary poster. To make a vocabulary poster, teachers can have ELLs and other students work in cooperative groups. Have each group of students cut out pictures from magazines and label them to create large posters of categories of common vocabulary words. Categories might be food, clothing, body parts, colors, animals, playground scenes, family groups, classroom, street scenes, house and furniture, or transportation. Display the posters in your classroom.

- Read aloud to your new ELLs daily. This reading must be accompanied by pictures, gestures, or dramatic voice to convey meaning. This is also great practice for mainstream first and second graders who are learning to read.

- Have your ELL students practice their English using a computer program or a book with a cassette tape. Be careful with this activity by having an appropriate time frame so that the ELLs won't be alone by themselves all day along. This is because they also need time to interact with peers in order to learn English.

- Have a daily conversation session with your ELLs. Teachers can model some questions with answers for the ELLs to have conversation with you. For example, you can ask them about items and surroundings in the classroom, such as "Is there a desk in the room?" Then you can progress to "Is there a book or a pencil on the desk?" This will help increase their speaking ability through daily conversation.

Tip 4: Additional Activities for ELLs

- ELLs need to know the school environment. Teachers can guide ELLs to make flash cards of the items that are often seen in classrooms and school. Teachers can also ask peer tutors to work with the ELLs with these additional activities:

    1. Introduce the classroom vocabulary to new students, point to some real objects in classrooms, and say each word in English.
    2. Have ELLs repeat these words verbally. Have each word written down on the cards in English and the native language or draw a picture of the object.
    3. Ask ELLs to point to each item as you name it. Or you point to an item while they name it.
    4. Indicate an item and ask ELLs, "What is this?" Gradually guide ELLs to know the classroom vocabulary. If ELLs are literate in their native language, teachers can use the school words as a basis for reading and writing activities in English.
    5. Have ELLs write these words with a sentence for each card, with the sentence pattern that you provide. For example, "This is a _____."
    6. Provide ELLs with a folder for keeping their cards and work together. Organizing the work will enable ELLs to more easily refer to the cards in other activities.
    7. If necessary, teachers can provide ELLs with a second set of cards. Have them use the cards to make flash cards, concentration games, and sorting activities.

- Once ELLs are familiar with the classroom vocabulary, teachers can play games with the ELL. For example, if your ELLs already know the names of some small items in your classroom, you can play this game:

1. Put 6 to 10 items on a table and cover them with a cloth. Items may include a pen, pencil, eraser, marker, crayon, rubber band, stapler, ruler, scissors, book, paper, etc.

2. Give the students a few minutes to look at the items. (The length of time will depend on the age and ability of the students.)

3. Have students cover their eyes while you remove one item.

4. Allow students to guess what was removed. The student who guesses correctly gets to remove the next item.

In all, teachers can find interesting ways to engage ELLs and encourage their participation. It is in classrooms that ELLs have the opportunity to interact with their English-speaking peers and to experience the new language. Involving the ELLs' participation can also help them overcome many challenges on their journey from their home language and culture to the English-dominant culture and new school environment. This also gives them the confidence and helps them become socially proficient and academically successful. Thus, teachers must make the effort and find ways to engage ELLs.

Working on Teacher-Student Relationships

Positive teacher-student relationships are the foundation of a successful classroom and particularly one that includes English language learners. According to research, a positive teacher-student relationship is the most powerful weapon for teachers to foster a favorable learning climate, and it is also associated with positive learning outcomes (Boynton & Boynton, 2005; Mohr & Mohr, 2007; Thompson, 1998). Therefore, working on positive teacher-student relationships is important for improving learning for ELLs and all students. When students feel that teachers value them and care for them as individuals, they are motivated and will participate in learning and classroom activities. They are also more likely to be respectful and caring for each other when they feel that important adults in their lives respect them and genuinely care about them.

Teachers must continually reflect on their teaching and update their practice to address the needs of ELLs and all students and place a strong emphasis on the human side of teaching, that is, working on positive teacher-student relationships. As educators, we know that learning occurs in the context of a social environment. The relationships accompanying a range of social behaviors among students can have a major impact on how well ELLs learn English and how well all students learn overall. No students can achieve in an unwelcoming, hostile environment. Thus, teachers must be good role models, foster a positive teacher-student relationship in classrooms, and communicate positive expectations so that students will be respectful and caring for each other. For example, ELL students should not be made fun of when they speak English with an accent. If this happens, they can withdraw and not participate, which further interferes with their academic achievement.

Teachers can develop strong and powerful relationships with ELLs and all students by integrating some strategies through positive interactions with students in classrooms daily (Alford & Nino, 2011; Boynton & Boynton, 2005; Mohr & Mohr 2005). The purpose is to build a supportive learning environment and to enhance achievement for ELLs and all students. Although teachers can choose many different strategies, these three are especially powerful in helping to build a positive teacher-student relationship in classrooms: (a) communicating positive expectations, (b) correcting students in a constructive way, and (c) demonstrating caring.

First, *communicating positive expectations* means that teachers foster positive interactions and communicate to students high behavioral and academic expectations to all students, including ELLs. Teachers need to communicate clearly that you expect them to do well and tell them that they can do well. Every child needs a significant adult in his or her life who believes in him or her (Boynton & Boynton, 2005; Kerman et al., 1980). Sometimes the parents may not be able to fulfill this role. Thus, teachers have the unique opportunity and privilege to communicate daily to their students that you believe in them. When a student is told that you know he or she will behave appropriately because he or she was successful yesterday, you help build confidence in that student and increase his or her chance for success. After a student demonstrates good behavior or academic achievement in a specific situation, telling her that you knew she would be successful instills confidence in that student through your positive expectations. This also applies to ELLs who need confidence and motivation to perform well through the positive expectations that you communicate with them daily.

Second, *correcting students in a constructive way* is a way to provide a fair and meaningful consequence for a student's inappropriate behavior. Yet teachers must remember that it is important to communicate that you care for and respect the students and you do so because you expect them to be successful. In fact, teachers can build positive relationships by correcting students in a constructive way. For example, it is not constructive if the student thinks, "I hate my teacher. I'm going to be sure I don't get caught next time." The correction process will not be productive if students are corrected in a manner that communicates bitterness, sarcasm, low expectations, or disgust (Boynton & Boynton, 2005; Kerman et al.,

Table 4.3. Correcting Students in a Constructive Way

Steps	Procedures	Caution
Step 1. Before Action	• View what happened. • Predict the student's feeling. • Think of alternative actions.	Think of a private location for correction.
Step 2. During Action	• Meet the student and explain the established rule and policy as it applies to the situation. • Let the student know that all students are treated the same with respect to the consequence. • Let the student know that you are disappointed in having to invoke this consequence due to his or her action. • Communicate an expectation that the student will do better in the future.	Treat students as you want your own children treated, stay calm, and avoid frustration.
Step 3. After Action	• Touch base with the student. • Acknowledge postdisciplinary success and encourage continued success. • Be persistent.	Remain friendly.

1980). Instead, if students are allowed to keep their dignity and the correction focuses on improvement instead of punishment, you increase the chance that the students will reflect on their behavior and choose their behavior more wisely next time. A three-step process of correcting students in a constructive way is listed in Table 4.3. Teachers need to view the situation, think of alternatives, and take actions with caution for positive outcomes.

Third, *demonstrating caring* means that you demonstrate that you sincerely care for your students through actions and words. Caring is one of the most powerful ways to build positive relationships with your students. When teachers care, students are more likely to enjoy coming to school and performing well. Demonstrating caring can also be is a preventive approach to discipline problems (Boynton & Boynton, 2005; Kerman et al., 1980). When students feel cared for, they are more likely to be willing to comply with classroom rules and policies. Sometimes it is unfortunate that students mistakenly believe that their teachers do not care for or like them. Most teachers do care but sometimes fail to communicate this valuable message. Teachers can use many strategies to demonstrate caring. The following are especially effective ways for teachers to show students that you care about them:

- Showing an interest in your students' personal lives
- Walking and talking
- Greeting the students by the door in the morning
- Touch base with students daily
- Exchanging teacher-student letters

Showing an interest in your students' personal lives is a powerful way to communicate with your students that they are important and cared for. Take time and talk with students on a daily basis. This can easily be done by checking in with a few students each day, either before class, while they are working at their desks, or after class. Asking students about their experiences inside and outside of school can help build a genuine relationship. The students will know that their teacher is interested in their lives. You can also ask about their families, about their hobbies, a recent trip, or a sports activity. Be careful to share equal time with all students when you use this strategy so that no student feels that there is *favoritism*. You can use the information you have learned about your students to further develop some learning activities, such as having students write a journal or draw pictures for younger children about the places they visited or describe about their hobbies and sports.

Walking and talking with your students is another powerful way to communicate with ELLs and all students how much you care about them. Having one-on-one conversations with students about their goals, interests, struggles, and so on can be difficult to do during class time. One way to quickly connect with students is to take a brief walk around the school campus (Ferlazzo, 2012; Haynes, 2007). This 5-minute conversation could take place before or after school, or even during a teacher's prep period if an arrangement is made with a student teacher. These talks can strengthen the teacher-student relationship and help you to get to know new ELLs or to deal with students who are having behavior or learning challenges. Students feel cared for when teachers can have individual time with them and listen to them. Be sure to maintain eye contact and paraphrase if needed, which helps students feel that you are genuine.

Greeting students at the door and welcoming them in the morning as they enter the classroom is a quick and easy way to show students that they are important and that you are glad to see them. This procedure also helps generate a positive feeling with the students for a good start of the day because the teacher has made personal contact with each and every student. Research indicates that this approach is a proactive classroom management procedure for a productive day because it builds a on positive note and advocates for a positive way to begin the day and the school year (Allday & Pakurar, 2007; Wong & Wong, 1998). Teachers can use verbal greetings to each student, such as praising a student for walking in quietly or simply saying, "Hello, how's it going, Fernando?" or "Thank you for walking in quietly, Anna." Or teachers can use nonverbal greetings, such as patting the student on the back, giving the student a thumbs up, high 5, fist bump, head nod with eye contact, or even a wink. In addition to positive greetings and interactions, teachers can take this opportunity to briefly exchange information with each student. For example, after saying hello, teachers can ask students to look at the daily schedule, to check their name as being present on the attendance list, or check if they are at the right place when it is the beginning of the school year.

Touch base with students daily is another way to demonstrate caring for the students and letting them know that they are important. Most teachers work hard at improving teaching and improving student learning. Creating a positive atmosphere is a powerful way to help improve student learning. Touching base with students on a daily basis is an important way that teachers can continue to promote a caring school culture, which can result in student success. Students are more successful when they feel safe. When you see students display strong emotions (e.g., when they are happy, excited, or angry), you have an opportunity to build positive relationships by asking how they are doing and what is going on with them. Use statements such as, "Are you all right?" and "Can I help with anything?" to let students know they are cared for, valued, and noticed. In addition, when you pay attention to students, they understand that they are recognized and valued. This does not mean that you have to agree with all their actions, but that you let them know that you are paying attention to them by touching base with them daily. You can communicate empathy by telling students that even though it's wrong to hit someone, for instance, you understand the emotions behind an incident.

Exchanging teacher-student letters is another way to improve teacher-student relationships. Teachers can introduce themselves by writing a brief letter to the class during the first week of school. This letter can serve as a model for students to follow as they write back to the teacher. The teacher's letter could be simplified depending upon the level of the class, and the teacher could give beginning students the sentence frames to scaffold their letters.

For example, students can start with *My name is* _____. *I am* _____ *years old. I was born in* _____. This activity helps teachers learn about students and also provides a sample of each student's writing. Teachers can stay connected to students by exchanging letters during the school year. Sometimes teachers simply encourage students to write in the form of reflections or responses to questions on a weekly basis. The teacher can structure the journal prompt or questions as an invitation for students to share their feelings, concerns, and questions about the class and about their lives outside the classroom. For example, ask what classroom activity they liked the best this week and why. What are their weekend plans? Reading student reflections can help teachers "take the pulse" of the class, that is, which activities are being enjoyed, areas of confusion, pacing issues, and so on. Teachers can make adjustments, offer feedback, and address any concerns. Teachers also gain important information about what is going on in their students' lives and can use this information as "talking points" when they speak one-on-one with students. These letters and reflections can also be used as a formative assessment.

These are just a few ways that you can demonstrate to your students that you care about them. As indicated earlier, teachers should never underestimate the power of demonstrating caring. The importance of caring helps build strong positive relationships that in turn help enhance student learning and also help prevent discipline problems. Use these strategies to consistently communicate your positive expectations and build the positive teacher-student relations and they will work wonders. In all, teachers must foster positive relationships with students through daily interactions with them. Not only does this contribute to a positive class-room environment, but it also improves student learning and contributes to the quality of school life for both you and your students.

Involving Parents and Family Support

Involving parents and family support is an important way to engage ELLs. Family support builds relationships that strengthen the develop-mental journey with families. It helps the family construct a solid founda-tion, which fosters the growth of its members and children's learning. Family is important in the Hispanic culture. Families have a strong sense of interdependence, mutual respect, and co-parenting (Haynes, 2007). Grandparents, godparents, aunts, uncles, and older siblings may help raise ELLs. This extended family might live at home, visit frequently, or live nearby. Hispanic families may travel back and forth between their native country and the United States. Understanding this family structure helps you gain trust from the immediate and extended family members when involving family support.

If you really want to know your ELLs, you need to know their parents and extended families. Hispanic parents in the United States tend to make big sacrifices for the future of their children. They often move far from home and work long hours so that their children can have a better educa-tion and succeed in life. Therefore, it is no surprise that these parents have high expectations and aspirations for their children's success in school. Yet, due to some circumstance, the family may be reluctant to meet with you. In this situation, you need to respect their wishes and understand that they may have good reasons for this. However, many parents do want to meet you. If they do, you can introduce yourself to them. Hispanic parents in the United States care deeply about their children's education, but they may not be used to taking an active role. It is up to the teacher to explain that in the United States it is common that teachers invite the parents to be in touch, come to school for conferences, help with reading and homework at home, and make decisions together with the school.

Sometimes ELL parents may work several jobs or do not have the means of transportation to come to schools. Yet this doesn't mean the parents don't want to be involved or that they don't have high aspirations for their children. Research indicates that two thirds of Latino teens say their parents play an active role in their education, and 8 of 10 say their parents urge them to go to college (Cummins, 2004; Goodz, 2004). In many cases, parents of ELLs speak a language other than English. This creates a barrier to developing a collaborative relationship for the benefit of these children. Yet there are some strategies that teachers can use to help communicate with parents of ELLs in an effective way. The following strategies can be used to build a collaborative relationship and help improve learning for ELLs.

Mail letters home before the school year starts to say hello, preferably in the ELL student's home language, and tell the ELL's parents that you are eager to meet them. *Make phone calls* to ELLs' parents from classrooms to tell them something specifically good about their children, such as "Anna did so well on the multiplication quiz today!" These phone calls help teachers reflect on each child's progress and also make sure everyone has the opportunity to get a positive call. It can make a big difference in a parent's attitude. *Go to their home* if you can't get them on the phone. You can call home first: "I'd like to work out a plan to make your child successful." Parents love to hear about children's success. Once you are there at the kitchen table, you can tell the parents that you want to empower their child and ask, "What might be the best way to address your child's learning style?"

Sometimes teachers can learn a few basic words and everyday expressions in Spanish for brief communication with parents and family members. This may be a small gesture for you, but using Spanish phrases can mean a great deal to your ELLs and their families. Making the effort shows that you respect and value their language. Learning some basic Spanish-English cognates and common classroom words and phrases will help you gain this trust. If needed, you can take a Spanish class to learn more Spanish to improve communication with Hispanic families and parents. By going through the process of learning a second language, you will better understand the challenges faced by your ELLs, who have to learn English and subject matter at the same time. You will also become more aware of effective strategies for teaching your students. This will help build positive relations with ELL families.

You can also learn about the students' culture and know where your ELL students come from. You also need to move beyond the "Latino and Hispanic" label. The ELL may be a Mexican student or a second-generation Mexican American. Or he or she may be from Central America, a Caribbean island, or South America. Your students and their families have interesting histories and a rich cultural heritage to share. Sometimes teachers can make an effort to learn more by reading about their ELL students' countries, regions, and customs. Teachers can find this information in books, articles, and on the Internet. Reading encyclopedias or travel guidebooks will give you a basic overview of their countries. Teachers can bring their cultures into the classroom by inviting ELL family members for show-and-tell, storytelling, food tasting, dancing, and such. Doing this will likely raise the self-esteem of ELL students and generate greater respect from their class peers. A solid relationship between the school and the home is essential for the educational development of children. Parents play a vital role in helping their child to learn the skills necessary to succeed in school. Teachers and schools have an obligation to reach out to parents and the community in order to open and maintain a healthy relation and keep positive contact in a collaborative way between the school and the home.

SUMMARY

This chapter discusses the importance of engaging ELLs and their participation. Useful tips are provided to help teachers get to know their ELLs and to engage their school participation. The chapter also discusses the importance of building a positive teacher-student relationship and the importance of involving the parents and family support. Despite the need to use and develop their English-language proficiency, ELLs are sometimes silent and reluctant to participate. It is important for teachers to provide a supportive environment to engage them in participation that increases their learning success. We hope that the information and strategies in this chapter can help teachers work with ELLs in a positive way in classrooms.

REFERENCES

Alford, B., & Nino, A. C. (2011). *Leading academic achievement for English language learners: Guide for the principals*. Thousand Oak, CA: Sage.

Allday, R. A., & Pakurar, K. (2007). Effects of teacher greetings on student on-task behavior. *Journal of Applied Behavior Analysis, 40*(2), 317–320.

Boynton, M., & Boynton, C. (2005). *Educator's guide to preventing and solving discipline problems*. Alexandria, VA: ASCA.

Cazden, C. (2001). *Classroom discourse: The language of teaching and learning*. Portsmouth, NH: Heinemann.

Cummins, J. (2004). Knowledge, power and identity in teaching English as a second language. In F. Genesee (Ed.), *Educating second language children: The whole child, the whole curriculum* (pp. 33–58). New York, NY: Cambridge University Press.

Ferlazzo, L. (2012, April 17). Seven tips for building positive relationships with English-language learners. *Edutopia*. Retrieved October 2012, from http://www.edutopia.org/blog/building-positive-relationships-ELL-larry-ferlazzo-katie-hull-sypnieski

Goodz, M. (2004). Interactions between parents and children in bilingual families. In F. Genesee (Ed.), *Educating second language children: The whole child, the whole Curriculum* (pp. 61–81). New York, NY: Cambridge University Press.

Haynes, J. (2007). *Getting started with English language learners: How educators can meet the challenge*. Alexandria, VA: ASCA.

Kerman, S., Kimball, T., & Martin, M. (1980). *Teacher expectations and student achievement*. Bloomington, IN: Phi Delta Kappan.

Jalongo, M. R., & Li, N. (2010). Young English language learners as listeners: Theoretical perspectives, research stands, and implications for instruction. In B. Spodek & O. Saracho (Eds.), *Contemporary perspectives on language and cultural diversity in childhood education* (pp. 95–115). Charlotte, NC: Information Age.

Li, N., Howard, C., & Mitchell, Y. (2011). What a case study reveals: Facing the new challenge and learning the basics in L2 acquisition. *The National Teacher Education Journal, 3*(2), 57–69.

Mohr, K. J., & Mohr, E. S. (2007). Extending English-language learners' classroom interactions using the response protocol. *The Reading Teacher, 60*(5), 440–450.

Saracho, O. N., & Spodek, B. (2010). Language and cultural diversity in early childhood education. In B. Spodek & O. Saracho (Eds.), *Contemporary perspectives on language and cultural diversity in childhood education* (pp. 1–17). Charlotte, NC: Information Age.

Stipek, D. (2002). At what age should children enter kindergarten? A question for policy makers and parents. *SRCD Social Policy Report, 16*(2).

Thompson, R. A. (1998). Early socio-personality development. In W. Damon (Series Ed.) & N. Eisenberg (Vol. Ed.), *Handbook of child psychology: Vol. 3. Social, emotional, and personality development* (5th ed., pp 25-104). New York, NY: Wiley.

Yoon, B., & Kim, H. K. (2012). *Teachers' roles in second language learning: Classroom applications of sociocultural theory*. Charlotte, NC: Information Age.

Wong, H. K., & Wong, R. T. (1998). *The first days of school*. Mountain View, CA: Harry K. Wong Publications.

PART III

BASIC VOCABULARY

CHAPTER 5

ACADEMIC WORDS FOR ELLS

CASE SCENARIO

Soraya is a sixth grader and she came to the United States with her family from the Dominican Republic. Her parents spoke some English at home with the children, but they both worked from home. Soraya spent most time with her maternal grandparents who spoke to her only in Spanish. Soraya's oral English proficiency was tested at the beginning level. She also had limited academic English vocabulary and word knowledge. She was required to attend the ESOL class and met her ESOL teacher daily at her new school. She stayed in her mainstream classrooms after her ESOL class period. What Soraya struggled with most was reading and writing. This affected her learning subject content because she could not understand instruction or respond to the questions in content lessons. Her teacher kindly provided her a bilingual dictionary. Yet Soraya often became frustrated because of multiple meanings of an English word for her to choose and use in the right context. Even though she was good at mathematics in her home country, she often failed mathematic exams now. As result, she didn't do well in standardized testing either. Her teacher tried the best to help her as she could. Yet it appeared to be especially difficult for her to understand those academic words in content areas, such as social studies, mathematics, and science.

Teachers may find that many ELLs are in the same situation as Soraya. They are challenged to understand academic English words. Due to the

A Book for Every Teacher: Teaching English Language Learners
pp. 105–141
Copyright © 2015 by Information Age Publishing

cultural differences, they may not know the multiple meanings of an English word used in different contexts. For example, "foot" can refer to the body part below the ankle; yet it also refers to the measurement of one foot a being equal to 12 inches or 0.3048 of a meter; also, it can mean the leg of a piece of furniture, especially when shaped or modeled or the bottom of a slope, hill, and stairs; it can be used as a verb and in idioms, such as "*walks with a light foot*" or "*She footed the rest of her way down the hill.*" Yet an ELL may know only the basic meaning and definition of this word. Academic vocabulary is made up words and phrases that consist of general academic words that ELLs might see in different subjects, specialized academic words that are related to a specific subject content area, and technical academic words that are specifically related to a topic in a subject or a technical area (Egbert & Ernst-Slavit, 2010). In this chapter, basic academic words that are important for ELLs to learn are introduced with strategies for teaching ELLs at the beginning level. These academic words include these categories: numbers, shapes and colors, subject content words, and common descriptive words used in classrooms and schools.

Numbers

Numbers are expressed usually by a word, symbol, or figure representing a particular quantity and used in counting and making calculations and for showing order in a series or for identification and for showing order in a series or for identification. Numbers are used in many ways, for example, in telling temperature, phone dial numbers, counting money, and banking. ELLs will encounter numbers when they come to school and classrooms on the first day. Academically, numbers are used in many ways in school and classrooms. For example, students will use numbers to tell the time and date, do calculations in mathematics, learn the timeline of historical events in history lessons, and in many other content area lessons. To effectively teach ELLs numbers, it is important that teachers find efficient ways of teaching ELLs and all students so that they can learn numbers efficiently. The following method helps teach students learn to count numbers from 1 to 1,000 in as quickly as five days at the beginning of school (see Table 5.1).

Teachers need to have a whiteboard, chalkboard, or chart paper. In fact, the Post-it-note chart paper with colored markers will work well. The key point is to help students see the numbers as they are written both in word format (e.g., *one*, *two*, and *three*) to see how numbers are spelled and in Arabic numeric form (e.g., *1*, *2*, and *3*).

Table 5.1. Teaching Numbers From 1 to 1,000

Day 5	Day 3	Day 4	Day 1	Day 2
100 one hundred		1 one		11 eleven
200 two hundred	20 twenty	2 two		12 twelve
300 three hundred	30 thirty	3 three		13 thirteen
400 four hundred	40 forty	4 four		14 fourteen
500 five hundred	50 fifty	5 five		15 fifteen
600 six hundred	60 sixty	6 six		16 sixteen
700 seven hundred	70 seventy	7 seven		17 seventeen
800 eight hundred	80 eighty	8 eight		18 eighteen
900 nine hundred	90 ninety	9 nine		19 nineteen
1,000 one thousand		10 ten		

Day 1: Learn Numbers 1–10

1. Introduce numbers from 1 to 10 by using hand gestures to teach each number and help ELLs count each number as the number is written on the board/chart paper (see Table 5.1). Teachers can ask students to follow while the numbers are counted and written. Guide students to pronounce each number from 1 to 10.

2. Ask students to incorporate their hands and practice the numbers several times until they are familiar with the sound and able to count them. ELLs might struggle with "th" (ð) sound in "three." Focus on rehearsal with hand gestures and sound.

3. Confirm these number words from 1 to 10 and be sure students are able to count each of the numbers fluently. Incorporate TPR, sound, graphics, and pictures if needed in order to help students. Count up and count down (i.e., 1 to 10 and 10 to 1). In all, make sure that ELLs are able to count the numbers fluently and confidently.

Day 2: Learn Numbers 11–19

1. Help students review the numbers from 1 to 10 learned in Day 1. Be sure that the students know these numbers well and can count/recognize them. Check understanding by asking the students tell the numbers as they are pointed randomly.

2. Introduce new numbers from 11 to 19. Use the same procedure as used in Day 1. Ask the students to pay attention to the differences

of the word ending, that is, "*-teen*" as from *thirteen* to *nineteen,* and help students to pronounce them correctly.

3. Confirm the numbers from 11 to 19 with multiple practices. Review the numbers from 1 to 19 and ask ELLs to count up and count down with fluency as each number is pointed to randomly. Be sure they can count and recognize each number from 11 to 19.

Day 3: Learn Numbers 20–90

1. Help students review the numbers from 11 to 19. Be sure they can count the numbers fluently and practice as needed. Also, check understanding for numbers from 1 to 10.

2. Introduce new numbers from 20 to 90. Use the same procedure in Day 2. Ask the students to pay attention to the differences in how each number ends, that is, "-ty" as from *twenty* to *ninety.* Practice as needed to count up and count down these numbers.

3. Help students to compare the difference by pointing out the endings between 20 and 90 and 13 and 19, that is, the difference between "*-teen*" and "*-ty.*" Encourage them to count each number and practice in multiple ways with visual aids (Table 5.1).

4. Confirm the numbers 20–90, 11–19, and 1–10. ELLs should say each number as they are pointed to randomly. Remind them again of the differences in the endings between "-ty" and "-teen" as in *thirty* and *thirteen*.

Day 4: Learn Numbers 21–99

1. Review numbers 20–90, 11–19 and 1–10. Provide visual aids (Table 5.1) and make sure that ELLs can count all the numbers fluently as they are pointed to.

2. Introduce new numbers from 21 to 99. As shown in Table 5.1, Day 4 is between Day 1 and Day 3. Begin with numbers from 21 to 29. Using a pointer, start with "20" and move the pointer to "1" and say "twenty-one." Use the same method for 22–29.

3. After 22–29, move the pointer to "30." Ask students how to say the numbers from 31 to 39 and practice each number with the pointer. By this time, students should be able to count the numbers without much difficulty. Move to the numbers 41–99 and practice.

4. Review, practice, and confirm all the numbers. Point at a number randomly, for example, "59," and ask students to speak aloud. Students can also write the numbers by their hand gestures.

Day 5: Learn Numbers 100–900

1. Review numbers from 1 to 99 with the visual support (Table 5.1). Practice these numbers randomly by asking students to count the numbers aloud as they are pointed to randomly.

2. Introduce the new numbers from 100 to 900. Focus on the spelling, "*hundred.*" Repeat the procedures in Day 4. Start with *one hundred twenty* to *one hundred ninety.*

3. Help ELLs add single numbers to the numbers. For example, "one hundred twenty-one," "one hundred twenty-two." Use the same procedure for "two hundred thirty-one" until "nine hundred ninety-nine." Then move the pointer to the final number 1,000.

4. Guide students how to say 101 through 109. Write it on the board, "one hundred and one" and remind students to add "and" between numbers. Review all the numbers from 1 to 1,000.

Not all students learn at the same pace. Teachers need to observe the progress and be sure that students are confident before moving on to introduce new numbers. After students learn the concept of how numbers work, it will be easier for them. Providing visual aid support is important to using this strategy and helps students learn the numbers.

Extended Activity

To help ELL students learn numbers, teachers can incorporate other interesting visual aids. Another extended activity to teach numbers is "A Hundred Chart" posted in the classroom on the word wall (see Table 5.2).

Table 5.2. A Hundred Chart Method for the Word Wall

1	2	3	4	5	6	7	8	9	10
11	12	13	14	15	16	17	18	19	20
21	*22*	23	24	25	26	27	28	29	30
31	32	*33*	34	35	36	37	38	39	40
41	42	43	*44*	45	46	47	48	49	50
51	52	53	54	*55*	56	57	58	59	60
61	62	63	64	65	*66*	67	68	69	70
71	72	73	74	75	76	*77*	78	79	80
81	82	83	84	85	86	87	*88*	89	90
91	92	93	94	95	96	97	89	*99*	100

"The word wall" is a literacy tool of an organized collection of words displayed on the classroom wall. This chart can be created with the first row from 1 to 10, the second row from 11 to 20, the third row from 21 to 30 until the 10th row from 91 to 100. This visual chart helps students conceptualize how numbers are related. Students can see the numbers in horizontal and vertical patterns, compare and look for patterns in the numbers (e.g., 11, 22, 33, 44, 55, 66, 77, 88, and 99). It also provides an easy way to practice addition, subtraction, multiplication, and division. In all, teachers can use it creatively.

Shapes and Colors

Shapes. Shape is the external look, appearance, or outer characteristic of an object. ELLs need to know the names of different shapes, especially those related to academic work. Using visual aids, picture cues, and hands-on activities are effective ways to teach ELLs different shapes and describe the shape of an object. The following are the basic words about shapes that ELLs may encounter in subject content areas.

1. *Words for plane figures*: Plane figures refer to any two-dimensional (2-D) shapes such as lines, circles, squares, or triangles that can be drawn on a surface (see Figure 5.1).
2. *Solid figures*: Solid figures refer to any three-dimensional (3-D) shapes that have width, depth, and height. Examples of solid figures are cone, cube, cylinder, sphere, and rectangle. The following figures can appear and are used in math and geometry lessons (see Figure 5.2).

Teachers can incorporate many activities to teach ELLs about different shapes. Many websites provide shape worksheets and activities for teaching ELLs. Teachers can find printable worksheets for ELLs of all levels. The following website provides free worksheets and activities at http://www.eslprintables.com/vocabulary_worksheets/general_vocabulary/shapes/. Teachers can also incorporate an activity called *My Shape Book* to help ELL students learn about shapes. This method has been used in preschools and early grades (see the link for an example: http://www.tls-books.com/minishapebook.pdf). It also helps build on ELLs' vocabulary. The steps to help students creating a shape book are (a) cut different shapes out of construction paper; (b) paste the same shapes of different sizes on page; (c) leave enough space on each page for writing the word, drawing the shape, counting sides and corners of a shape, or drawing

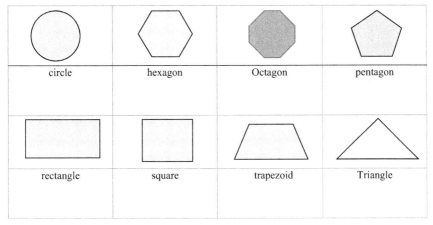

Figure 5.1.

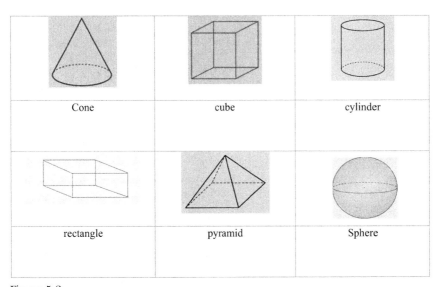

Figure 5.2.

objects that have the similar shape (see Figure 5.3). When helping students learn about shapes, the teacher can also encourage students to write and describe each shape on the page. Students can add a new page to their shape books when a new shape is learned.

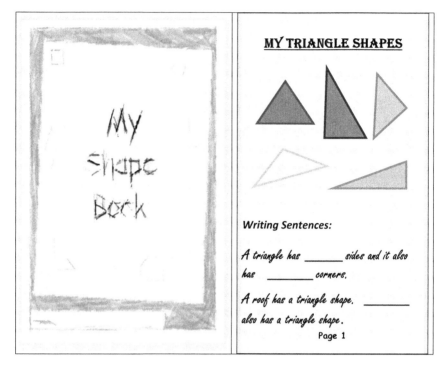

Figure 5.3.   My Shape Book. Students can add more pages as they learn new shapes.

Extended Activity

Based on ELLs' English proficiency level, teacher can extend the shape book activity for teaching shapes. For example, teachers can take ELLs for a walk around the school or neighborhood to observe the shapes of buildings and describe the shapes observed. Prepare a clipboard, a pencil, and some drawing paper for each student. If possible, find a few buildings for them to draw that differ in size, shape, or aesthetic details. Encourage them to notice the different geometric shapes that compose each building. Bring the group together to share and discuss what they have drawn and added these shapes to My Shape Book.

Colors. Color is a visual perceptual property and derives from the spectrum of light interacting in the eye with the spectral sensitivities of the light receptors. Color derives from the spectrum of light interacting in the eye with the spectral sensitivities of the light receptors. Colors include basic colors and neutral colors. Basic and neutral color words are introduced here and each color has a real object that matches the color to help ELLs learn color words. Additional activities are provided for ELLs of different proficiency levels.

1. *Basic color words*: Basic colors refer to the primary, secondary, and tertiary colors. The primary colors are red, yellow, and blue. The secondary colors, a mixture of two primary colors, are green, orange, and purple. Tertiary colors are combinations of primary and secondary colors, such as red-orange, yellow-orange, yellow-green, and blue-green (see Figure 5.4).

2. *Neutral color words:* Neutral color literally refers to a color that does not attract attention or appear to be without color. Yet, in many applications, they refer to the undertones of color, such as beige, ivory, taupe, black, and gray (see Figure 5.5).

Activities

Teachers can help the ELLs learn color words with in the following activities:

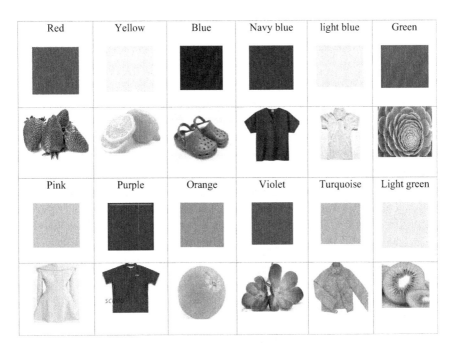

Figure 5.4.

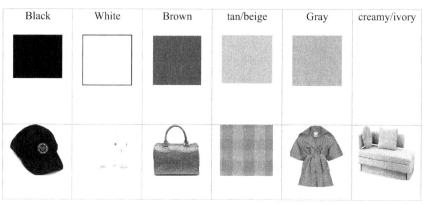

Black	White	Brown	tan/beige	Gray	creamy/ivory

Figure 5.5.

1. *Beginning level*: Incorporate the Total Physical Response (TPR) approach in Chapter 3 and ask students to respond to the teachers' command such as

   (a) Touch your shoulders with your hands if you're wearing blue.
   (b) Clap your hands twice if you're wearing green.
   (c) Walk to the front of the room if you're wearing red.
   (d) Walk to the back of the room if you're wearing orange.

2. *Intermediate level*: Guide ELLs in the following activities:

   (a) Ask ELLs to use color words to describe the color of the objects in school and classrooms and talk about these colors with their peers in classrooms.
   (b) Encourage ELLs to draw the shapes of different colors with colored markers and name a real object that matches the shape and color (i.e., red for apple and circle). Incorporate visual aids for colors and shapes provided in this section.

3. *Advanced level*: Teachers can encourage students to talk about how colors are represented in their home cultures that may different from the United States. Students can also describe how color is associated with moods and represents feelings. For example, the color blue indicates calmness; red is associated with excitement, and green is for peace.

Subject Content Words

Subject content, such as history, geography, math, or science, is what students study in order to acquire a body of knowledge. Subject content words refer to those academic words related to a subject content area. In this section, the commonly used academic words, such as those words used in mathematics, science, and social studies, are introduced.

Mathematics. Mathematics is the subject of study that deals with logic, shape, quantity, and arrangement. Math is often seen as a pure subject from equations to abstract concepts. Yet math is something all around us and is related closely to our daily lives, such as using calculators, mobile devices, architecture design, and engineering. In real life, people cannot live without mathematics. This is the reason that ELLs need to know math vocabulary and words related to math concepts or used in the real world. Math words may have special meaning when it is related to a math concept. For example, the word "right," which *can* mean the opposite of wrong or the opposite of left, refers to an angle with a specific connotation in mathematics. In this section, basic math words related to both concepts and real-world applications are introduced.

1. *Words in Equations*: An equation means that two things are equal. It is often represented with an equal sign "=" such as $7 + 3 = 10$.

   (a) Addition (+): add, sum, find the total amount or numbers, plus, total
   (b) Subtraction (-): subtract, take away, deduct, minus, loss, find the difference,
   (c) Multiplication (x): multiply, combine, reduplicate, reproduce, times
   (d) Division (÷): divide, separate, split, dividend, divisor, remainder

2. *Money Concept Words*: See Figure 5.6.

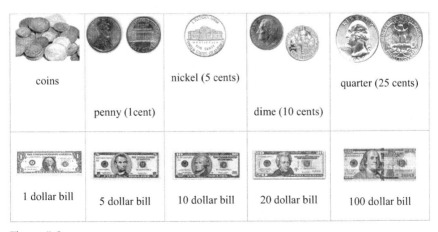

coins	penny (1cent)	nickel (5 cents)	dime (10 cents)	quarter (25 cents)
1 dollar bill	5 dollar bill	10 dollar bill	20 dollar bill	100 dollar bill

Figure 5.6.

3. *Words in Geometry:* Geometry is the branch of mathematics concerned with the properties and relations of points, lines, surfaces, solids, and higher dimensional analogs (see Figure 5.6).

(a) Points: Read as *Point A and Point B*

(b) Line: Read as *Line A and B*

(c) Line segment: Read as *Line segment A and B*

(d) Rays AB: Read *as Ray AB*

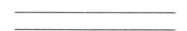

(e) Parallel: Read as *parallel lines*

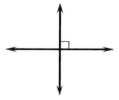

(f) Perpendicular: Read as *perpendicular lines*

(g) Angle: An angle is formed by two rays, sharing a common endpoint, called the vertex of the angle. An acute angle is less than 90°; an obtuse angle is greater than 90° but less than 180°

(h) Right angle: A right angle is an internal angle which is equal to 90°

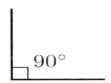

4. *Words for Capacity:* Capacity is the a maximum mount that something can contain.

| gallon | quart | pint | cup | tablespoon |

1 gallon = 4 quarts = 8 pints = 16 cups; 1 cup = 8 ounces; 2 cups = 1 pint; 4 cups = 1quart

Activities

Capacity is a difficult concept to teach. Connecting to life experiences and using real objects and other visual aids can help ELLs learn the basic capacity concept and how to convert them. The *Mr. Gallon Man Activity* is helpful and has been used for teaching students capacity. Teachers can use this strategy, print the patterns, or encourage ELLs to create their own Mr. Gallon Man with illustrations. Here is a website link that allows you to print free Mr. Gallon Man patterns: http://www.theteacherweb-site.com/mrgallonmanproject-tools.pdf

1. *Weight and Length Measures*: America is a country that does not use the metric system. Yet ELLs from other countries may have used or are familiar with the metric system. The frequently used metric measuring words are listed below.

   (a) Length: Metric System

   > 1 millimeter = 1/1,000 meter
   >
   > 1 centimeter = 1/100 meter
   >
   > 1 decimeter = 1/10 meter
   >
   > 1 kilometer = 1,000 meters

   (b) Length: American/British Units

   > 1 inch = 1/36 yard = 1/12 foot
   >
   > 1 foot = 1/3 yard
   >
   > 1 mile = 1,760 yards = 5,280 feet
   >
   > 1 fathom = 6 feet

   (c) Weight: Metric System
   > 1 milligram = 1/1,000,000 kilogram = 1/1,000 gram
   >
   > 1 centigram = 1/100,000 kilogram = 1/100 gram
   >
   > 1 gram = 1/1,000 kilogram
   >
   > 1 kilogram = 1000 grams

   (d) Area measure: Metric System

   > 1 square centimeter = 1/10,000 square meter
   >
   > 1 square decimeter = 1/100 square meter
   >
   > 1 are = 100 square meters
   >
   > 1 square kilometer = 1,000,000 square meters

   (e) Area measure: American/British Units

   > 1 square inch = 1/1,296 square yard = 1/144 square foot
   >
   > 1 square foot = 1/9 square yard

1 acre = 4,840 square yards = 160 square rods

1 square mile = 3,097,600 square yards = 640 acres

(f) Volume and Capacity Measure

1 centimeter = 1/1,000,000 meter

1 milliliter = 1/1,000 liter

1 centiliter = 1/100 liter

1 deciliter = 1/10 liter

1 dekaliter = 10 liters

1 hectoliter = 100 liters

(g) Length and Weight: American/British Units

1 inch = 1/46,656 yard = 1/1,728 foot

1 foot = 1/27 yard

1 yard = 3 feet

1 ounce = 1/128 gallon = 1/16 pint

1 pint = 1/8 gallon = 1/2 quart

1 quart = 1/4 gallon

1 gallon = 128 oz.; 1/2 gallon = 64 oz.

2. *Telling the Time and Date*: Telling time and date is a skill that is as essential as any other real-life skill, such as addition and subtraction, in the digital world. There are different ways of teaching ELLs how to tell the time and date. See examples and activities below:

   (a) Quarter hour: 7:15 a.m.: Read as *seven fifteen* or *a quarter after seven*;
   (b) Three quarters: 10:45 a.m.: Read as *ten forty-five* or *a quarter to ten*
   (c) Half an hour: 2:30 p.m.: Read as *two thirty*.
   (d) Date: October 4, 2014: Read as *October the fourth, two thousand fourteen*
   (e) Date: 4 October 2014: read as *the fourth of October, two thousand fourteen*

Teachers need to explain to ELLs that ordinal numbers are used to pronounce dates. Practice the pronunciation of ordinal numbers, matching the ordinal numbers with words of the same pronunciation, such as *fourth/force*; *first/fast*; *third/bird*; *tenth/tense*, is helpful.

Note: a.m. is the abbreviation for *ante meridiem*, which means *before midday*; p.m. is the abbreviation for *post meridiem*, which means *after midday* in Latin. For example, *The park is open at 7:00 a.m. and closes at 7:00 p.m.*

Activities and strategies for introducing vocabulary words in math to ELLs:

(a) Use visual aids, such as hand clocks, number letters, or other objects

(b) Use BINGO game to teach students' skill at telling time. Teachers can write different times on a board or chart. Students select random times on the list and then write a different time in each square of Telling Time BINGO card.

(c) Resourceful websites: The se websites provide activities for telling time. Click the first link and scroll down to find free online time games that help ELLs of all levels learn to tell time. The games are matching analog to digital clocks, starting with o'clock times, then moving on to half past, then quarter to and past, followed by five minute intervals. The second link explains how to pronounce the time, and the third link gives pronunciation of the dates:

  o http://www.maths-games.org/time-games.html
  o https://www.khanacademy.org/math/arithmetic/telling-time-topic/telling-time/v/telling-time-exercise-example-1
  o http://www.speakenglish.co.uk/phrases/dates

Science

Traditional science lessons may be seen as teachers presenting students with science vocabulary words and asking the students to write the words, finding the definitions in a dictionary or the glossary of the textbook, matching the words to definitions, or using the words in a sentence. This teaching model presents isolation. English language learners have the added burden of trying to learn science in a language they have not yet mastered. Teachers can incorporate different activities to make learning interesting.

Words for amphibians and reptiles: Amphibians mean living two lives (on land and in water). Amphibians have no scales and breathe by means of gills and lungs. They live in damp places where their skin won't be dry. Examples of amphibians are frogs and toads. A reptile is an animal that has dry, scaly skin and breathes by means of lungs. Examples are snakes, lizards, crocodiles, and turtles (see Figure 5.7).

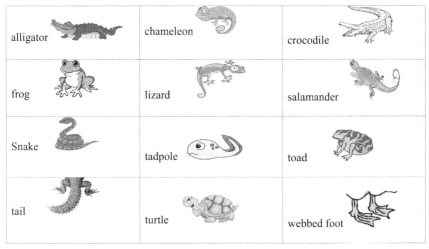

Figure 5.7.

Activities

Engage students in a research project and find out the differences and similarities between amphibians and reptiles. Teachers can also use a K-W-L chart or Venn diagram to organize ideas and enhance students' understanding. The Venn diagram, conceived around 1880 by John Venn, has been used to compare elements and show relationships. Teachers can use Venn diagrams (see Figure 5.8) to help students compare the differences and similarities between amphibians and reptiles as well as frogs and toads or alligators and crocodiles (see Figure 5.9).

Words for insects and arachnids: An insect refers to a small arthropod animal that has six legs and generally one or two pairs of wings, such as flies, mosquitos, or bees. An arachnid is an arthropod that is a joint-legged invertebrate animals, such as a spider.

Activities

Teachers can ask students to do the following activities:

(a) Categorize and classify animals from reading texts about insects and animals.
(b) Prepare a report about their findings in the categories such as insects and animals.
(c) Discuss animals and insects, for example, animal skin coverings and body parts.
(d) Incorporate reading selected children's books about a variety of animals.

Different   Same   Different

Figure 5.8.   Use a Venn diagram to compare the differences and similarities of the animals.

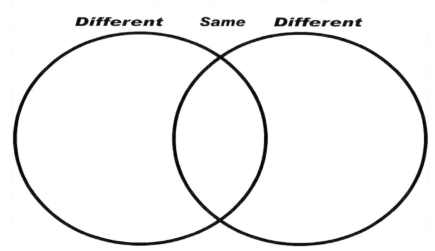

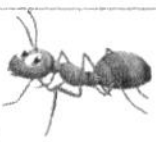

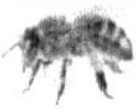

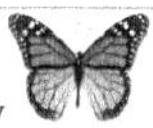

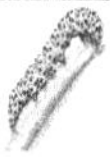

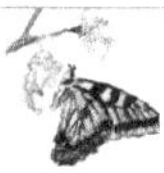

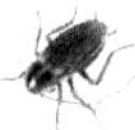

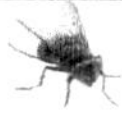

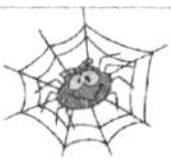

Figure 5.9.

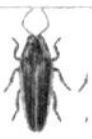

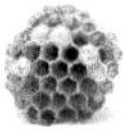

(e) Observe the change of caterpillars or other insects.
(f) Use visual aids to compare and contrast the differences and similarities between insects and animals observed and write a description.

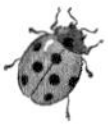

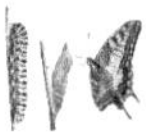

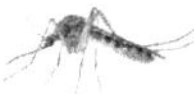

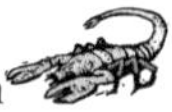

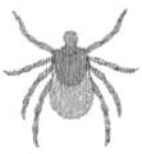

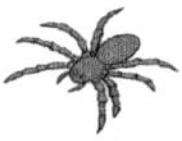

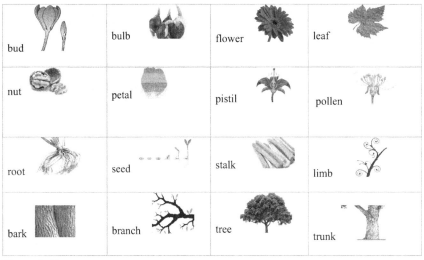

Figure 5.10.

(g) Incorporate drawings, paintings, and other art forms to tell stories about insects and animals you are familiar with and describe verbally.

Words for plants: Plants are a living organism, typically growing in a permanent site, absorbing water and inorganic substances through their roots (see Figure 5.10).

Activities

Teachers can ask students to do the following:

(a) Help ELLs plant flower seeds to observe how plants grow. Divide students into small groups for this project and watch the process, taking notes in journals.

(b) Conduct research and seek useful tips on how to grow plants in a scientific way, for example, plants need sun, water, and the proper temperature to help the process.

(c) Name categories of plants using graphic organizers (K-W-L, Venn diagram) to categorize plants. List familiar plants and unfamiliar ones.

(d) Describe the differences between these words: bud, bulb, petal, pistil; trunk, limb, and branch; leaf, root, and stalk, and so on.

head		hair		face		eye	
nose		ear		mouth		teeth	
lips		cheek		chin		neck	
shoulder		arm		elbow		wrist	
thumb		finger		fingernail		hand	
body		chest		back		leg	
kneel		foot		toe		thigh	

Figure 5.11.

Words for body features: They include those words that are regularly used to describe human body features, such as hair, eyes, arms, and legs (see Figure 5.11).

Activities

Students at the beginning level can do the following activities:

(a) Stand up and sing the "Head, Shoulders, Knees, and Toes" song. While singing, ask ELLs to touch different parts of body following the song.

(b) Students sit on the floor, and each student has at least one body flashcard. Say a random flashcard word (e.g., "ears"). All students with the ears flashcards must do the action. Continue with other words and different actions (e.g., jump up and down, turn around, stand up, sit down, touch toes, etc.).

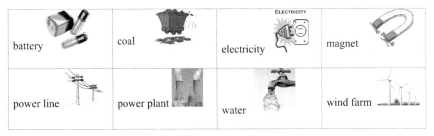

Figure 5.12.

(c) Use TPR and ask ELLs to respond to teachers' commend, such as, "Put your hands on your head," "Put up your right hands up if ... and your left hands up if ..." Or point to the nose, eyes, toes, legs, head, and shoulder for action.
(d) Practice using body part names in sentences: I use my hands to touch, my nose to smell, my ears to listen, my eyes to see, my mouth to eat, etc. Students can take turns.
(e) Ask students to close their eyes. Teachers make a noise with the body parts, for example, clap hands, snap fingers, click tongue. Then ask students to name the body part.

Words for energy: Energy refers to the power derived from the utilization of physical or chemical resources, especially to provide light and heat or to work machines (see Figure 5.12).

Activities

Ask students to do research about the importance of green energy. Discuss how to save energy by using the words above and also the function of energy. For example, the power line is used to conduct electricity. What is the function of wind farm, power plant, and such?

Social Studies. Teachers often find it challenging to make social studies interesting. Students also tend to see Social Studies as a subject that is not as important to their lives or future needs. Yet children love to discover why things are the way they are. Teachers can find ways to arouse their curiosity. Teaching with strengths and trying new things is the key. When we teach with passion, our excitement will be contagious to students, who will look at the content with a unique, individual passion. In this section, basic words from community and government to the environment are introduced with activity suggestions.

Words for community: Community refers to the group of people with diverse characteristics who are linked by social ties, share common per-

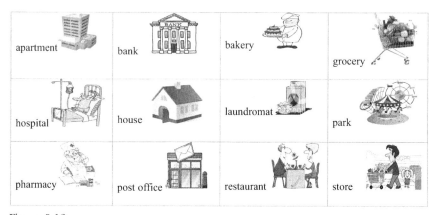

Figure 5.13.

spectives, and engage in joint action in geographical locations, such as a city, town, or neighborhood (see Figure 5.13).

Activities

Teachers can guide students to do the following:

(a) Use the shared events of students' lives in their community to discuss and write about what they have experienced,. For example, how was their experience to visit a doctor, eat dinner in a restaurant, mail a letter at the post office.

(b) Generate topics to discuss on a community service that the students and their families may need to use, such as banking, ordering food in a restaurant, going to park, with the purpose of helping ELLs familiarize the process.

(c) Teachers can verbally describe a place and provide basic features. Then ask ELLs to guess what this place is, such as, "This place is for financial activities, such as depositing or borrowing money or other activities."

(d) Prepare cards with pictures and names of different places where the community service is received. Ask each student to randomly select a card and take turns to describe the place on his or her card, such as, "This is a restaurant." "A restaurant is a place where people eat." "House of Pizza is my favorite restaurant."

Words for professions: A profession refers to an occupation that requires prolonged, specialized training and a formal qualification in order to provide objective counsel and service to others. This section provides those

Figure 5.14.

professions that ELLs may need the services of or need to know such as doctor, nurse, mail carrier, hairdresser, plumber, and policeman (see Figure 5.14).

Activities

Ask ELLs to complete the sentences. Then describe the experiences they may have had with or known about these professionals in real life and do a pair-share activity to describe these professions to their elbow partners:

    (a) A doctor is someone who ...
    (b) A teacher is someone who ...
    (c) A writer is someone who ...
    (d) A singer is someone who ...
    (e) A nurse is someone who ...
    (f) A chef is someone who ...
    (g) A policeman is someone who ...
    (h) A plumber is someone who ...

Figure 5.15

    (i) A hairdresser is someone who …

    (j) A pharmacist is someone who …

Words for government: Government refers to the governing body of a nation, state, or community, or it is the system by which a nation, state, or community is governed. This section provides basic vocabulary words related to government (see Figure 5.15).

Activities
Use worksheets to teach the branches of the government and government concepts, which can be obtained from https://www.teachervi-

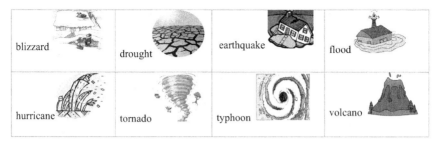

Figure 5.16.

sion.com/government/teacher-resources/6623.html. This website also provides many links to teach students, such as the three branches of the government, with popular government printable worksheets. Use online resources, such as videos, Google maps, and images to help ELLs understand the concepts related to government at different levels.

Words for natural disasters: An adverse natural event, such as a flood, earthquake, hurricane, or volcanic eruption that causes great damage or loss of life (see Figure 15.16).

Activities

Teachers can ask students to do the following activities:

(a) Engage students in discussion about the causes and consequences of those most commonly occurring natural disasters. Also, discuss nature's role versus the impact of human activity in contributing to natural disasters.

(b) List five different natural disasters and divide students into small groups with each group responsible for doing research on one disaster and present their findings.

(c) Use visual graphics, for example, sematic mapping or a Venn diagram, to brainstorm the related words associated with a disaster (see Figure 5.17 as an example).

Words for transportation: Transportation means the action of transporting someone or something from one place to another place or the process of being transported (see Figure 5.18).

Activities

Teachers can guide ELLs in the following activities:

(a) Ask each other this question and respond, "How did you get here today?" The purpose is to practice using different means

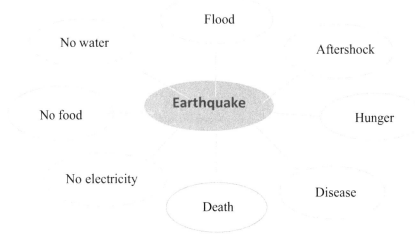

Figure 5.17. Use the semantic map to learn words associated with earthquakes.

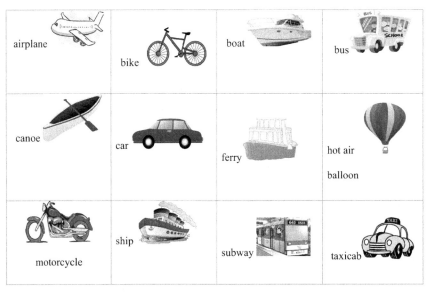

Figure 5.18.

of transportation and the response can be, "I got there _____ (on foot, bus, bicycle, car, train, boat)."

(b) Guide students in the role-play of buying tickets for going to some places by air, bus, or boat. The purpose is to help ELLs become familiar with the transportation process.

Figure 5.19.

> (c) Ask real questions related to students' life and talk about what transportation they have been using to travel, and describe their experiences.

Words for five senses: The five senses are touch, hearing, sight, smell, and taste. The five senses are important in reality because we use them to observe and to sense what is happening in the observable world around us (see Figure 5.19).

Activities

Ask the ELLs to do the following activities to help them understand the five senses:

> (a) The teacher points to the body parts and says, "We use our eyes to ...?" Ask students to respond and have more practice: "We use our ears to ..." "We use our hands to ..." and "We use our noses to ..."
>
> (b) Have one group of students lie on the floor with one ear to the ground while the other group jumps up and down to "hear" the vibrations and describe it.
>
> (c) Place about 10 common objects on a tray, for example, glue, scissors, eraser, pen, pencil, and ask ELLs to observe and tell what they "see" in the tray. Then hide the tray and remove one object and ask students what they "see" now.
>
> (d) Using the old technique of tin cans and string to play telephone, teachers can help ELLs do the same by using plastic cups tied with string to help students understand hearing.

Words for geographic features: These refer to the components of the Earth. Two types of geographical features are natural geographical features and artificial geographical features. Natural geographical features refer to landforms and ecosystems. Artificial geographical features are man-made, such as buildings (see Figure 5.20).

Activities

Teaching geographic literacy is essential to helping ELLs understanding the complex world. Guide students to do the following activities:

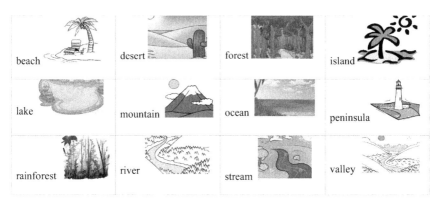

Figure 5.20.

(a) Working in pairs or small groups, compare the different features between a river and an ocean, a forest and a rainforest, an island and peninsula, a valley and a mountain. Tell the popular ones in their home country.

(b) Students fill in a Post-it note for each feature; summarize the differences. Also, write those popular names of rivers, mountains, lakes, or islands and post under a class map of the world. Each group can also discuss their findings.

(c) Prepare students for a BINGO game by listing geographic features or topics related to students' culture and backgrounds. When students have a horizontal or vertical row of examples, they have "Bingo."

Words for continents and oceans: Continent refers to one of the main landmasses of the globe, such as, the sevens (Europe, Asia, Africa, North America, South America, Australia, and Antarctica). Ocean refers to the large expanse of sea, and each is divided geographically (the Atlantic, Pacific, Indian, Arctic, and Antarctic oceans) (see Figure 5.21).

Activities

Teachers can guide students in learning by introducing them to geographic features with visual aids, such as a map (see Figure 5.4) or globe. Ask students to do the following:

(a) Guide ELL students to respond to these questions: *The United States is in which hemisphere (Northern or Southern Hemisphere)? Which continent is in the Southern Hemisphere (Asia or Australia)?*

(b) Practice these sentences in pairs: *Where are you from? I am from _____, which is located in _____ (continent) and close to the _____ Ocean.*

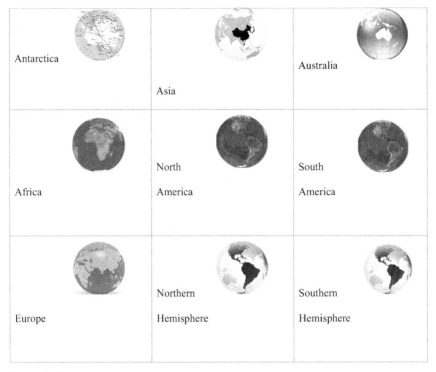

Figure 5.21

(c) Using worksheets, ask ELLs to label the continents and oceans. Then describe the location of a continent or an ocean on the map or globe. For examples, "The *Atlantic Ocean* is surrounded by the continents of *Africa, Europe, North America,* and *South America*." "The *Pacific Ocean* is between the continent of *North America* and *Asia*." "What about the *Arctic Ocean* or *Indian Ocean?*" See Figure 5.22.

American 50 states, abbreviation, and capitals: In the United States, there are 50 states and each state has a capital city and also an abbreviation. Please see Table 5.3 for all the 50 states with the capital cities and abbreviations.

Activities

Teachers can use the information in Table 5.3 and the map of continents and oceans (Figure 5.22) to engage students in the following activities:

Continents and Oceans of the World

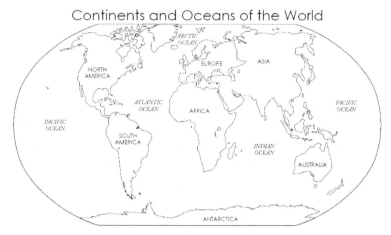

Figure 5.22.

**Table 5.3.   The 50 States of the United States
With Abbreviations and Capital Cities**

State	Abbr.	Capital	State	Abbr.	Capital
1. Alabama	AL	Montgomery	26. Montana	MT	Helena
2. Alaska	AK	Juneau	27. Nebraska	NE	Lincoln
3. Arizona	AZ	Phoenix	28. Nevada	NV	Carson City
4. Arkansas	AR	Little Rock	29. New Hampshire	NH	Concord
5. California	CA	Sacramento	30. New Jersey	NJ	Trenton
6. Colorado	CO	Denver	31. New Mexico	NM	Santa Fe
7. Connecticut	CT	Hartford	32. New York	NY	Albany
8. Delaware	DE	Dover	33. North Carolina	NC	Raleigh
9. Florida	FL	Tallahassee	34. North Dakota	ND	Bismarck
10. Georgia	GA	Atlanta	35. Ohio	OH	Columbus
11. Hawaii	HI	Honolulu	36. Oklahoma	OK	Oklahoma City
12. Idaho	ID	Boise	37. Oregon	OR	Salem
13. Illinois	IL	Springfield	38. Pennsylvania	PA	Harrisburg
14. Indiana	IN	Indianapolis	39. Rhode Island	RI	Providence
15. Iowa	IA	De Moines	40. South Carolina	SC	Columbia
16. Kansas	KS	Topeka	41. South Dakota	SD	Pierre
17. Kentucky	KY	Frankfurt	42. Tennessee	TN	Nashville
18. Louisiana	LA	Baton Rouge	43. Texas	TX	Austin
19. Maine	ME	Augusta	44. Utah	UT	Salt Lake City
20. Maryland	MD	Annapolis	45. Vermont	VT	Montpelier
21. Massachusetts	MA	Boston	46. Virginia	VA	Richmond
22. Michigan	MI	Lansing	47. Washington	WA	Olympia
23. Minnesota	MN	St. Paul	48. West Virginia	WV	Charleston
24. Mississippi	MS	Jackson	49. Wisconsin	WI	Madison
25. Missouri	MO	Jefferson City	50. Wyoming	WY	Cheyenne

Note: Washington, District of Columbia (DC) is the capital of the United States.

Figure 5.23.

Figure 5.24.

(a) Describe the capital city by using, for example, "The capital city of Arizona is Phoenix."
(b) Describe the location of states for example, "Arizona is located southeast of California."
(c) Practice writing an address, such as, 300 Magnolia Street, Orangeburg, SC 29115.

Words for environment: Environment refers to the surroundings, conditions, or natural world in which a person, animal, or plant lives or operates (see Figure 5.24).

Activity

Teachers can engage students to do the following activities:

(a) Guide students to talk about the issues related to water conservation or recycling. Ask students to discuss what things can be done in school and classrooms and at home to protect the environment?

(b) Students work in pairs to list things that can be recycled in school and at home to protect the environment and save energy, for example, "Turn off the light when leaving," "Turn off the water when finished using," "Recycle glass, cans, and paper," "Plant trees and gardens."

Descriptive Words in Classrooms

Words about schools and subjects. These include words that are regularly used to describe schools and subjects, such as elementary or middle school, and subject names (see Figure 5.25).

Activity

Teachers can help students understand these words about schools and subjects by introducing interesting educational activities. The following is an example:

(a) *Hunting Game:* Prepare 10 big flashcards with pictures and names of school subjects on each card. Hide these flashcards around the classroom while students have their eyes closed. Ask students to hunt for these cards. Then work in pairs to write or explain the subject they found and get a reward.

(b) *Drill Practice:* Ask ELLs to speak verbally with sentences such as *I like* _____ *(a subject) because I am really good at* _____ *(the subject). I also like* _____ *(a subject) because* _____ *(give a reason).*

Words for school materials and supplies: These refer to items and small equipment commonly used by students in the course of their studies. Yet they may include not only stationery but also items such as pocket calculators, display boards, or compasses (see Figure 5.26).

Activities

Guide the students to do the following activities:

(a) Play a fun wheel game to help ELLs practice words related to school supplies. This game helps teaching especially young or

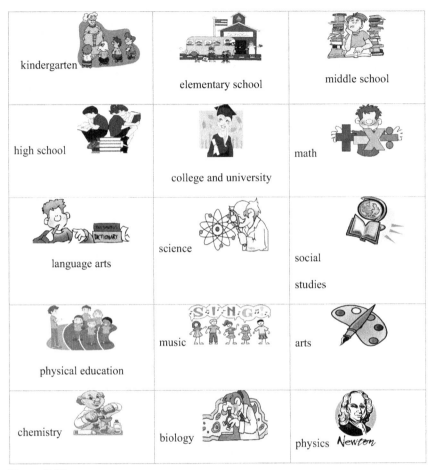

Figure 5.25.

beginner ELLs. This link is useful: http://www.eslgamesplus
.com/school-vocabulary-game-practice-school-supplies-
subjects-school-tools-and-actions/

(b) Help ELLs identify objects and supplies in the classroom and
model them to say, *This is* _____ *(e.g., paper clip) and
it can clip the paper together, this is* _____ *(e.g., envelope) and it
is for mailing a letter, and this is* _____.

(c) *Activity "What Kelly has in Her Bag"*: Use Figure 5.27 and ask
ELLs to describe items in her school bag. ELLs can also name/
describe items in their own bags.

Figure 5.26.

Figure 5.27.

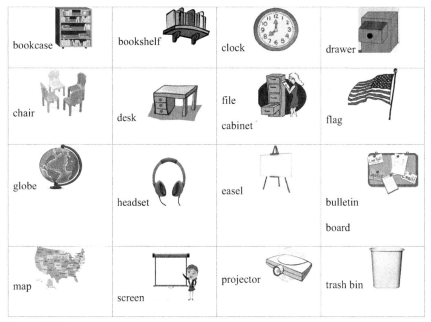

Figure 5.28.

Words for classroom furniture and equipment: Furniture and equipment include words regularly used in classrooms, such as school chairs, desks, or bookcases (see Figure 5.28).

Activities

Teachers can guide students to do the following activities:

(a) Point to objects in the classrooms and ask students to tell the names.

(b) Help students prepare labels for objects in the classroom or different learning centers and guide them to label these objects.

Other common words used in classrooms: There are other common words that are often used in classrooms but are not in the above categories listed in this section (see Figure 5.29).

Activities

Teachers can engage ELLs to do the following:

(a) Use the TPR method to model these words and students respond to each command.

Figure 5.29.

(b) Use visual aids, for example, K-W-L, semantic map, or Venn diagram, to organize information and practice the use of words, for example, raise hand, listening, speaking.

SUMMARY

This chapter introduces basic academic words commonly used schools and classrooms, such as words related to numbers, shapes, colors, words used in subject content, and words used in classrooms. Meaningful activities and strategies about how to introduce and teach these academic words are discussed. Academic words are important components for ELLs in learning L2 and content knowledge. The academic words listed in this chapter are intended to help ELLs at the beginning level or intermediate level lay a foundation for their understanding of academic content and improve their chances for learning success.

REFERENCES

Egbert, L. J., & Ernst-Slavit, G. (2010). *Access to academics: Planning instruction for K–12 classrooms with ELLs.* New York, NY: Pearson.

CHAPTER 6

BASIC DAILY WORDS FOR ELLS

CASE SCENARIO

Jose is a fifth grader and 12 years old from Mexico. He lives with his father and a younger brother. According to him, his mother had to return to Mexico and left him and his sick brother behind. He looks worried and frustrated sometimes. In a conversation, he expressed that he liked school here and his favorite subject was math. However, he also expressed that he needed to know more English words to understand lessons. What he meant was that he needed to expand his word knowledge to understand the lesson content and to read the text and understand the instruction for his homework and assignments. Jose explains that he has a lot of homework but it is hard for him to complete these assignments because he cannot read and comprehend the material. Although Jose is a fifth grader, his reading level is at 0.9, which is equal to a kindergarten reading level. Looking through Jose's folders in each of his content areas shows that his grades are mostly below 60 on a 100 point scale. To help improve his grades, Jose needs to know basic daily English words so that he can understand instruction for schoolwork. Once he understands the instruction, he seems to know the content and can give correct answers. This shows that he knows his grade-level material. Yet it is hard for him to read and sound out the words due to limited word knowledge. To increase his daily vocabulary words becomes one of the most important tasks for him to improve his English and to cope with schoolwork.

A Book for Every Teacher: Teaching English Language Learners
pp. 143–167
Copyright © 2015 by Information Age Publishing

The above scenario represents a most challenging issue that many ELLs face. Life has been difficult for them due to the transition from culture to culture. Above this difficulty, they must learn English to understand instructions for schoolwork. Many of them lack basic daily words to cope with school routines. To facilitate this process and ease the struggle they face, teachers can help ELLs expand their English vocabulary, starting with basic daily English words to help them understand instruction and routines in school. This chapter introduces the basic daily words that ELLs need to know. These daily vocabulary words includes greeting words, direction words, words about food and cafeteria, words about families and relatives, and about weather and sports. ELLs need to know these daily words to cope with life and schoolwork so that they can be prepared and can learn academic content.

Greetings

Greetings are the words and expressions or signs of welcome or recognition. Greetings can also be a message that expresses good wishes to someone. Basic greeting words and expressions are important because friendly greetings are a part of Western culture. Teachers can show ELLs that there are many ways to say greetings. For example, "Hello" in English is a basic word of greetings. There are many ways to say "Hello." People say "Hi," "Hey," or "I am glad to see you," "Nice to meet you" or "How are you?" or "How have you been?" Sometimes people say a quick *hello* as they are passing somebody. At other times, people may say a greeting to lead to a conversation. The common ways of saying greetings are listed in Table 6.1. At many times, people want to use greetings as conversation starters, and some of these expressions may include but are not limited to the following:

- *I am glad to see you.*
- *It's nice to meet you.*
- *How are you?*
- *How are you doing?*
- *How have you been?*
- *How are things?*
- *How's it going?*
- *What's the latest?*
- *What's up?*
- *What's up with you?*

- *What's happening?*
- *Did you have a good trip?" (If the person greeted traveled to the meeting place)*
- *How was the trip?*
- *How was the flight?*
- *How was the traffic?*
- *How were the roads?*

From the above example, we can see some expressions are formal, while others are informal. The expressions, such as "What's up," "What's the latest," or "How's it going," are not very formal. They intend to ask about something new in life to the person greeted. Friends and family members usually greet each other in a casual way, while formal greetings are used in formal settings and situations, such as in a school environment. There are also time-specific greetings, such as greetings in the morning, afternoon, and evening. Some common expressions are "Good morning," "Good afternoon," or "Good evening," or simply say "Morning." See common ways of saying greetings in Table 6.1.

Teachers can explain to ELLs that in English-speaking countries it is normal to make "small talk" in certain situations, such as at a social event or waiting somewhere. Small talk is a casual form of conversation used to break the ice or to fill an awkward silence between people. Even though ELLs may feel shy, teachers can encourage them to consider saying some

Table 6.1.   Ways to Say Daily Greetings

Greetings	Simple "Hello" Greetings	Conversation Starter Greetings	Time-Specific Greetings
Common words and expressions	• Hello • Hey • Hi • Hey, there • Well, there	• It's nice to see you • I am glad to see you • How are you? • How have you been? • How are things? • How is everything? • How was the trip/flight/ road?	• Good morning • Good afternoon • Good evening • Good day
Informal words and expressions	• Howdy? • Hallo? • Alo! • Halo? • Aloha	• Good/great/nice to see you • What's the latest? • What's up? • What's up with you? • What's going on? • What's happening? • Long time no see.	• Morning • Afternoon • Evening • How are you today?

Table 6.2.   Using Small Talk in Different Situations for Conversation

Talking about the weather	• Beautiful day, isn't it? • We couldn't ask for a nicer day, could we? • Did you bring this sunshine? • I hear they're calling for thunderstorms this weekend. • It looks like it's going to snow. • It sure would be nice to be in Hawaii right now. • Can you believe all of this rain we've had? • How about this weather?
Talking about news	• Did you listen to the news today? • Did you hear about that the car accident on the 5th Avenue? • What do you think about the school election? • I read in the paper today that the Sears Mall is closing. • I heard on the radio today that they are going to build a new shelter facility in town. • How about the Ravens? Do you think they're going to win?
Talking about weekends	• Are you looking forward to the weekend? • Have you planned for something nice? • I can't wait until the weekend for nice weather. • Has it been a long week? • It looks like a nice weekend for a picnic in the park. • What do you think you'll do for this nice weekend?
At a school event	• So, how do you like your new school? • Are you enjoying it here? • What is your favorite subject? • You look very nice in that dress/suit. • I love your dress. Can I ask where you got it? • Do you like the speech from the guest speaker?
Out for a walk	• What's your puppy's name? • How old is your baby? • The tulips sure are beautiful at this time of year, aren't they? • How do you like the new park? • Nice day to be outside, isn't it?
Waiting somewhere	• I didn't think it would be so busy today. • You look like you've got your hands full (with children or goods). • The bus must be running late today. • It looks like we are going to be here a while, huh? • I'll have to remember not to come here on Mondays. • How long have you been waiting?

"small talk" and greetings. Just as there are certain times when small talk is appropriate, there are also certain topics that people discuss during these moments. People usually select a neutral topic, such as weather, sports, news, or public events (see Table 6.2).

The following greetings can be used in the classroom. Teachers can explain to ELLs that it is polite to greet a new student who joins the class.

Some tips for using greetings to start a conversation may include saying hello and exchange his or her names and nationalities before one or two lines of small talk about weather, surroundings, news, or events. Teachers can use the following sentence pattern to guide ELLs to practice:

- I'm from … (city or country)
- I hear it's beautiful/hot/expensive there.
- How do you like it here?
- How long have you been here?

Teachers need to explain to ELLs using "I'm from …" instead of "I come from …" that people sometimes refer to "come from" to things or animals and not to people. For example, people usually say: *The toys come from China. Milk comes from cows.* Teaches can guide ELLs to practice and act in a role-play with the following sentence pattern:

A: Hello. I'm Sara.
B: [shaking hands] Hi Sara, I'm Anthony.
A: Nice to meet you, Anthony. Where are you from?
B: Costa Rica. And you?
A: I'm from Mexico. I live in Mexico City.
B: Mexico City. Wow, I've always wanted to go there. I heard it is a beautiful city. How long have you been here in the United States?
A: I have just arrived this week. It's my first day of school.
B: Really? I think you'll like it here. The weather is nice and people are friendly.

Teachers need to explain to the ELLs that a specific situation also needs to be considered when engaging in a small talk. See Table 6.2 as a guide to different situations commonly used as small talk starters.

Directions

Direction words are the words and expressions to tell about directions, positions, and locations relevant to a surrounding or space. Some common directional and positional words are provided in Table 6.3. For the convenience of helping ELLs understand these words, these words are also grouped by synonyms and antonyms, with basic meanings and sample sentences provided.

Teachers can teach these directional words using different methods. Using rhyming words and animals should be interesting to younger ELLs.

Table 6.3. Direction Words With Meanings and Examples

Direction Words	Meanings	Example Sentences
• Above, below (antonyms)	• *Above*: At/in/to a higher place, level • *Below*: At/in/to a lower place, level; preposition, adverb, adjective	• Tony's apartment is above Annie's. • A hawk hovered above. • The temperature is below freezing. • This team is ranked much below.
• around	• On/at every side or all sides from; preposition, adverb	• A snake wrapped around a tree. • The tree was about 40 inches around.
• After, before (antonyms)	• *After*: Behind in a place, position, time; • *Before*: in front/ahead of or prior to a position or time; preposition, adverb, adjective	• The post office closes after 5 o'clock. • She believes in an afterlife. • The office won't open before 9 a.m. • I have never heard about it before.
• behind	• At/to/toward the back or rear of; preposition, adverb, noun	• Look for it behind the tree. • They were behind in this competition. • He was kicked in the behind.
• Beside, besides, next to (synonyms)	• *Beside*: At side of or next to; preposition • *Besides*: in addition to or apart from; preposition, adverb • *Next to*: nearest in space, time, position; preposition	• Your remark was beside the point. • He was beside himself today. • No one besides his parent will do this. • No one besides will do this for him. • He parked beside her car.
• between	• In/to/across/through the position, space; preposition, adverb	• The cats hide between two bushes. • I was caught in between.
• Bottom, top (antonyms)	• *Bottom*: the lowest part, point, level; the far end or part; noun • *Top*: The uppermost part, point, surface, end; noun	• Water is at the bottom of the well. • A bird is on the top of the tree. • She is at the top of her career.
• Down, up (antonyms)	• *Down*: From a higher to a lower place, position; preposition, adverb • *Up*: From a lower to a higher place, position; preposition, adverb	• A boat was floating down the river. • He walked down the trail. • They rowed the boat up the river. • He looked up at the sky. • She was up all night studying.

Far, near (antonyms)	*Far*: To/at/from a great distance, time, space; adjective, adverb *Near*: To/at/within a short distance, time, space; adjective, adverb	• A cat stood far behind the tree. • That is a far country. • They lived near a farm. • He stayed in a near location.
Front, back (antonyms)	*Front*: The forward part or surface; noun, adjective *Back*: the side or part opposite the front, reverse side; noun, adjective	• He parked in front of the house. • The front yard was pretty. • The house has a large back yard
In, inside (synonyms)	*In*: Within the limits, bounds, or area; preposition, adverb *Inside*: within, interior; preposition, adjective, adverb, noun	• The sun goes down around 6:00 p.m. • He opened the door and stepped in. • The inside story is stunning. • The door is locked from the inside.
Left, right (antonyms)	*Left*: on the west side when a body or thing is facing north; adjective, adverb, noun *Right*: on the east side when a body or thing is facing north; adjective, adverb, noun	• He writes with his left hand. • The car turned left and disappeared. • The car turned to the right. • His right hand is strong.
middle	Central, the point/position at an equal distance from all the sides; noun, adjective	• He is in his middle age. • She stood in the middle of the crowd. • He parts his hair in the middle.
Off, on (antonyms)	*Off*: away from a course, position; preposition, adjective, adverb *On*: at a position above, supported by; preposition, adjective, adverb	• He turned off the oven. • The bird hopped off the barn. • She turned on the TV. • She sat on the chair.
out, outside (synonyms)	*Out*: from the inside or center of something to the open; preposition, adjective, adverb *Outside*: to/on the external side; preposition, adjective, adverb	• Out of this door is the garage. • The sun came out. • The garage is outside this door. • Outside in the yard is a treehouse.
over	*At/to/in* a position above or higher; preposition, adjective, adverb	• The cat jumped over the fence. • A tree hung over the cliff.
through	From one end, side to an opposite end, side; preposition, adjective, adverb	• The train went through the tunnel. • The boy climbed in through the window.
Under, underneath (synonyms)	*Under*: in/to a lower position; *Underneath*: below a position or surface; preposition, adjective, adverb	• She put a rug under the table. • She hid the key underneath the rug.

For example, teachers can use some positional words to guide ELLs to understand word meanings while playing with rhymes. Children can also draw pictures about the position of each of the animals.

Where Is My Pet?
I see an eel is *in* a meal.
The meal is *between* deals.
I see a chimp *on* a bike
A monkey is going *for* a hike
A dog is running *to* the hog.
The hog is *after* the frog.
A frog hides *behind* a log.

I also see a cat sleep *under* the hat.
A rat is *underneath* the mat.
A monkey is *outside* the house.
A donkey is *next to* cows.
A snake is *off* to the lake,
I finally find my pet turtle,
My turtle is jumping *over* the hurdle.

Teachers can also use useful website links to print out many free worksheets for teaching directional and positional words and for interactive activities. Some of these links even provide sounds and visual aids for teaching positional and directional words:

- http://www.eduplace.com/math/mw/models/overview/k_2.html
- http://www.pinterest.com/mycahlyn/positional-words/
- http://www.pinterest.com/cherl48/preschool-prepositions-positional-directional-etc/
- http://www.twigglemagazine.com/February-activities/pet-rhyme.html
- http://www.sightwordsgame.com/directional-positional-words/
- http://www.sparklebox.co.uk/maths/shape-space-measures/position.html
- http://www.k-3teacherresources.com/position-words.html
- http://lifelonglearnersinprep.blogspot.com/2013/03/positional-language-activities.html

Food and Cafeteria

Food refers to any nutritious substance that people or animals eat or drink, or that plants absorb in order to maintain life and growth. Cafeteria is a dining room in a school or a business in which students or customers serve themselves or are served from a counter. These are other categories of daily words that ELLs need to know. They need to know these words not only when having lunch in the school cafeteria daily but for going out with the families during the weekend or they need these daily words since they may appear in the reading text. Food is a part of culture and ELLs, especially those who are newly arrived, often find it difficult to select words due to cultural differences between home and school. Teachers need to communicate with the peers to be kind and helpful. Peers can also introduce some basic words related to food that are used daily in the school cafeteria. Some of these daily words related to the food and cafeteria are listed in Table 6.4. They are grouped in fast food, oven-baked foods, grilled, and other food categories.

We can see that food has different categories. Fast food is typical of American food when people do not have much time and need something to be prepared and served quickly. A typical fast food meal in the United States includes a hamburger, French fries, and a soft drink. Due to early European colonization of the Americas, American food has absorbed many foreign ingredients and cooking styles. During the late 19th and early 20th centuries, the large numbers of immigrants further brought various cooking styles. Thus, American food has developed and expanded into a rich diversity by absorbing different styles and ingredients from many places around the world.

For instance, pizza is based on the traditional Italian dish, brought by Italian immigrants to the United States. Hot dogs and hamburgers are both based on traditional German dishes. Many types of the top American food today have foreign ingredients. For example, fajitas originated from a Mexican dish called grilled skirt steak (*faja* in Spanish), which was originally cooked over a campfire, wrapped in a tortilla, and served with grilled onions, green peppers, shredded cheese, and sour cream. Cornbread is a popular Southern staple, as is "soul food," which finds its origins in many cultures, including Native American. Meatloaf is a common American dish made of ground meat formed into a loaf, mixed with egg and breadcrumbs, then baked or smoked; yet it originated from a traditional German dish or a cousin to the Dutch meatball.

Teachers can have many ways to teach food words. Some teaching tips may include asking ELLs to talk about food and tell the type of foods they like and dislike, using the sentence pattern, *I like …* and *I don't like …* after learning a food unit. Teachers can also use the Pair Food activity (see Figure 6.1) to ask the students to match food with the correct names by drawing lines or writing the numbers or names of the food underneath each food image. Teachers can also engage the students in an authentic activity of making a sandwich or a hot dog to learn food words by doing.

Table 6.4.   Food Words With Ingredients and Pictures

Food Name	Definition/Ingredients	Pictures
Fast Food		
BLT	A bacon, lettuce, and tomato sandwich	
Hamburger	A sandwich with one or more cooked patties of ground meat placed inside a sliced hamburger bun	
Hot dog	A cooked sausage, traditionally grilled or steamed and served in a sliced bun	
Lobster roll	A sandwich filled with lobster meat soaked in butter and served on a hot dog bun/roll	
Pizza	An oven-baked, flat, round bread typically topped with tomato sauce, cheese, and various toppings	
Reuben sandwich	A hot sandwich made of corned beef, Swiss cheese, Russian dressing, and sauerkraut	
French fries	Potatoes cut into strips, deep-fried, and served as a typical side dish	
Buffalo wings	Chicken wings deep-fried, unbreaded, and coated in a vinegar-based cayenne pepper hot sauce and butter	
Fried chicken	Breaded, deep-fried chicken thighs, drumsticks, breasts, or wings	
Philly cheese steak	A sandwich made from thinly sliced pieces of steak and melted cheese, onion, and peppers on a long roll	

(Table continues on next page)

Table 6.4.   (Continued)

Food Name	Definition/Ingredients	Pictures
Oven baked food		
Apple pie	A fruit pie filled with apples served sometimes with ice/whipped cream on top	
Baked beans	A dish containing beans, sometimes baked but usually stewed in a sauce	
Barbecue ribs	Pork or beef ribs served with barbecue sauce and usually eaten by hand	
Biscuits and gravy	Soft biscuits covered in sausage gravy; a popular breakfast dish in the South	
Chicken pot pie	A baked savory pie containing chicken meat and vegetables	
Chocolate-chip cookies	Cookies with chocolate chips as an added ingredient	
Cornbread	A generic name for a number of quick breads containing cornmeal	
Corn dog	A hot dog coated in a thick layer of cornmeal batter and deep fried in oil, although sometimes baked	
Crab cakes	A cake with crab meat and other ingredients, such as bread crumbs, milk, mayonnaise, eggs, onions, and seasonings	

(Table continues on next page)

Table 6.4.   (Continued)

Food Name	Definition/Ingredients	Pictures
Meatloaf	A dish of ground meat formed into a loaf shape, mixed with egg and breadcrumbs, then baked or smoked	
Smithfield ham	A specific type of the country ham, originated in the town of Smithfield in Virginia	
Sourdough bread	Bread made by long fermented dough using natural yeasts with a mildly sour taste	
Thanksgiving turkey	A large roasted turkey as the center of the American Thanksgiving dinner, served with other traditional foods	
Sirloin steak	Steak cut from the back portion of the animal	
Grilled and Other Food		
Muffin	An individual sized quick bread similar to a cupcake in size and cooking methods	
Brownies	A flat baked square or bar of chocolate sometimes containing nuts	
Cupcake	A small cake baked in a small thin paper or aluminum cup with icing and decorations	
Clam chowder	A creamy soup containing clams and broth with diced potatoes as well as onions	

(Table continues on next page)

Table 6.4.   (Continued)

Food Name	Definition/Ingredients	Pictures
Coleslaw	A salad consisting primarily of shredded raw cabbage dressed with mayonnaise or butter-milk	
Enchiladas	A corn tortilla rolled and filled with meat, cheese, beans, potatoes, vegetables, or sea-food	
Fajitas	A Mexican dish with grilled skirt steak wrapped in a tortilla and served with grilled onions, green pepper, shredded cheese, and sour cream	
Grits	A ground corn food of Native American origin, common in the Southern United States and eaten at breakfast	
Jerky	Lean meat trimmed of fat, cut into strips, and dried to prevent spoilage	
Smoked salmon	A salmon fillet smoked and sometimes served on bread with cream cheese, sliced red onion, lemon, and capers	
Olympia oysters	Oysters of the Pacific coast; the name derived from the 19th century oyster industry near Olympia, Washington.	
Spicy deviled eggs	Hard-boiled eggs with the yolk mixed with spices and served in the halved egg whites	
Macaroni and cheese	Macaroni in a cheese sauce baked in the oven or prepared in a pan on the top of the stove	

(Table continues on next page)

Table 6.4.   (Continued)

Food Name	Definition/Ingredients	Pictures
Nachos	Corn chips served with a cheese sauce and sometimes other spicy ingredients	
Potato chips	Thin slices of potato, deep fried or baked; commonly served as an appetizer, side dish, snack	
Dessert		
Cheesecake	A sweet dish with two or more layers; the thickest layer consisting of a mixture of soft, fresh cheese, eggs, and sugar; the bottom layer is often a crust	
Key lime pie	An American dessert made of Key lime juice, egg yolks, and sweetened condensed milk in a pie crust	
Banana split	An ice cream dessert with a banana cut in half lengthwise and scoops of ice cream and other toppings	
Strawberry shortcake	A sweet cake with sliced strawberries mixed with sugar whipped cream, and vanilla	

Teachers can also collect some food magazines and cut out food pictures to make a food-word dictionary and practice with students. Many websites allow printing out free worksheets to teach food words with interesting activities and online games. Some of these links are

- http://www.eslprintables.com/vocabulary_worksheets/food/
- http://busyteacher.org/classroom_activities-vocabulary/ food_and_drinks/food-worksheets/
- http://busyteacher.org/8824-food-pair-work-activity.html
- http://busyteacher.org/8111-mixed-food-multiple-choice.html

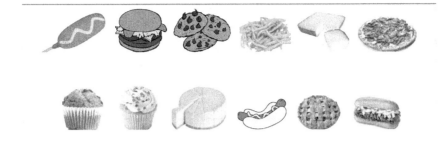

1. Hot Dog   2. Cheese steak   3. Apple pie   4. Cheesecake   5. Cornbread   6. Corn dog

7. Pizza   8. Chocolate-   9. Cupcake   10. Hamburger   11. French fries   12. Muffin

                  chip cookies

Figure 6.1.   Pair the food activity: Draw lines or write the number to match the food names.

- http://supersimplelearning.com/songs/original-series/one/are-you-hungry/
- http://www.anglomaniacy.pl/foodTopic.htm
- http://www.enchantedlearning.com/themes/food/spelling.shtml
- http://www.wikisaber.es/Contenidos/LObjects/bb1/act5e/act5e.html

Families and Relatives

Family is a term that usually refers to the basic social unit that consists of parents and their children. Or it can refer to a bigger group of related people, including grandparents, aunts, uncles, cousins, and so on. A relative is a person connected by blood or marriage. Families and relatives are an important part of life for the people from Asian and Hispanic-speaking cultures and thus they are important for ELLs. Immediate family members are usually those who are the first-degree relatives or close blood-relatives who may include a spouse, parent, brother and sister, son and daughter. Extended family members, who are also blood-related and who are the second-degree relatives, may include grandparents, aunts, uncles, cousins, nephews, and nieces. Those relatives who are also blood-related but called the third-degree relatives may include great-grandparents or great-grandchildren. The sibling-in-laws are usually those who are related through marriage. Common words related to the families and relatives who are blood related or who are related through marriage are listed in Table 6.5 with a brief definition.

Table 6.5.   Words Related to Families and Relatives

Aunt	The sister of one's father or mother or the wife of one's uncle
Brother	A man or boy in relation to other sons and daughters of his parents
Cousin	A child of one's uncle or aunt
Daughter	A girl or woman in relation to her parents
Father	A man in relation to his natural child or children
Grandchild	A child of one's son or daughter
Granddaughter /son	A daughter/son of one's son or daughter
Grandfather /mother	The father/mother of one's father or mother
Grandparent (s)	A parent of one's father or mother; a grandmother or grandfather
Great-grandchild	A son or daughter of one's grandchild
Husband	A married man considered in relation to his wife
Ex-husband	A woman's former husband, from whom she is now divorced
In-laws	Relatives by marriage
Son-in law, etc.	The husband of one's daughter
Mother	A woman in relation to a child or children to whom she has given birth
Niece	A daughter of one's brother or sister or one's brother-in-law or sister-in-law
Nephew	A son of one's brother or sister or one's brother-in-law or sister-in-law
Parent	A father or mother
Sister	A woman or girl in relation to other daughters and sons of her parents
Son	A boy or man in relation to either or both of his parents
Step-father	A man married to one's mother after the divorce or the death of one's father
Step-daughter,	A daughter of one's husband or wife by a previous marriage
Twin	One of two children born at the same birth
Twin sister/ brother	One of two girls/boys born at the same birth
Uncle	The brother of one's father or mother or the husband of one's aunt
Widow (woman)	A woman who has lost her husband by death and has not remarried
Widower (man)	A man who has lost his wife by death and has not remarried
Wife	A married woman considered in relation to her husband
Ex-wife	A man's former wife, from whom he is now divorced

First-, Second-, and Third-Degree Relatives

- A first-degree relative is defined as a close blood relative which includes the individual's parents, full siblings, or children
- A second-degree relative is defined as a blood relative which includes the individual's grandparents, grandchildren, aunts, uncles, nephews, nieces or half-siblings
- A third-degree relative is defined as a blood relative which includes the individual's first-cousins, great-grandparents or great grand-children (Source: http://www.bcbst.com/mpmanual/First_and_Second_Degree_Relative.htm)

Teachers can guide students to practice words related to families and relatives once ELLs know the definition. For example, ask them to write about their families with the title of *My Family* or *Who I am*, with the beginning sentence: *My name is …, I live with my family that includes….* Teachers can also encourage students to create their own family trees as an activity to practice the words about families and relatives and to talk about their families. The family tree may start with the grandparents, to parents, uncles, aunts, siblings, cousins, and nephews. An example of the family tree is provided in Figure 6.2.

Guess My Family is another interesting activity. Teachers can use this activity to practice words about families and relatives. Students can take turns to describe one member of their family sentence by sentence, start-

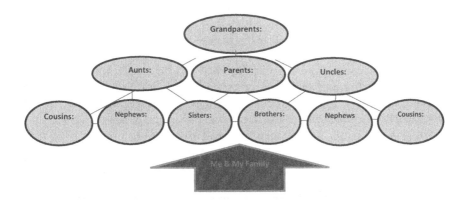

My family includes these members: Write down their names.

Figure 6.2.   Teachers can use My Family Tree to practice the words related to family members orally or ask the Ells to draw their own family tree and tell the story.

ing with less obvious clues like hobbies or countries they have lived in or visited, until someone guesses who that person is. To extend each turn, teachers may take away points for wrong guesses or only allow one guess per student. Some websites also allow the practice of words about families and relatives with interesting activities:

- http://www.anglomaniacy.pl/familyTopic.htm
- http://edition.tefl.net/ideas/vocab/vocabulary-practice/
- http://busyteacher.org/classroom_activities-vocabulary/familyfriends-worksheets/
- http://www.englishexercises.org/buscador/buscar.asp?nivel=any&age=0&contents=family#a

Weather and Sports

Weather refers to the state of the atmosphere at a place and time with regard to heat, dryness, sunshine, wind, rain, and such. *Sports* is a term that refers to an activity that involves physical exertion and skill in which an individual or team competes against another or others for entertainment. Weather and sports are an important part of culture for American people. They need to know about the weather to travel and to go to work. They watch different sports and games and are enthusiastic fans for some sports. Yet ELLs may not know about how to talk about weather or enjoy the topics of sports due to lack in their daily vocabulary. The frequent words related to weather are provided in Table 6.6.

An interesting activity to teach weather words is the *Weather Reporter Activity*. Teacher can select several cities favored by students and ask them to do a weather search and report the weather in each of their selected cities as a weather reporter. This can be developed into a role-play for the students to dress up as a reporter and the class acts as travelers. For younger ELLs, teachers can use the *Cut & Paste Activity*. Search online and print some pictures of weather symbols (e.g., clouds, snow, rain, sun, thunder) and ask the students to cut out these weather pictures. Write down on a poster board different weather names and ask the students to paste each picture in the right place. Teachers can also engage students in a talk-and-write activity. Ask the students to talk about the weather in the country or hometown where they live and then write about it using as many words related to the weather as possible; or teachers can provide basic words for students to include in their writing.

Sports are an important part of the American culture. Some of the nation's most popular team sports developed in North America are Amer-

Table 6.6.   Commonly Used Words Related to the Weather

Vocabulary	Meaning	Example Sentence
avalanche *noun*	a rapid slide of snow down a mountainside	The skiers were warned about a possible *avalanche*.
below freezing *preposition/adjective*	temperature less than 0 degrees Celsius/(32F)	It's supposed to go *below freezing* before the weekend.
blizzard *noun*	a severe snowstorm with high winds and low visibility	The airplane couldn't takeoff because of the *blizzard*.
breeze *noun*	a light wind	There is a gentle *breeze* in the air.
Celsius *noun*	measurement of temperature (0 degrees is freezing/100 degrees is boiling)	In the summer, the average temperature here is 20 degrees *Celsius*.
chilly *adjective*	uncomfortably cool or cold	It's a bit *chilly* today, so I think you should wear a coat.
clear *adjective*	when there are no clouds in the sky	On a *clear* night you can see a lot of stars.
cloud/cloudy *noun/adjective*	condensed water vapor floating in the atmosphere/the sky	It may look *cloudy* in the morning, but the sun will come out by noon.
cold adjective	relatively low temperature compared	It was freezing *cold* for the parade this evening.
cold spell *adjective + noun*	a period of weather colder than normal	They're calling for a *cold spell*, so we put off our camping trip.
cool *adjective*	temperatures between warm and cold	The days were boiling hot, but the nights were *cool* and comfortable for sleeping.
degrees *noun*	measurement for temperature	I feel the heat because it's about forty *degrees* Celsius outside.
drizzling *continuous verb*	a fine, mistlike rain	I can't walk the dog because it is *drizzling* now.
drought *noun*	a long period with no rainfall and a shortage of water	Forest fires are a serious danger during a *drought*.
Fahrenheit *noun*	measurement of temperature (32 degrees is freezing/212 degrees is boiling)	It was 100 degrees *Fahrenheit* when we got to San Francisco.
flood *noun*	overflow of rainwater	The *flood* was so bad, our basement was full of water.
flurries *noun*	a small swirling mass of very light snowfall	There are a few *flurries* but the roads are OK.
fog/foggy *noun/adjective*	thick water vapor that blocks one's vision or restricts visibility	We couldn't see the bridge because of the *fog*.

(Table continues on next page)

Table 6.6.   (Continued)

Vocabulary	Meaning	Example Sentence
forecast *noun/verb*	a prediction of weather	According to the 5-day *forecast*, it's going to rain this weekend.
frost *noun*	ice crystals formed by below-freezing temperatures	These flowers are so strong they can withstand *frost*.
frostbite *noun*	a skin condition caused by overexposure to the extreme cold with reddish skin with white spots	I lost my hat while I was skiing, and I ended up with *frostbite* on my ears.
hail *noun*	small pieces of ice/frozen rain that fall during a storm	The *hail* damaged some of the trailer homes.
humid/humidity *adjective/noun*	moisture in the air	It feels a lot hotter than it actually is because of the *humidity*.
hurricane *noun*	a tropical storm with very strong wind and heavy rain; called a typhoon in Pacific Ocean	Half of the buildings on the island were flattened by the *hurricane*.
ice/icy *noun/adjective*	frozen water	The roads are *icy*, so please avoid driving down any hills.
lightning *noun*	a flash of high voltage electricity between a cloud and the ground or within a cloud, typically with thunder	The outdoor pool always closes when the lifeguards see *lightning*.
mild *adjective*	warm and gentle temperature in a cold season	It's quite *mild* out so I didn't bother with a hat or mittens.
meteorologist *noun*	an expert who studies weather and weather patterns	The *meteorologist* predicted that the cold spell would be over by now.
overcast adjective	clouds covering a large part of the sky with no sun visible	The sky is *overcast* now, but the sun is supposed to come out by late today.
precipitation *noun*	rain or snowfall	There is very little *precipitation* in the desert.
puddle *noun*	a small pool of rainwater	Children were splashing and playing in *puddles* with their rubber boots.
rain/rainy *noun/adjective*	condensed water that falls to the ground	My hair is all wet and messy from the *rain*.
raindrop *noun*	a single measurement of rain	I love catching *raindrops* on my tongue.
rainbow *noun*	an arc of colors formed in the sky after a rainfall	By legend, you can find a pot of gold at the end of a *rainbow*.

(*Table continues on next page*)

Table 6.6.   (Continued)

Vocabulary	Meaning	Example Sentence
raining cats and dogs *idiom*	an expression describing heavy rainfall	They canceled the football game because it was *raining cats and dogs*.
season *noun*	a time of year characterized by certain weather conditions	My favorite *season* is fall, because I love the colors of the changing leaves.
shower *noun*	a brief and light rain fall	They've been calling for rain *showers* all week, but so far it's been dry.
sleet *noun*	rain that freezes as it falls or a mixture of rain and snow	All-weather tires are best if you have to drive in *sleet*.
slush/slushy *noun/adjective*	partially melted snow or ice	The snow turned to *slush* as soon as it started to rain.
smog *noun*	fog combined with smoke and other atmospheric pollutants	You really notice the *smog* downtown in this type of humidity.
snow/snowy *noun/adjective*	water vapor frozen into ice crystals that fall in white flakes	It is already *snowing* up in the mountains that is great for ski this year.
snowstorm *noun*	a heavy snowfall	All of the schools were closed because of the *snowstorm*.
sun/sunny/sunshine *noun/adjective/noun*	a period in which the sun is not blocked by clouds	We hope to have *sunshine* on the day of the beach picnic.
sunburn *noun*	a red/pink skin condition caused by being in the sun too long	The bald man got *sunburn* on his head.
temperature *noun*	the degree of atmospheric heat or cold as measured by a comparative scale	Let's check the *temperature* before we get dressed for a walk.
thermometer *noun*	an instrument for measuring the temperature of the air	The *thermometer* said it was already thirty degrees Celsius this morning.
thunder/thunder-storm *noun*	a loud rumbling heard after a lightning flash due to the expansion of rapidly heated air or the conditions that cause it	Let's close all of the windows before the *thunderstorm* is coming.
tornado *noun*	a violently destructive rotating vortex of wind	The *tornado* picked up everything in its path, including animals and cars.
wind/windy *noun/adjective*	a perceptible current of the air caused by atmospheric pressure	It's too *windy* to play golf today.
wind chill factor *noun*	the temperature felt on the skin due to the flow of cold air; wind chill temperatures are always lower than actual air temperature	It's minus 2, but with the *wind chill factor* it feels like minus 15.

ican football, basketball, and ice hockey. Sports are also closely associated with education in the United States, with most high schools and universities having their own sports teams. College sports competitions play an important role in the American sports culture. In many cases, college athletics are more popular than professional sports. It is important for the ELLs to know the basic words related to major sports. Words related to the major sports are provided in Table 6.7.

To teach sports words, teachers can find some interesting sports pictures and do the *Cut & Paste Activity* to score the student teams for high or low scores with rewards. Teachers can also use many websites for interesting activities and worksheets to teach sports words. The following are a few examples: www.eslgamesplus.com/sports-vocabulary-esl-game-car-racing-rally-game/ is interesting and engaging for elementary students. To use puzzles words activities, teachers can go to http://puzzles.about.com/od/sportswordsearches/ig/Sports-WS/. Also, teachers can also go to the busyteacher.org site to print many free worksheets for classroom activities at all grade levels to practice vocabulary related to sports and hobbies.

SUMMARY

This chapter introduces basic daily vocabulary. These words include words related to daily greetings, directions, food and cafeteria, families and relatives, and weather and sports. To be successful in school, ELLs need to know these daily words so that they can function in school and participate in classroom activities. These words also help them cope with life more easily in new environments socially and academically as they start a journey in the United States.

Table 6.7. Words Related to Major Sports in the United States

Sports Name	Definition	Picture
American football	Game played by two teams of 11 players on a rectangular field 120 yards long and 53.33 yards wide with goalposts at each end. The offense team attempts to advance an oval ball down the field	
Badminton	Game with rackets in which a shuttlecock is played back and forth across a net	
Baseball	Game played between two teams of nine on a field with a diamond-shaped circuit of four bases, played mainly in the United States, Canada, and Latin America	
Basketball	Game played between two teams of five players in which goals are scored by throwing a ball through a netted hoop	
Bowling	A player rolls a ball down a lane with the goal of knocking over pins	
Boxing	A sport of fighting with the fists and padded gloves in a roped arena according to prescribed rules	
Cricket	A bat-and-ball game played between two teams of 11 players on a field; each team takes turn to bat, attempting to score runs; each turn is known as an innings.	
Exercise	Engaging in physical activity to improve or maintain health and fitness	
Golf	Game played on a grass course; a small hard ball struck with a club into a series of 18 holes in the ground to complete the course with the fewest possible strokes	Golf Bags

(Table continues on next page)

Table 6.7.   (Continued)

Sports Name	Definition	Picture
Gymnastics	A sport involving the performance of exercises requiring physical strength, flexibility, power, agility, coordination, grace, balance, and control	
Hockey	Game with 11 players on each of two teams attempting to score by hitting a hard rubber puck with a hockey stick at the opposing team's goal.	
Horse racing	The sport in which horses and their riders take part in races, typically with substantial betting on the outcome	
Motor racing	Competitive events of motor sports involving the use of motor vehicles, such as racing cars or motorcycles, including off-road racing such as motocross	
Pool/billiards	Sports played on a felt-covered table with six pockets along the rails, into which balls are deposited as the main goal of play	
Racket sports	The sports that players use rackets to hit a ball or other object (e.g., tennis, badminton, racketball)	
Rowing	A sports in which athletes race against each other in narrow boats (shells) on rivers, lakes, or the ocean	
Sailing	Using sailboats for recreation or sport such as yacht racing	
Soccer	Game played by two teams of 11 players with a ball not touched with the hands or arms except by the goalkeepers; each team trying to kick the ball into the other's goal	

(Table continues on next page)

Table 6.7. (Continued)

Sports Name	Definition	Picture
Swimming	The sport of propelling oneself through water using the limbs	
Table tennis	An indoor game based on tennis, played with small paddles and a ball bounced on a table divided by a net	
Tennis	Game in which two or four players strike a ball with rackets over a net stretched across a court	
Volleyball	Game for two teams of six players with a large ball hit by hand over a high net to score points by making the ball reach the ground on the opponent's side of the court	

CHAPTER 7

TRADITIONS AND HOLIDAYS

CASE SCENARIO

Leon is a tenth grader. He came to the United States 3 years ago with his family, which included his mom, dad, a younger brother and a younger sister. Compared to his classmates, he looked more mature. This was because he was about 2 years older than his peers. Due to limited English proficiency, he was placed in a lower grade level when he came and also in lower-track classes in all subject areas. Although he had been in the United States for 3 years, he still could not express himself clearly in English. He was sensitive and withdrawing in school. At home, he was a good child, trying his best to do homework even though he could not completely understand the assignments. As the oldest child, he had to take care of his younger siblings when his parents were away for work. His parents had high expectations for him. Without much education themselves, they made every effort to save enough money to send Leon to the best university in the country, Harvard. Yet they did not know that Leon was struggling with understanding basic lesson content due to his limited English proficiency. Teachers must deal with behavioral problems in those lower track classrooms. Yet Leon seldom had a behavioral issue. He even got good grades in those classes due to low expectations and low academic standards. So he was a good student in these classrooms. That's why his parents thought that Leon could go to Harvard, not knowing his track status. How can teachers help the ELLs like Leon to fulfill their dreams?

A Book for Every Teacher: Teaching English Language Learners
pp. 169–182

Many ELLs face the same problems as Leon does. Although they may have been in the United States for years, these ELLs cannot understand subject content and perform unsuccessfully in schools due to limited English proficiency. Limited English words are one of the major factors that contribute to their L2 development. Thus, it is crucial that teachers build a language-rich classroom environment and help build on their daily words. If teachers serving ELLs in mainstream classrooms can help ELLs enlarge their basic English vocabulary in this respect, it will contribute significantly to their school success. English vocabulary is the foundation for ELLs to read texts and to understand instruction in classrooms. There is some basic vocabulary that all ELLs needs to know in order to function successfully in school and life. As mentioned in the previous chapter, daily words involving numbers, colors, animals, families, school places, and school and classroom terms are used often. Traditional holiday vocabulary is also an important category. This chapter will introduce these basic vocabulary words related to traditions and holidays with strategies to help teach ELLs at the beginning level and build a foundation for the ELLs' academic success.

Tradition and Holiday Words

The United States is a country that is developed and embedded with Western cultures and traditions but it is also infused with many other diverse cultural traditions such as those from Native American, African, Asian, Polynesian, and Latin American cultures (Bromley, 2007; Greenwood, 2004, pp. 29–52). American culture started over 10,000 years ago with the migration of Paleo-Indians, who were among the first to inhabit the Americas during the glacial periods from the Asian continent as well as from Oceania and Europe. This land is what we call the United States of America today. The United States has unique cultural characteristics in terms of dialect, music, arts, social habits, cuisine, and folklore. The United States is an ethnically and racially diverse country because of large-scale immigration from many ethnically and racially different countries throughout its history. The natives, settlers, and immigrants have all played a role in the formation of the United States. This has resulted in a wide range of cultural traditions and therefore many traditional holiday words. Major traditions and holiday words are listed in Table 7.1. Some lesson ideas are also provided to help teachers introduce these traditions and holiday words and help ELL students. For the convenience of introducing these words, they are grouped according to month from January to December, explaining the holiday name, date, and celebration activities.

Table 7.1.   Major Holidays and Traditions in the United States

Name	Date	Tradition and Activity
New Year's Day*	January 1	Festivities include counting down to midnight (12:00 a.m.) on the preceding night, New Year's Eve often with a fireworks display and party. The ball drop at Times Square in New York City has become a national New Year's tradition. It also marks the traditional end of the Christmas and holiday season.
Martin Luther King, Jr. Day* (National Day of Service)	Third Monday in January	Honoring Dr. Martin Luther King, Jr., a civil rights leader born on January 15, 1929. More recently, the 1994 King Holiday and Service Act was passed to encourage Americans to transform the King Holiday into a day of citizen action and volunteer service, which has gained in popularity.
Valentine's Day	February 14	Celebrates love and friendship. Valentine's Day is named after early Christian martyr St. Valentine. It was established in 496 AD. Today, it is a tradition that people celebrate love and romance, exchanging cards, flowers, candy, and other gifts.
Presidents Day*	Third Monday in February	Celebrates the birthdays of American presidents George Washington and Abraham Lincoln. In 1971, it was changed from February 22, Washington's true birthday, to the third Monday in February. Federal offices, schools, post offices, and many banks are closed.
Easter Sunday	Date varies from March to April	Traditionally celebrated on the first Sunday after the first paschal full moon on or after the vernal (spring) equinox. It celebrates the resurrection of Jesus Christ on the third day after his crucifixion as described in the New Testament. People decorate hard-boiled eggs and give baskets of candy, toys, and so on, especially to children to indicate rebirth of life.
Memorial Day*	Last Monday in May	Honors soldiers who died serving their country and those who died from the Civil War onward. It also marks the unofficial beginning of the summer season. Traditionally, it was on May 30 and shifted by the Uniform Holidays Act 1968.
Independence Day*	July 4	Celebrates the signing of the Declaration of Independence from British rule in 1776 by the thirteen original American colonies. Fireworks celebrations are held throughout the nation.
Labor Day*	First Monday in September	Celebrates the American labor movement and is dedicated to the social and economic achievements of workers. It also marks the unofficial end of the summer season.

(Table continues on next page)

Table 7.1. (Continued)

Name	Date	Tradition and Activity
Columbus Day*	Second Monday in October	Honors Christopher Columbus and his traditional discovery of the Americas. In some areas it is also a celebration of Italian culture and heritage.
Veterans Day *	November 11	A day to honor all veterans of the United States Armed Forces, whether or not in a conflict. It was briefly moved to the fourth Monday in October under the Uniform Monday Holiday Act of 1971, but was moved back to November 11 to restore its coincidence with the date of the World War I armistice.
Halloween	October 31	It is to celebrate Eve of All Saint's Day. Decorations include jack o'lanterns. Costume parties are also part of the holiday. Kids go "trick-or-treating" to neighbors who give away candy. Not generally observed by businesses.
Thanksgiving Day *	Fourth Thursday in November	American holiday originated to give thanks for the blessing of the autumn harvest and of the preceding year. Tradition includes the sharing of a turkey dinner. This tradition also starts the holiday season. Several other places around the world observe similar celebrations.
Christmas *	December 25	Celebrates the birth of Jesus Christ. Yet many nonreligious people observe it. Schools, banks, post offices, government offices, and most businesses are closed on Christmas.

In addition, more details of these major holidays are provided in the next section, such as origins and celebrations.

American Traditions and Holidays

The 4th of July or Independence Day is a major national holiday celebrating the signing of the Declaration of Independence from British rule. The Declaration of Independence is a document announcing, on July 4, 1776, that the thirteen American colonies would be no longer a part of the British Empire but form a new nation, the United States of America. John Adams was a leader pushing for independence. After voting for independence, Congress focused its attention on the Declaration of Independence, which had been prepared by a Committee of Five with Thomas Jefferson as its principal author. Congress debated and revised the wording of the Declaration, finally approving it on July 4, 1776. Independence Day is commonly associated with fireworks, parades, barbecues, carnivals, fairs, picnics, concerts, baseball games, family reunions, and political speeches and ceremonies, in addition to various other public and private events.

Christmas is a major holiday celebrated on December 25. By legend, it is the celebration of the birth of Jesus Christ, whom most teachings of Christian denominations believe to be the Son of God. Christmas is also observed by many nonreligious people in the United State and celebrated widely by millions of people around the world. People celebrate Christmas by singing carols, sending cards, and giving gifts. Government offices, schools, banks, post offices are closed. The day and night before Christmas is called Christmas Eve. The Christmas and holiday season starts at Thanksgiving and lasts until New Year's Day.

Columbus Day honors Christopher Columbus and his discovery of the Americas. It is celebrated on the second Monday in October. Christopher Columbus (1451–1506) was an Italian explorer, navigator, and colonizer. He completed four voyages across the Atlantic Ocean to the Americas with the first in 1492, which resulted in the discovery of America from a European point of view. These voyages generally led to the European awareness of the American continents and to the Spanish colonization of the New World.

Easter is a Christian holiday to celebrate the resurrection of Jesus Christ on the third day after his crucifixion as described in the New Testament. It is usually the Sunday following the Paschal full moon with the date varying from March 22 to April 25. People traditionally decorate hard-boiled eggs and give baskets of candies, fruits, toys and so on, especially to children. According to traditions, eggs, rabbits, hares and young animals are thought to represent the rebirth and return to fertility of nature in the spring.

Martin Luther King, Jr. Day is a federal holiday in honor of King's birthday celebrated on the third Monday in January. Dr. King (1929–1968) was born on January 15, 1929, and assassinated on April 4, 1968, in Memphis, Tennessee, when he was planning for a national event called the Poor People's Campaign. Dr. King was a clergyman, activist, humanitarian, and civil rights leader. He is best known for his role in achieving civil rights while using nonviolent civil disobedience. On October 14, 1964, Dr. King received the Nobel Peace Prize for combating racial inequality through nonviolence. In the final years of his life, King expanded his focus to include poverty and the Vietnam War.

Memorial Day is a federal holiday to honor soldiers who died serving the country and those who died from the Civil War onwards. Memorial Day was officially proclaimed on May 5, 1868, and was first observed on May 30, 1868. It is now celebrated on the last Monday in May because of the National Holiday Act of 1971, to ensure a 3-day weekend for federal holidays. People usually visit cemeteries and place American flags on graves in national cemeteries. Memorial Day also unofficially marks the start of the summer season and people think of their summer vacation.

Labor Day is a federal holiday in the United States celebrated on the first Monday in September. Yet, in many other countries, Labor Day occurs on May 1. In the United States, it is celebrated to honor the American labor movement and dedicated to the social and economic achievements of workers. It also marks the unofficial, symbolic end of the summer.

New Year's Day celebrates the beginning of the year. New Year's activities include counting down to midnight (12:00 a.m.) on the preceding night, New Year's Eve. New Year's Eve is the last day of the year. People celebrate the new year at New Year's Eve with evening social gatherings to dance, eat, drink, and display fireworks to mark the new year. The celebrations generally go on past midnight into New Year's Day. The ball drop at Times Square in New York City has become a New Year's tradition in the United States. New Year's Day is also the traditional end of the Christmas holiday season and is celebrated worldwide.

Presidents Day is a federal holiday that was started to celebrate George Washington's birthday on February 22, but was changed to the third Monday in February in 1971. George Washington (1732–1799) was the first President of the United States, serving two terms (1789–1797). He also presided over the convention that drafted the U.S. Constitution. Washington's birthday is commonly referred to as Presidents' Day, yet President Abraham Lincoln's birthday is also in February, which is why it is called Presidents' Day. Federal offices, schools, post offices, and banks are closed to observe this holiday.

Thanksgiving Day is celebrated mainly in the United States and Canada as a day of giving thanks for the blessing of the fall harvest and of the preceding year. It is celebrated on the fourth Thursday in November by federal legislation in 1941 and has been an annual tradition in the United States by presidential proclamation since 1863. Thanksgiving tradition includes the sharing of a turkey dinner accompanied by many other traditional foods. This day also marks the traditional start of the holiday season.

Valentine's Day is a day to celebrate love and friendship. Valentine's Day is named after an early Christian martyr St. Valentine and was established in 496 AD. According to legend, St. Valentine was imprisoned for performing weddings for soldiers who were forbidden to marry and for those who were persecuted under the Roman Empire. During his imprisonment, he healed the daughter of his jailer. Before his execution, he wrote her a letter "From your Valentine" as a farewell. Today, Valentine's Day is associated with romantic love. Modern traditional celebration of love and romance includes the exchange of candies, cards, flowers, and other gifts.

Veterans Day honors America's veterans for their patriotism, love of country, and willingness to serve and sacrifice for the country. The Uniform Holiday Bill was signed on June 28, 1968, to ensure a three-day weekend for federal employees by celebrating four national holidays on Mondays: Washington's Birthday, Memorial Day, Veterans Day, and Columbus Day. However, it was thought that these extended weekends would encourage travel, recreational and cultural activities instead of honoring veterans. Therefore, Veterans Day was restored to November 11 to be consistent with the historical significance of the date.

Lesson Ideas With Words for Traditions and Holidays

Vocabulary is an important factor contributing to ELLs learning English. This is because the ELLs' word knowledge determines their level of reading comprehension and understanding of subject content. In order to understand subject content, they must have the knowledge of basic vocabulary to read texts and understand instructions daily in classrooms. Thus, it is important that teachers teach vocabulary and word concepts through explicit instruction to build their comprehension so that they can deposit new words daily into their vocabulary bank.

The basic principles for teaching ELLs vocabulary include these key areas:

- Teach how to *pronounce* the new vocabulary.
- Help understand the *definition* or meaning of the word in context.
- Connect the word to the student's *existing knowledge* and experiences for the specific understanding and comprehension of the meaning.
- Provide *guided practice* on the new vocabulary through a variety of strategies, such as paraphrasing, mapping, acting out, or role-playing.
- Help *add* the new vocabulary to their word bank or student-made dictionaries.
- Practice the vocabulary and help ELLs use it *independently*.

Teachers can teach tradition and holiday vocabulary based on these principles by introducing and practicing the pronunciation of the names of the holidays and celebrations, explaining the meanings of the holidays in context, and guiding students to read and practice the new vocabulary independently. For example, in January, teachers can teach holiday words around New Year's concepts by introducing the pronunciation associated with the New Year's vocabulary and then teaching the New Year's concepts and explaining the meaning, such as New Year's Day is the first day of the year and a holiday in the United States. Schools, banks, post offices, government buildings, and many stores are closed on New Year's Day. Teachers can connect the students' existing knowledge and experience by asking how they celebrate the new year in comparison to the traditional activities of people in the United States. In addition, New Year's Day is also a good time for people to think about changes they want to make to better their lives. To extend the New Year' Day concept, teachers can guide ELLs to think about a New Year's resolution and make their own New Year's resolutions.

Specifically, teachers can ask these questions about New Year's Day and help build vocabulary through interaction. At the same time, it helps increase the ELLs' understanding of New Year's traditions. See some sample questions to ask are in Table 7.2.

Teachers can also incorporate a variety of activities to build on ELLs' vocabulary and words related to New Year's concepts. Some examples may include doing these activities:

Table 7.2. Questions for Interaction Related to New Year's Concepts

Students Working in Pairs and Small Groups

Teachers can interact with the ELLs with these questions:

- What is it like for the New Year's celebration in your country?
- What are interesting things families do on New Year's Day in your country?
- Do people stay up late on the New Year's Eve?
- How about children? Do they stay up late too?
- What activities do people do to celebrate New Year's Eve? For example, do you eat special meals, give presents, visit the relatives, or wear new clothes?
- What is the traditional food for the families in the New Year in your country?
- What other activities or things do people do?
- People often make New Year's resolutions at this time. These are some things people may resolve to do:
  ○ Eat healthily
  ○ Do more exercise
  ○ Lose weight
  ○ Quit smoking
  ○ Learn a new language
  ○ Improve themselves by working hard
- What is your plan for your New Year this year?
- Are you looking forward to the new year? Have you ever made a New Year's resolution? If you have, what is your New Year's resolution? Can you share?

- New Year's Crossword Puzzle Game
- New Year's Bingo Activity
- New Year's Resolution Worksheet Activity
- New Year's Around the World Activity

The following links are useful, and teachers can use and print out free worksheets for activities:

- http://www.elcivics.com/holiday-lessons-usa.html
- http://www.eslprintables.com/vocabulary_worksheets/holidays_and_traditions
- http://www.eslprintables.com/vocabulary_worksheets/holidays_and_traditions/new_year/
- http://www.elcivics.com/new-years-resolution-worksheet.pdf
- http://www.elcivics.com/new-years-cards.pdf
- http://www.elcivics.com/months-of-the-year.pdf
- http://seasonal.theteacherscorner.net/new-years/

February is the Black History Month. Teachers can teach lessons about famous African Americans, such as Martin Luther King, Sojourner Truth, George Washington Carver, Rosa Parks, Madame C.J. Walker, Malcolm X, Dr. Charles Drew, and others. Or teachers can teach concepts about Groundhog Day and Super Bowl Sunday, which also happen in February. These are some new concepts that the ELLs need to know due to their limited opportunities to interact in the social environment. In March and April, teachers can introduce St. Patrick's Day and the concepts about the Daylight Saving Time, spring, and the Easter Bunny. For more traditional words and events, teachers can find them listed by month in Table 7.3.

Other Useful Traditional Words

In addition to words associated with the above holidays, other useful words for special events also need to be introduced to ELLs and help them learn about American culture while learning vocabulary. The words for traditions and special events are also listed in Table 7.3. Teachers can use different strategies to introduce these words. The basic principles of teaching ELLs vocabulary are important. Teachers can help them know how to pronounce the new words, explain the definition or meaning of the words in context, connect the words to their existing knowledge and experiences for understanding the word meaning, and provide them with

Table 7.3.   Other Words Related to Special Events or Traditions

Date	Event	Note
January 20	Inauguration Day	Occurs every year that coincides with a presidential election. The president is elected in November, but he doesn't take office until the following January 20. The president gives an inaugural speech after taking the Oath of Office in a ceremony.
February 1–28	Black History Month	February is a month to celebrate and recognize the contributions of African Americans. Black History Month was created in 1926 in the United States to be "Negro History Week" in the second week of February because this week coincided with the birthday of Abraham Lincoln on February 12 and of Frederick Douglass on February 14, both of which Black communities had celebrated.
February 2	Groundhog Day	By legend or folklore, if a groundhog comes out of its hole and sees its shadow then there will be six more weeks of winter weather. If it is cloudy and it sees no shadow, there will be an early spring. Groundhogs are small brown furry animals, living in burrows in the ground.
First Sunday in February	Super Bowl Sunday	The Super Bowl is the annual championship game of the National Football League (NFL), the highest level of American professional football. Super Bowl Sunday is the Sunday on which the Super Bowl is played. Football is a popular American sport played by two team of 11 players in each team. The players wear helmets, shoulder pads, and team uniforms.
March 8	International Women's Day	March is Women's History Month. It is a special time to recognize and honor the contributions of women.
First Sunday in April	Daylight Saving Time Begins	In 2007, the United States passed the Energy Policy Act of 2005 with an adjustment in time to save energy. Typically, at 2 a.m., clocks are moved forward one hour adding to the amount of daylight. Not observed in all states.
March 17	Saint Patrick's Day	Saint Patrick's Day is an Irish-based holiday. In the United States, it is celebrated mainly to recognize Irish and Irish American culture. People usually wear green color, watch parades, and eat corned beef.
Third week in March	First day of Spring	Also known as the vernal (spring) equinox, occurring between March 20 and the 23, depending on the year. Spring is time a time of rebirth, when flowers bloom, plants sprout, and trees get leaves. In spring, people wash windows, clean closets, and paint houses. Some people have garage sales.

(Table continues on next page)

Table 7.3. (Continued)

Date	Event	Note
April 1	April Fool's Day	A day when people play practical jokes, sending someone on a "fool's errand," or trying to get people to believe ridiculous things. By legend, in ancient Roman, people celebrated New Year's Day on April 1. Due to reform, it was shifted to January 1. Yet many people were confused and continued to celebrate New Year's Day on April 1. Thus, they were made fun of by sending on "fool's errands" or being tricked for something false.
April 22	Earth Day	It is celebrated to encourage protection of the environment. People do things such as clean beaches; recycle cans, bottles, and newspapers; donate money to environmental groups; sign petitions; and teach others about the importance of protecting the environment. Teachers give lessons about the environment. It was established in 1970 by Gaylord Nelson, a U.S. senator from Wisconsin.
Second Sunday in May	Mother's Day	It is a special holiday to honor mothers. Adult children usually take their mothers to a restaurant for breakfast or lunch. Younger children often cook breakfast for their mothers on Mother's Day. Mothers receive flowers, cards, and gifts on this special day.
Third Sunday in June	Father's Day	It is a special day to honor fathers. Fathers receive cards and gifts on this special day.
Third week in June	First Day of Summer	Also known as the summer solstice, occurring between June 20 and the 23, depending on the year. Summer is traditionally a time to relax and have fun. Most schools are closed and some people get a few weeks off from their jobs. It's a great time to go new places and try new activities. Summer is the most popular season for going on a cruise, spending time at the beach, golfing, playing baseball, rafting, hiking, gardening, and grilling food outside.
September 22	First day of Fall	Also known as the autumnal (fall) equinox, occurring between September 20 and the 23, depending on the year. The colors of autumn are orange, green, yellow, and brown. In autumn, people rake leaves, eat apples, wear sweaters, drink cider, bake pies, read books, and take long walks
October 24	United Nations Day	The United Nations is an international organization, established after World War II to keep the world at peace. It is located in New York City. It is also called the *UN* and its role has expanded to include encouraging respect for human rights and reducing poverty.

(Table continues on next page)

Table 7.3.   (Continued)

Date	Event	Note
Last Sunday in October	Daylight Saving Time Ends	Setting clocks back one hour at 2 a.m. ends Daylight Saving Time, bringing an earlier dawn and dusk.
Tuesday after the first Monday in November	Election Day	The day set by law for the general elections of public officials. It occurs on the Tuesday after the first Monday in November. This does not necessarily mean the "first Tuesday" in a month because the first day of a month can be a Tuesday.
November 11	Veterans Day	An American holiday to honor people who have completed military service or who are currently serving in the military. It is a federal holiday, so schools, banks, post offices, and government buildings are closed. If it occurs on a weekend, observance is moved to the previous Friday or following Monday. Generally marked by parades and other festivities to honor Armed Forces veterans.
November–December	Hanukkah	Hanukkah (or Chanukkah) is an 8-day Jewish holiday, also called the "Miracle of Lights" or "Festival of Lights." The dates on which it is celebrated are determined by the Jewish calendar—the 25th day of Kislev through the second or third day of Tevet. It is a time when Jews celebrate the rededication of the Second Temple in Jerusalem, which took place after the Jews defeated the Syrians in the 2nd century BC and regained control of the temple. The festival is observed by the kindling of the lights of a menorrah, the nine-branched *Hanukiah*, one additional light on each night of the holiday, progressing to eight on the final night.
Third week in December	First day of Winter	Also known as the winter solstice, occurring between December 20 and the 23, depending on the year. During winter, people in cold climates shovel snow, make snowmen, snowboard, ski, sit by the fireplace, drink hot chocolate, and shop for holiday gifts.

guided practice on the new vocabulary through a variety of strategies, such as paraphrasing, mapping, acting out, role-playing, or creating student-made dictionaries to expand their vocabulary.

Words for Special Events and Seasons

To help ELL students understand American culture, some popular events and seasonal words should also be introduced to them. A special event can refer to an activity or series of activities, specific to an identifiable time and place that are most often produced in conjunction with community organizations, held on public property, and generally occurring throughout a year. Many words related to special events have been listed in Table 7.3 for special days and events, such as Inauguration Day, Groundhog Day, Super Bowl Sunday, Earth Day, and Election Day. The seasonal words are also listed in Table 7.3, such as spring, summer, fall and winter. In addition, ELLs need to know words about months.

To teach ELLs the words related to these special events and seasonal words, teachers can follow the basic principles on teaching vocabulary, that is, help ELLs understand the definition, pronunciation, and meanings in context for these words. Yet different strategies can be used to teach these words. Some ELL content picture books are very helpful, and teachers can also incorporate worksheets for teaching seasonal words to English language learners. This website provides interesting worksheets: http://www.eslprintables.com/vocabulary_worksheets/seasons/. Teachers can also incorporate arts as a tool to teach ELLs. Integrating the arts and artmaking into teaching and learning not only arouses students' interest but helps them develop and deepen their understanding of their environment and human experiences. Art can be combined with reading, writing, speaking, and listening when teaching ELLs and all students.

SUMMARY

Chapter 7 introduces the basic daily words on American traditions and major holidays as well as special events. Vocabulary is a foundation that helps ELLs to read instructions, understand texts, and learning information. It contributes to their overall learning of English and achieving academic success. There are some basic words and vocabulary that all ELLs need to know to be successful in social and school environments. Due to the importance of the vocabulary, teachers need to teach vocabulary through explicit instruction with several basic steps. In addition to the major traditions and holiday words, there are also other traditional words and special events that teachers need to introduce to ELLs. Some lesson ideas are provided for teachers to work with the ELLs in learning American culture while teaching vocabulary.

REFERENCES

Bromley, K. (2007). Nine things every teacher should know about words and vocabulary instruction. *Journal of Adolescent & Adult Literacy*, 7(2), 528–537.

Greenwood, S. C. (2004). *Words count: Effectively vocabulary instruction*. Portsmouth, NH: Heinemann. Retrieved from http://www.heinemann.com/shared/onlineresources/e00648/chapter1.pdf

PART IV

RELEVANT INFORMATION

CHAPTER 8

INFORMATION
FOR PROFESSIONALS

CASE SCENARIO

Hillcrest was a rural school district located in a southeastern state where there was a high increase in ELL population. One ESOL teacher who had a master's degree in elementary education but with an ESOL endorsement served this school district's 79 ELLs, who received a pull-out ESOL language support service. Most mainstream teachers in this district had little or no training on how to work with ELL students. Therefore, the ESOL teacher played an important role serving ELLs while collaborating with mainstream teachers with ELLs. She was the connection between the ELLs and the mainstream teachers and provided any possible support and assistance as needed to help their ELLs, including even serving as a translator to communicate with the ELLs' parents, if needed. For the mainstream teachers, it was a challenge teaching ELLs, who did not speak English but were enrolled in their classrooms. What made the situation even worse was that the teachers had no knowledge of how to interact with ELLs. Without resource and support, the mainstream teachers felt helpless as to where to start and what to do with their ELLs in classrooms. It was expected that they turned to the ESOL teacher for assistance. On the other hand, the ESOL teacher faced the challenge of managing her time serving all the ELLs in K–12 grades, coordinating the work with teachers on how to teach ELLs, and often performing many other functions. As a result, the ESOL teacher was often burdened with providing

A Book for Every Teacher: Teaching English Language Learners
pp. 185–225
Copyright © 2015 by Information Age Publishing

language support for her ELLs who had L2 proficiency from Pre-Production to Intermediate Fluency. It was difficult for her to provide additional support in the subject content areas. The question then was who is responsible for ensuring that ELL students are supported in the school district across the subject content areas?

The above scenario occurs in many school districts throughout the United States. Due to the fast increase in the ELL school population in all K–12 classrooms, it has become more and more challenging for teachers to have the knowledge required on how to teach ELL students. A systematic change in education is also on the way across the nation regarding *what* students should be learning and *how* teachers should be evaluated (Samson & Collins, 2012). For example, most states have adopted the Common Care Standards as the benchmark for what all students should know nationwide at each of K–12 grade levels. Therefore, it becomes more important to ensure the academic success of the K–12 ELL students.

Who Is Responsible for Teaching ELLs?

Traditionally, the responsibility for teaching students who do not speak English belongs primarily to ESOL teachers or the teachers in the bilingual program. (NEA, 2013). In many states, ELLs have access to language and content instruction, but the instruction may not be in core academic classes, such as language arts, mathematics, social studies, and science. Yet, due to the large numbers of ELLs who are currently enrolled in schools, this responsibility has been shifted in recent years, so all general education teachers are required to be adequately prepared for teaching ELLs. Under federal laws, ELLs must be provided appropriate English language development support services and be assessed annually until they meet a state's criteria for proficiency in English on specific language tests in order to exit the required language support services (Antunez, DiCerbo, & Menken, 2000; NEA, 2013; Peregoy & Boyle, 2008).

Unfortunately, many ELLs are not properly identified and are transferred out of services prematurely and placed in mainstream classrooms with no additional support (Huba & Freed, 2000; NEA, 2013). This is not only harmful to ELLs but inconsistent with what the law requires. For example, the Elementary and Secondary Education Act (ESEA) requires ELLs to be provided with ample support in core academic content instruction. This means that general education teachers who are responsible for core content are also responsible for providing effective, comprehensible instruction to ELLs. Although this requirement has been in place, appropriate professional development training is needed to support teachers. With the Common Core on its way to implementation, teachers are faced with an even more challenging role.

Common Core and the Challenging Role of Teachers

Common Core

The Common Core refers to a set of high quality academic standards in mathematics and English language arts/literacy (Common Core, 2012; Fenner, 2013). The Common Core Standards were created to ensure that all students graduate from high school with the skills and knowledge necessary to succeed in college, career, and life, regardless of where they live. As of October 2014, there are 43 states, the District of Columbia, four territories, and the Department of Defense Education Activity that have voluntarily adopted the Common Core Standards and have moved forward for implementation (see Figure 8.1). For years, the United States is a

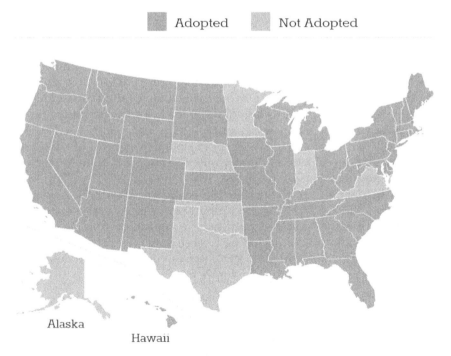

Figure 8.1. States that have adopted CCSS. For more information related to CCSS or to review the current status of the states that have adopted the CCSS, please see http://www.corestandards.org/

nation that has state regulations but no consistent goals and requirements in place nationwide related to educating K–12 students. Due to the need for consistent learning goals across states, state school leaders and governors, which compose the Council of Chief State School Officers (CCSSO) and the NGA Center (National Governors Association), coordinated a state-led effort in 2009 to develop the Common Core State Standards (CCSS). Designed through collaboration among teachers, school leaders, administrators, and other experts, the CCSS provides a clear and consistent framework for teachers and educators.

The Standards were created also out of concern for the academic progress of American K–12 students, who need to show vigor, especially when compared to their international peers. American students must meet high standards in subject areas such as math and science, but often lag in scores when compared to international students. College remediation rates have been high (Common Core, 2012). One of the causes was the absence of common academic standards. They vary from state to state with no consistency in terms of what students should know and what to achieve at each grade level. Therefore, the CCSS were created to define the knowledge and skills that students should gain throughout their K–12 education in order to graduate from high school and be prepared to succeed in entry-level careers, introductory academic college courses, and workforce training programs.

The Standards focus on core concepts and procedures, beginning from the early grades (McCormick-Lee & Fenner, 2011). This gives teachers the time needed to teach them and it gives students the time needed to master them. The Standards also draw on some important international models and are research-based from multiple sources, such as educators from kindergarten to college levels, from state departments of education to assessment developers, and from professional organizations to parents, students, and members of the public. While the standards set grade-specific goals, they do not define how the standards should be taught or which materials should be used to support students. It is up to states and districts to recognize that they need to have a range of supports in place to ensure that all students, including English language learners, can master the standards. Therefore, the states need to determine and define the full range of supports appropriate for their students.

Challenging Role of Teachers

As the CCSS is on the road to being implemented, K–12 teachers are facing a challenging role teaching ELLs. Since the CCSS requires that *all* students be held to the same high expectations, ELL students are included in this expectation. However, what teachers need to consider is that ELLs will need additional time, appropriate instructional support, and aligned assessments as they acquire both English language proficiency and content area knowledge (Marchand-Martella, Klingner, & Martella, 2010; McCormick-Lee & Fenner, 2011). ELL students are a most heterogeneous group, with differences in cultural background, first language, socioeconomic status, prior schooling, and English language proficiency. To effectively work with these students, the appropriate diagnosis of each student must be in place in order to adjust instruction accordingly and monitor student progress. For example, ELLs who are literate in a first language (L1) that shares cognates with English can use L1 vocabulary knowledge when reading in English; ELLs who have high levels of schooling often bring the L1 knowledge and concept already developed when reading in English. Yet ELLs with interrupted schooling may need background knowledge as a prerequisite to perform a specific learning task.

Dr. Diane Staehr Fenner and Dr. Karlene McCormick-Lee provide much insight in their presentation, *The Road to the Common Core State Standards: Building a Bridge for ELLs*, which was originally presented at the Learning Forward Conference related to CCSS and ELLs. Dr. McCormick-Lee is a K–12 education leader who focuses on successful education reform initiatives and implementation of large-scale data for improving programs and performance. Dr. Fenner is an educator and researcher, with expertise in the instruction, assessment, and support of ELLs, with an extensive instructional background in K–12, including teaching and assessing ELLs (McCormick-Lee & Fenner, 2011). They both believe that ELLs' ability to access the CCSS and achieve on the CCSS-based assessments largely depends on their ability to acquire academic language. In Chapter 2, it is also discussed that cognitive academic language proficiency (CALP) is critical for ELLs in understanding subject content. Therefore, K–12 teachers need to collaborate with ESOL teachers and ensure that ELLs can acquire academic language proficiency in order to access academic content knowledge in subject areas.

Obviously, K–12 teachers are facing more challenges today in terms of teaching ELLs. Teachers must be simultaneously teachers of both challenging content and academic language under the CCSS requirements. The role of ESOL teachers will shift to being an expert consultant and advocate as CCSS is on the road to implementation. In February 2013, TESOL International Association brought 30 ESL teachers and administrators, education experts, researchers, and thought leaders from Maryland and the District of Columbia to start a conversation on how the Common Core State Standards would change the roles of the ESL teachers (Fenner, 2013). As one of the ESOL teachers stated at this meeting, the Common Core is both a challenge and an opportunity for teachers to continue bringing the learning needs of ELLs to the center of the conversation about student achievement, and all teachers must help their students synthesize materials through diverse media, facilitate a high level of interaction, and weave together content objectives to help ELLs' academic success.

Recently, consensus seems to have been reached based on several key research findings for teaching ELLs. They include the need to emphasize the development of oral language skills and the need to focus on academic language and culturally inclusive practices (Samson & Collins, 2012). Unfortunately, this knowledge is often excluded in the requirements of teacher education programs, in state certification exams, or in school-based teacher evaluations. With the CCSS requirements, this information becomes more necessary for teachers to know in order to teach ELLs effectively. Therefore, what general education teachers should know to better serve ELL students are these three basic areas: ELLs' oral language development, academic language, and cultural diversity and inclusivity (see Table 8.1).

There is no doubt that under the CCSS requirements, both content area teachers and ESOL teachers face the challenge of teaching academic language and content knowledge to ELLs. As the CCSS is on its way to implementation, teachers in the subject content areas need guidance from ESOL teachers in order to provide effective instruction to ELLs. New instructional strategies must be designed with learning materials

Table 8.1.   All Teachers of ELLs Must Understand These Three Areas of Basic Knowledge

Teacher Competency Areas	*Required Teachers' Knowledge and Understanding*
Oral language development	Teachers must have knowledge and understanding of language as a system and of the role of the components of language and speech, specifically sound, grammar, meaning, coherence, communicative strategies, and social conventions.
Academic language	Teachers must have knowledge of academic language and of the particular type of language used for instruction as well as for the cognitively demanding tasks typically found in textbooks, classrooms, assessments, and those necessary for engagement in discipline-specific areas.
Cultural diversity and inclusivity	Teachers must have knowledge and understanding of the role of culture in language development and academic achievement. Cultural differences often affect ELL students' classroom participation and performance in several ways. The norms for behavior, communication, and interactions with others that ELL students use in their homes often do not match the norms that are enforced in the school setting.

Source: Based on Samson and Collins (2012).

that have depth and rigor (Fenner, 2013). Based on ELL students' language proficiency levels, authentic lessons that incorporate the CCSS need to be designed and implemented. The content objectives need to be based on the ELLs' academic language level. K–12 teachers will need to teach grammatical structures and academic languages to ELLs in collaboration with ESOL service. ESOL teachers also need to collaborate with K–12 teachers in order to help ELLs learn academic language and have access to content knowledge as required by the CCSS. It is a collaborative effort indeed for the CCSS to be implemented and reach intended goals.

Trends and Programs in L2 Teaching

The debates on second language (L2) teaching have continued for decades on the direction of teaching ELLs. In the past 15 years, several crucial factors have combined to affect current perspectives on teaching English as L2: (a) the decline of methods, (b) a growing emphasis on the bottom-up and top-down skills, (c) creation of new knowledge about English, and (d) integrated and contextualized teaching of multiple language skills (Carasquillo & Rodriguez, 2002; Hinkel, 2006). Today, the debate on L2 teaching is even more heated on how ELLs should be served under the CCSS requirements. Through working with ESOL teachers in school districts, we know that ESOL teaching is also changing; yet teaching four language skills is still the center focus. Many ESOL teachers develop their own materials to work with ELL students. ESOL teachers are often challenged by heavy workloads with many duties, as well as having to work with ELLs for a short period of time in the L2 support programs. Yet, under the CCSS requirements, ESOL teachers are required to develop curricula tied to Common Core State Standards at K–12 schools and to work collaboratively with K–12 teachers in mainstream classrooms (Fenner, 2013).

Even before the CCSS requirements, the shift in instructional practices related to L2 teaching took place. Traditionally, L2 instruction for K–12 ELLs focuses on the linguistic aspects (Stoller, 2004; Xanthou, 2010). Yet, since the 1980s, with the trend of integrating educational theories and linguistics knowledge in L2 teaching, the correlation between subject content knowledge and students' language development has gained much attention. L2 theory studies play an important role in this shift. For example, Cummin's (1984, 2000) theories on basic interpersonal communication skills (BICS) and cognitive academic language proficiency (CALP) provide a theoretical framework for understanding the importance for ELLs to develop academic language in order to have access to content knowledge. Until now, many ESOL teachers seem to still focus teaching on four language skills: listening, speaking, reading, writing (Mancilla-Martinez & Lesaux, 2011; Perez & Holmes, 2010) when ELLs are served in the ESOL classrooms. When ELLs return to their mainstream classrooms, they struggle in math, science, and social studies with the textbooks written at the grade levels. As a result, there is a gap between the L2 teaching and content knowledge. An ESOL teacher generally travels to several schools on a daily basis to provide ESOL services for ELLs. This has been the practice for many school districts and adds to the challenges that ESOL teachers have in addressing the needs of ELLs. Therefore, it is necessary that ESOL teachers and K–12 mainstream teachers collaborate and work together in order to solve the problem of curriculum alignment (Hinkel, 2006; Honigsfeld & Dove, 2010).

Different Programs for ELLs

Due to law requirements, ELLs must be provided with L2 support services. Although different types of programs exist, several general types are commonly used in many schools. The programs in L2 support services introduced here are those commonly known programs: *bilingual programs, inclusion programs, pull-out programs, sheltered instruction,* and *content-based ESOL programs.* In general, *bilingual programs* require that teachers be trained in and be competent in teaching students through both their native language and English. *Inclusion programs*, as the name suggests, require placing ELLs in mainstream classrooms with L2 support. *Pull-out programs* are traditional programs to pull ELLs out of the mainstream classroom for instructional support. *Sheltered instruction* refers to grade-level content instruction in which the classroom teacher provides modified instruction by teaching the grade-level content. *Content-based ESOL programs* refer to structured immersion, sheltered English, and Specially Designed Academic Instruction in English (Brown, 2004; Reed & Railsback, 2003). All these programs share the same goal of teaching ELLs both English language and academic content. Teachers use a variety of strategies, such as gestures, visual aids, graphic organizers, and simplified English, to teach students and help them learn content knowledge.

Bilingual Programs

Bilingual programs usually refer to a program in an English-language school system in which students with little fluency in English are taught in both their native languages and English (Ovando & Collier, 1998; Ovando, Collier, & Combs, 2003; Thomas & Collier, 2002). There are several types of bilingual programs. For example, *transitional bilingual programs*, also called *early-exit bilingual programs*, are common in early elementary grades, and instruction in the first language is used for 2 or 3 years in the program. *Maintenance bilingual programs*, also called *late-exit programs,* usually have students for a longer period of time or even throughout elementary school. *Two-way bilingual programs* are also called *dual language programs.* In this model, English language learners are grouped based on a single language background in the same classroom with native English speakers. These programs are supposed to have a nearly 50-50 balance between ELLs and native English speakers, with instruction divided equally between English and the other language. Students remain in these programs throughout elementary school. Despite differences, the main purpose of a bilingual program is to build a bridge and help ELLs become proficient in their native language and English. Bilingual programs will gradually transition ELLs to English-speaking classrooms. The programs benefit ELLs by meeting students' linguistics, academic, and cultural needs while preparing ELLs with the grade-level content, the move to English-only classrooms, and adaptation to school culture and environment

With the Bilingual Education Act of 1968, bilingual education has received much attention and support. Yet bilingual education programs have also received criticism. For example, due to the short duration of early-exit programs, many ELLs are not ready for mainstream classrooms when they are dismissed from the program. Others criticize bilingual education as having little evidence to show that it is more effective than all-English programs (Ovando et al., 2003; Thomas & Collier, 2002). Nevertheless, bilingual education has been practiced for many decades, and a good bilingual program does benefit ELLs. For example, a bilingual program that offers instruction in content areas at grade levels for students through both languages helps ELLs better understand content knowledge. In the program, the use of the first language can take as much as 90% of instruction time for beginners; as students move to higher grade levels, English and L1 can be shared equally for instruction time, that is, the instruction in the L1 can be reduced to 50% (Ovando & Collier, 1998; Ovando et al., 2003; Thomas & Collier, 2002). Thus, despite criticism, the bilingual model is believed to help ELLs gain knowledge through their L1 because it makes English more comprehensible; ELLs also gain literacy through their L1, which can be transferred into the L2, and it gives ELLs confidence in their schoolwork.

Inclusion Program

Inclusion is a term originally used to include students with special needs within the general education setting. However, politics and budgets have motivated the decision to mainstream ELL students (Harklau, 1994; Platt, Harper, Mendoza, 2003). For example, in an effort to save costs, some schools and states have created mandatory full-inclusion programs, where ELLs are immersed in a regular-paced English classroom with peers who are fluent in English (Clair, 1995; Harklau, 1994; Reeves, 2004). This doe helps reduce the costs of ESOL specialists while still engaging ELL students in an atmosphere for learning. However, there are bodies of literature about ELL students in inclusion programs indicating that ELLs have more effective social interactions in ESOL classrooms than inclusion classrooms, and that ELL students are also more academically successful in ESOL classrooms than in inclusion classrooms. In other words, ELLs are not as socially or academically engaging in inclusion programs. For example, California is one of the states that has implemented the *full inclusion* approach, requiring that all public schools instruct ELLs solely in English. This approach is supported by Proposition 227, which provides ELLs with $50 million each year for additional English tutoring support. Yet, when an ELL has never been exposed to L2 but is forced to stay in fluent-English classrooms, it is not helpful to that ELL.

However, inclusion is also supported by literature. Some suggest that the best way to attain L2 fluency is through inclusion in an English-speaking environment and that inclusion has more positive results (Coelho, 2004; Hill & Flynn, 2006; Reeves, 2004). For example, by using differentiated instruction, full inclusion helps engage ELLs. Teachers in inclusion programs are expected to incorporate a wide range of learning modalities (visual, auditory, kinesthetic, etc.) in designing instruction. Teachers can use traditional tools used to support ELL students, such as graphic organizers and visual aids, to help those students who are proficient in English learn a concept in a new way. While inclusion has literature support, some other educators believe that inclusion is not the best ways to teach either ELLs or mainstream students because it slows down the English-speaking students (Callahan, 2005; Montgomery, Roberts & Growe, 2003; Norrid-Lacey & Spencer, 2000). In addition, the literature on tracking shows that ELL students are often disproportionately tracked into low-level classrooms. Once they are placed in a low track, ELLs often have difficulty acquiring the language and content knowledge necessary to demonstrate their ability to enter a different track.

ELL students typically need additional resources and support to adjust to the various linguistic complications in learning a new language. Thus, immersing ELLs in a regular-paced English class with students who are fluent in English may not be as beneficial to them as in the ESOL room unless appropriate support is in place. Teachers in inclusion programs also may not have time to take into consideration ELLs' needs, especially if an ELL does not know English. It is also a concern that teachers of the full-inclusion model are not prepared to successfully help ELL students acquire a new language. For example, K–12 classroom teachers in the inclusion model need to meet state certification requirements or be provided curriculum and materials for working with ELLs (Murillo & Smith,

2008; Wright, 2010). Furthermore, classroom teachers should provide the same type of instruction that ESOL teachers provide for ELLs in a pull-out program. Therefore, the pros and cons of inclusion programs will continue to be debated among educators and researchers.

Pull-Out Programs

The pull-out program originates from special education that takes either gifted students or students with disabilities out of the regular classroom during the typical school day and places them in alternative programs (Gelzheiser, Meyers, & Robert, 2010; Harklau, 1994; Reeves, 2004). For ELLs, it refers to the program in which ELLs receive assistance for a portion of the day through the pull-out component. When pulling out, ELLs go to the ESOL room for intensive instruction in English and also receive L2 support within content areas while they spend the majority of their day in mainstream classrooms with English-speaking peers. This allows ELLs to be a part of the student body within their school. The ESOL teacher pulls ELLs out of the regular classroom for mainly instruction on language arts, reading, and writing in the ESOL room. The length of time depends on the number of ELLs and their language proficiency level. ELLs can meet the ESOL teacher in the resource room on a daily basis, but sometimes it can be twice or three times a week.

Debate on the effectiveness of pull-out programs has remained ongoing. For example, some studies point out disadvantages of the pull-out model as follows: (a) shortened instructional time due to being in and out classrooms; (b) a hard time for students to connect the contents in the regular room to that of the pull-out program; (c) lower expectations and easier assignments from the regular teachers; and (d) ELLs are segregated in the pull-out setting (Cook & Zhao, 2011; Ovando & Collier, 1998). In addition, scheduling is not easy for the ESOL teacher because ELLs are pulled out from more than one classroom. ESOL teachers find it hard to communicate with mainstream teachers. Yet, despite the disadvantages, the advantages of a pull-out program are identified by researchers (Cook & Zhao, 2011; Ovando et al., 2003; Reeves, 2004). First, students can get one-on-one help in a small class–sized setting. Second, the pull-out program provides an environment for ELLs to be more relaxed. It is easy for ELLs to build a relationship with the ESOL resource teacher in a small class–sized setting. Finally, ELLs feel safe and comfortable in small groups. For example, ELLs can verbalize their ideas more in the ESOL room than in the big class–sized group. Although research findings about pull-out programs reveal both advantages and disadvantages and have both positive and negative effects, pull-out programs have been implemented across the United States in schools where other programs are not available. The pull-out model provides a supportive learning environment for ELLs to learn the L2 and school culture.

Sheltered Instruction

Sheltered instruction is an approach for teaching ELL students by integrating language and content instruction with two main goals for sheltered instruction: to provide ELLs with access to mainstream, grade-level content, and to promote L2 development for ELLs (Echevarria & Graves, 2007; Echevarria, Vogt, & Short, 2010; Hill & Björk, 2010). In the sheltered instruction model, mainstream teachers are required to provide modified instruction by using grade-level content objectives so that the content will be meaningful and comprehensible to ELLs. ELL students learn content knowledge at their grade level and at the same time develop academic English language skills. The Sheltered Instruction Observation Protocol (SIOP) lesson model is discussed in Chapter 3, with eight interrelated components from lesson preparation and delivery to strategies and assessment.

Another teaching model is the use of Sheltered Instruction Observation Protocol (SIOP). This research-based model serves as a guide for mainstream teachers on how to prepare and develop a lesson with language and content objectives appropriate to ELLs. When classroom teachers write content objectives, the objectives must relate to the development of a concept, an idea, or a skill that reflects the grade-level curriculum standards. When adding language objectives, teachers need to consider what language component is needed to support ELLs and all students for access to content knowledge. As effective strategies in the SIOP Model, teachers need modeling, helping students make connections between content and personal experiences or existing schemas, differentiated instruction, writer's workshop, cooperative learning, high level of student engagement, supplementary materials, technology integration, and so on. Teachers are required to incorporate these eight interrelated components in a SIOP lesson: lesson preparation, building background, comprehensible input, strategies, interaction, practice/application, lesson delivery, and review/assessment. For more details related to these components, please review the SIOP content in Chapter 3 and also visit the SIOP website at http://siop.pearson.com/about-siop/index.html.

Content-Based ESOL Programs

Content-based ESOL programs can refer to structured immersion, sheltered English, and Specially Designed Academic Instruction in English (Brown, 2004; Hill & Flynn, 2006; Reed & Railsback, 2003). They all share the same goal of teaching English language learners both English language and academic content. Teachers use a variety of strategies, such as gestures, visual aids, and simplified English, to help students access content knowledge. In traditional ESOL classes, most time is spent learning how to speak in imagined situations, focusing on social language competency; however, language learning in content-based ESOL programs provides purposeful, meaningful, and authentic opportunities for ELL students (Brown, 2004; Short, 1993). Thus, content-based ESOL programs benefit ELLs in that ELL students learn age-appropriate content knowledge that reflects the content learning in the mainstream; and ELL students read authentic texts, not simplified or contrived texts written for ESL students only. Thus, learning is more meaningful and situated, and ELLs learn the language meaningfully, for example, not just how to construct expository writing but writing about a science experiment result based on the content lesson, and then the language and vocabulary knowledge is more closely linked with academic content knowledge.

For a content-based ESOL program to be effective, ESOL teachers need to collaborate with mainstream teachers and know what content units ELL students are studying in various subjects. Once a content area is selected, the teacher needs to decide on what concepts in the units from the chosen content area to be explored in depth rather than breadth. This means an ESOL teacher cannot teach an entire curriculum of fifth-grade science or social studies. The teacher should pick one lesson that is interesting to ELL students or that is important to their content learning. The teacher then should choose content area reading materials based on ELLs' L2 proficiency. Since content area reading is full of difficult syntax and semantics, it is a good idea that materials selected are slightly below the ELLs' actual grade level. Finally, the teacher needs to design thematic unit lessons. To deal with a specific topic in an in-depth manner, lessons should have a series of related lessons in the same topic. For example, if recycling is the topic, teachers can design the first lesson to learn basic vocabulary related to recycling and build background knowledge by connecting to their students' personal lives related to the major concepts of recycling. The second lesson will be appropriate to learning about the recycling process and the importance of recycling. The third lesson can be designed for an experimental recycling project to engage ELLs in doing. The fourth lesson can ask ELLs to write an essay on recycling, and the fifth lesson can ask students to share their projects or publish their essays in the classroom newsletter. In content-based ESL programs, scaffolding is critical when ELL students learn abstract concepts. Hands-on activities and visual aids are an important part of scaffolding because they facilitate students in learning concepts.

Assessing ELLs and Related Issues

ELL students who are still in the process of developing L2 proficiency face challenges related to assessment and standardized testing, which also brings challenges for teachers on how to appropriately assess their work (Peregoy & Boyle, 2008). ELLs are a special group of students in terms of providing, designing, and administering assessments, especially in the large scale of formal assessment. Statistically, ELLs represent 1 in 4 students by the year 2025. Nationally, about 80% of ELLs are native speakers of Spanish, but overall, ELLs speak about 400 different home languages (Pitoniak et al., 2009). With increasing emphasis on accountability in general, the need to produce valid and fair assessments for ELLs has become a matter of important national concern.

Assessment should be the process of gathering information from multiple and diverse sources in order to develop a deep understanding of what students know, understand, and can do with their knowledge as a result of their educational experiences; the process culminates when assessment results are used to improve subsequent learning (Huba & Freed, 2000). Learning how to plan, implement, and assess ELL students is not an easy task. Gottlieb (2012), the lead developer for World-Class Instructional Design and Assessment (WIDA) at the Wisconsin Center for Education Research, provides well-documented texts, *Common Language Assessment for English Learners* (2012) and *Assessing English Language Learners: Bridges From Language Proficiency to Academic Achievement* (2006) that examine the unique needs of the ELL population and provide strategies for implementing instructional assessment of both language and content. With depth and breadth, Gottlieb's texts (2006, 2012) explain how to equitably and comprehensively assess the language proficiency and academic achievement of ELLs. Specifically, mainstream teachers and educators can find this useful information:

- Rubrics, charts, checklists, surveys, and other ready-to-use tools
- Professional development activities
- An integrated approach to teaching standards, language, and content
- Guidance on how best to address standardized testing and grading

As teachers constantly face the issue of assessing students, it is important for them to know that the ELLs' academic performance must be appropriately assessed in order to determine whether an ELL's performance is related to language barrier or the lack of content knowledge. In order to assess ELLs appropriately, teachers need information related to

Table 8.2. Factors Affecting Assessment of ELLs

Factors	Affecting Variables	Examples
Language factors	• different linguistic backgrounds • different proficiency in L1 • different proficiency in L2	• 400 different native languages are spoken by ELLs nationally
Educational background factors	• different degrees of formal schooling in L1 • different degrees of formal schooling in L2 • different degrees of exposure to standardized testing in U.S. schools	• Refugee populations may enter U.S. schools with little or no formal schooling in any language
Cultural factors	• different degrees of acculturation to U.S. mainstream culture • different expectations of familiarity	• Students from low SES backgrounds may respond to questions differently

Source: Based on Pitoniak et al. (2009).

ELLs. Data gathered may include the language background of the family, the literacy level of the first language, the parents' education in the first language, and the benchmark score of the student's language proficiency level. This information does not seem to be directly related to a testing instrument. Yet these factors can affect ELLs' performance in testing. In the following section, key factors that are important to consider when assessing ELLs are discussed (see Table 8.2) as well as other issues related to assessing ELLs.

Factors Affecting Assessment of ELLs

Language Factors

First, ELLs may have *different linguistic backgrounds*. While the majority of ELL student in the United States come from Spanish-speaking backgrounds, it is estimated that there are about 400 different native languages spoken by ELLs nationally (Peregoy & Boyle, 2008; Pitoniak et al., 2009). It is important for teachers to keep in mind when considering accommodations in assessment of their ELL students. Second, ELLs may have *different levels of proficiency in English*. For example, ELLs may have various levels of oral and written English proficiency. Teachers should not assume that ELLs who can converse orally in English will have the literacy skills necessary to understand the written directions and instructions in a standardized test. Some ELLs may be proficient in oral English but not in the academic English needed to fully understand content area assessments. Studies show that the level of language proficiency has an influence on processing speed. In other words, compared with native speakers, ELLs generally take longer on tasks presented in English. It is also important for teachers to keep in mind when providing the assessment as well as when making decisions about testing accommodations. Third, ELLs may have *different levels of proficiency in native language.* This means that ELLs are different in their levels of L1 proficiency and literacy. Therefore, teachers cannot assume that all ELLs will understand written test directions in their native languages. This is also important for teachers to keep in mind when considering using L1 accommodations.

Educational Background Factors

ELLs may have *different degrees of formal schooling in native language* (Pitoniak et al., 2009). The degree of previous schooling affects not only L1 proficiency and literacy but also the level of content knowledge and skills. For example, students from refugee populations may enter the U.S. educational system with little or no formal schooling in any language. These students must learn English and content area knowledge simultaneously while also being socialized into a school context that may be extremely unfamiliar. Other ELLs may come to the United States with more formal schooling and have received instruction in the content knowledge of their L1. Second, ELLs may have *different degrees of formal schooling in English.* ELLs also vary in the number of years they have spent in schools where English is the language of instruction. A distinction may also be made between students who have studied English as a foreign language while in their home countries and students who have studied English as an L2 only in the United States. In addition, ELLs from migrant populations may spend many years in English-speaking schools but may also experience repeated interruptions and relocation to different cities in the United States in the course of their schooling, which may have an impact on both their English language proficiency and on their content area knowledge. Third, ELLs may have *different degrees of exposure to standardized testing.* Teachers need to know that not all ELLs have had the same exposure to the standardized testing as American students have. Students in some countries may have had no exposure to multiple-choice questions, while other ELLs may never have seen a constructed-response question. Even ELLs from educationally advantaged backgrounds or high levels of English proficiency may not be used to large-scale standardized assessments and thus may be at a disadvantage in these testing situations.

Cultural Factors

Cultural factors can affect assessing ELLs appropriately (Pitoniak et al., 2009). ELLs may have *different degrees of acculturation into U.S. mainstream culture.* ELLs come from a wide range of cultural backgrounds, and cultural differences may place ELLs at a disadvantage in a standardized testing situation. For example, lack of familiarity with mainstream American culture can have potential impact on test scores for ELLs. Students who are unfamiliar with American culture may be at a disadvantage compared to their peers because ELLs may hold different assumptions about the testing situation or the educational environment in general, have different background knowledge and experience, or possess different sets of cultural values and beliefs and therefore respond to questions differently. ELLs from cultures where cooperation is valued over competition may be at a disadvantage in testing situations in U.S. schools where the goal is for each individual student to perform on his or her own. Students from economically disadvantaged backgrounds may also respond to questions differently and may have background knowledge and experiences that are different than expected by a test developer.

Planning the Assessment

Assessment as a benchmark tool provides feedback on the students' progress, and this feedback can help teachers redesign instruction to meet students' academic needs. When preparing for assessing ELLs, one of the important things to consider is the purpose of assessment. Assessments have different purposes. For example, one test may be used to evaluate students' readiness to advance to the next grade, while another test evaluates students' need for remediation. It is important to outline the specific interpretations that will be made based on the scores. For example, tests used as a criterion for determining high school graduation will affect ELL students differently than tests designed to inform instructional decisions (Gottlieb, 2006, 2012; Pitoniak et al., 2009).

When planning for assessment of ELLs, teachers also need to consider another important thing: how English language skills interact with the test construct. For example, when constructing for a math test, teachers need to consider whether it is intended to be a test of mathematics, in which case the test should require minimal or no English proficiency; or a test of the ability to do mathematics within an English-language educational environment, in which the student ability to comprehend word problems in English may be part of the construct. Similarly, when giving a test, attention needs to be paid to how much of the vocabulary of the discipline in English is part of the assessment. If English proficiency is part of the test construct, then plan carefully to determine what level of English proficiency should be expected of students. When determining the language proficiency to be included in the test, teachers need to make an effort to consult ESOL teachers or professionals with backgrounds in educating ELLs.

According to Pitoniak et al. (2009), it is also important to consider these basic elements when planning for assessment: *domain of knowledge and skills, number and types of test items, relative weights of tasks and skills,* and *assessment forms.* Domain of knowledge and skills mean that each state is likely to have documented content standards for the subject area to be assessed and even performance standards and other documents that define the domain and their expectations for student achievement. These documents should be reviewed carefully in order to know the degree to which each standard requires students' ability to read, write, speak, or listen in English to be.

Number and types of test items means that when all other things are equal, tests with more items will yield more reliable scores. Reliability refers to the extent to which scores obtained on a specific form of an assessment can be generalized to scores obtained on other forms of the assessment, administered at other times, or scored by some other raters (Pitoniak et al., 2009). Therefore, it is important to provide ELLs with multiple opportunities to show what they know and can do. Then, *relative weights of tasks and skills* needs to be considered. The weight of a task or test-content category is generally decided by the importance of the assessed task relative to other tasks on the test and the degree to which the tasks tap content described in the state's standards. Tasks that require more time to complete (e.g., longer responses written in English) receive more weight in an assessment. Such weightings may disadvantage ELLs; thus, develop a careful rationale for weighting to apply to all students' responses, taking both content knowledge and language skills into consideration. Finally, *assessment and response forms* should be considered. Assessment specifications describe how the tasks will be presented to the students and how the students are expected to respond. Printed test booklets and answer sheets on which students mark responses and write constructed responses are very common in the K–12 school environment. Just as including a variety of item types in an assessment provides multiple ways for ELLs to show their knowledge, some educators believe that incorporating different types of media (such as video or sound) in an assessment format may also benefit ELLs.

Types of Assessment for ELLs
When assessing ELLs, one critical question to ask is how to select proper assessment types in order to yield valid and fair assessment results. The first step is to identify ELLs' language and academic needs (Colorín Colorado, 2007; Gottlieb, 2012). This step is the basis for the development of a proper program of instruction. When ELLs' needs are not identified, the program they are placed into may lack the instructional components to help them in language proficiency and academic achieve-

ment. Thus, initial assessment will include a proper assessment of your ELLs' needs by identifying ELLs' *home language preferences*, *educational background*, *English proficiency level*, and *academic content knowledge in English*. Many states and school district mandates require that the families of ELLs complete *a home language survey* in their primary language (or if not available, in English) as soon as they register in the district. This home survey is usually given in the front office when ELLs and their parents first arrive. The survey has questions to identify ELLs' home and preferred language. For the most part, home language surveys will ask these questions:

- Is English your first language?
- Can you speak another language? If yes, what language?
- What language do you speak most often with your friends?
- What language do you speak most often with your family?

In addition to knowing ELLs' home language, teachers also need to find out about ELLs' educational background, literacy skills, and previous experience with English (Colorín Colorado, 2007; Gottlieb, 2012). Questions to be asked may include the following:

- How many years were you in school in your native country? In the United States?
- What was the last school you attended?
- What grade were you in at the last school you attended?
- What are the names of the other schools you attended?
- Can you read in Spanish (or your native language)? How well?
- Can you write in Spanish (or your native language)? How well?
- How much help do you need to learn English?
- Where do you need the most help? Speaking? Listening? Reading? Writing?

Teachers also need to identify the academic experience of their ELLs. This information helps to identify his or her knowledge of content areas in English or Spanish (Colorín Colorado, 2007; Gottlieb, 2012). Although this may not be part of formal assessment, knowing ELLs' level of content area knowledge is important to plan the instruction for the student. Teachers may ask these following questions to find out about their academic knowledge:

- What subjects did you study in your old school(s)? What language(s) did you use?
- What books did you use in your other schools? In what language(s) were the books?
- Did you study in a bilingual program? If so, which subjects did you study in Spanish (or your native language) and which did you study in English?

Formative Assessment

Formative assessment refers to a wide variety of methods that teachers use to conduct in-process evaluations of student comprehension, learning needs, and academic progress during a lesson, unit, or course (Colorín Colorado, 2007; Cook & Zhao, 2011; Gottlieb, 2012; Huba & Freed, 2000; Pitoniak et al., 2009; Wikipedia, 2014). The purpose of formative assessment is to *monitor* student learning in order to provide ongoing feedback that can be used by teachers to improve their teaching and by students to improve their learning. In other words, formative assessment helps teachers identify students' strengths and weaknesses and identify the targeted areas that need work, such as where students are struggling so that the problem can be addressed. Since standardized tests in English may not always reflect ELLs' true content knowledge or abilities, formative assessments becomes important to provide an accurate picture of their skills, abilities, and ongoing progress through informal, authentic, or performance-based assessment.

Performance-Based Assessment

This type of assessment is based on classroom instruction and everyday tasks. Teachers can use performance-based assessments to assess ELLs' language proficiency and academic achievement through oral reports, presentations, demonstrations, written assignments, and portfolios (Cook & Zhao, 2011; Gottlieb, 2012; Huba & Freed, 2000). For example, the performance assessments can include both processes (e.g., several drafts of a writing sample) and products (e.g., project assignments). Teachers can use scoring rubrics and observation checklists to evaluate and grade their students. These assessment tools can help document ELLs' growth over a period of time. When using performance-based assessments, it is important to establish clear and fair criteria from the beginning. It is also helpful to develop these criteria in conjunction with ESOL teachers or specialists in the school district. Performance-based assessments promote a wide range of responses and do not typically produce one single, correct answer. Therefore, evaluation of student performance and products must be based on teacher judgment, using the criteria specified for each task. Teachers can also develop assessment and instructional activities that are geared to the ELLs' current level of English proficiency. Performance-based assessment activities can concentrate on oral communication and/or reading. Here are some example activities that teachers can use for assessing ELLs' oral English skills or even reading comprehension:

- Retelling stories
- Oral reporting to the whole class
- Reading with partners
- Telling a story with a sequence of three or more pictures
- Completing conversation with written prompts
- Completing incomplete stories
- Debating, either one-on-one or taking turns in small groups
- Providing instructions with visual or written prompts
- Brainstorming
- Playing games or role-playing

Portfolios

Portfolios are another way of assessing student work throughout the entire year. With this method, teachers can systematically collect descriptive records of student work over time that reflects growth toward the achievement of specific curricular objectives (Gottlieb, 2006; Huba & Freed, 2000; Perez & Holmes, 2010; Venn, 2000). Portfolios can include information, sample work, and evaluations that serve as indicators for student performance. By documenting student performance over time, portfolios are a better way to systematically assess student progress than just one measure alone. Portfolios can include

- Written samples; for example, stories, completed forms, exercise sheets, or descriptions
- Drawings representing student content knowledge and proficiencies
- Tapes of oral work, such as role-playing, presentations, or an oral account of a trip
- Teacher descriptions of student accomplishments, such as performance on oral tasks
- Formal test data, checklists, and rating sheets

Summative Assessment

Summative assessments are often *high-stakes* types. The purpose is to evaluate student learning at the end of an instructional unit by comparing it against some standard or benchmark (Cook & Zhao, 2011; Gottlieb,

2012; Huba & Freed, 2000; Wikipedia, 2014). This means that they have a high point value and provide evaluation of the final quality of teaching and learning with an overall grade or score. At the end of the school year, standardized testing and standardized language testing usually take place. A midterm or final exam, a final project or a final research paper can be examples of summative assessment. For ELLs, with the recommendations of the ESOL teachers and classroom teachers, the summative assessment often serves as an indicator to determine if an ELL will exit from the ESOL program. If the ELL stays in the same school district, the assessment data can be used as a recommendation for the beginning of the new school year. Research often indicates that ELLs' L2 proficiency goes down during the summer break. Thus, at the beginning of the new school year, assessing returning ELLs' L2 proficiency can help identify gaps in their learning.

Appropriately Assessing ELLs

ELLs' Language Development

Students learning an L2 usually move through five predictable stages: preproduction, early production, speech emergence, intermediate fluency, and advanced fluency (Haynes, 2014; Hill & Björk, 2008; Krashen & Terrell, 1983). How quickly each student progresses through these stages depends on many factors, such as language factors, educational background, and time spent in the L2 country. After ELLs have had the initial placement test, their language proficiency levels are usually provided for classroom teachers. In other words, teachers should have this information on file. Yet teachers sometimes may not know what each level means. The characteristics of the five stages of language acquisition are exemplified as follows (Haynes, 2014; Hill & Bjork, 2008).

Stage I: Preproduction Stage

This is the silent period and usually occurs during the first 6 months. ELLs may build up to 500 words in their receptive vocabulary but they are not yet able to speak. Some ELL students may repeat what the teacher says. Yet they are mainly listening, that is, not really producing language.

- ELLs at this stage are in a *silent period.*
- Repeat words but not produce language
- Listen attentively
- Respond to pictures and visual aids
- Build receptive vocabulary

- Learn basic oral greetings and related vocabulary words
- Need much repetition (TPR methods work well)
- Benefit from a *buddy* who speaks their language

Stage II: Early Production

This stage may last up to 6 months, and ELLs may develop a receptive vocabulary of about 1,000 words. ELLs can usually speak in one- or two-word phrases. They can use short language chunks memorized, although these chunks may not always be used correctly. Teachers can do the following activities:

- Ask *yes* or *no* questions and accept one or two word responses
- Use pictures and visual aids to build vocabulary
- Use simple books with predictable text
- Support learning with graphic organizers, charts, and graphs
- Give students the opportunity to participate in some of the whole-class activities
- Modify content information to the language level of ELLs
- Provide listening activities
- Simplify the content materials to be used
- Focus on key vocabulary and concepts
- Begin to foster writing in English through labeling and short sentences

Stage III: Speech Emergence

At this stage (Years 1–3), ELLs may have developed a vocabulary of 3,000 words and may be able to communicate with simple phrases and sentences. They may ask simple questions that are not grammatically correct. They may able to

- Sound out stories phonetically
- Read short, modified texts in content area subjects
- Complete graphic organizers with word banks
- Understand and answer questions about charts and graphs
- Match vocabulary words to definitions
- Study flashcards with content area vocabulary
- Participate in pair and choral reading activities
- Understand teacher explanations or directions that are not complicated

- Draft brief stories based on personal experience
- Write in dialogue journals

Stage IV: Intermediate Fluency

ELLs at this stage (Years 3–5) should have a vocabulary of 6,000 active words. They begin to use more complex sentences when speaking and writing and are willing to express opinions and share their thoughts. They are also able to

- Ask questions to clarify what they are learning in class
- Work in grade-level math and science classes with some teacher support
- Use strategies from their native language to learn content in English
- Have errors as they try to learn English grammar and sentence structure
- Will translate written assignments from native language
- Are able to synthesize what they have learned and to make inferences
- Understand more complex concepts

Stage V: Advanced Fluency

This stage takes about from 5 to 7 years for ELLs to achieve and obtain cognitive academic language proficiency (CALP) in an L2, as discussed in Chapter 2. ELLs at this stage will have the ability to perform in content area learning. They should

- Have exited from ESOL and other support programs
- Function appropriately in mainstream classrooms
- Read academic
- content materials independently
- Write academic papers in content areas
- Understand and use some idioms, slang, and proverbs

Hill and Björk (2008) provide further explanation in their book, *Classroom Instruction That Works with English Language Learners: Facilitator's Guide*, about the five stages of L2 development (see Table 8.3 for more details). The authors also illustrate these language development stages by using a classroom example. For example, when teaching the picture book called *The Three Little Pigs* to ELL students, teachers can phrase the questions based on the ELL's L2 proficiency at each stage as follows:

- *Stage 1*: *Preproduction*: Ask questions by pointing at pictures in the book with demonstrations, such as, "Show me the wolf," "Where is the house?"

- *Stage II*: *Early Production*: Ask questions that need *yes* or *no* or with one or two word answers: "Did the brick house fall down?" "Who blew down the straw house?"

- *Stage III*: *Speech Emergence*: Ask *why* and *how* with short sentence responses, for example, "Why did the third pig built a brick house?" "How does the story end?"

- *Stage IV*: *Intermediate Fluency*: Ask "What would happen if …?" and "Why do you think so?" or "What could the two other pigs have done to survive?"

- *Stage V*: *Advanced Fluency*: Ask students to retell the story using literacy elements as clues; for example, plot, setting, theme, but leaving out unnecessary details.

To appropriately assess ELLs, teachers need to know the factors that affect the assessment of ELL students, be prepared for planning of assessment, and also be familiar with both formative and summative assessment tools. It is important to assess ELLs with adequate data in order to design instruction, plan lessons, and support ELLs in gaining academic language development that gives them access to the content area knowledge and skills necessary for them to achieve the intended goals. Assessing ELLs' integrated language skills and content knowledge is imperative. For example, when using a K-W-L-S graphic organizer, teachers can identify what students know, what kind of existing knowledge students have, what they want to learn, what they have learned, and what they still want to know. When collecting such data, teachers have not only identified ELLs' writing skills but have also diagnose the linguistic gap that ELLs may have. Even when asking ELLs to share their writing with a partner or in class, teachers can assess students' oral skills in L2. In all, teachers need to use both the formal and informal resources available to assess ELLs appropriately in assisting their learning.

ELL Population Data and Statistics

According to the definition from the Migrant Policy Institute, English language learners refers to those students who participate in appropriate programs of language assistance, such as English as a Second Language, High Intensity Language Training, and bilingual education (Jeanne & McHugh, 2010). Official data from the National Center for Educational

**Table 8.3.   Examples of Teacher Prompts
for Each Stage of L2 Development**

Stage	Characteristics	Time Frame	Teacher Prompts
I: Preproduction	ELLs: • Have minimal compre-hension • Do not speak • Nod "Yes" and "No" • Draw and point	0–6 months	• Show me … • Circle the … • Where is …? • Who has …?
II: Early Production	ELLs: • Have limited compre-hension • Use one- or two-word responses • Use key words, familiar phrases • Use present-tense verbs	6 months–1 year	• Yes/no questions • Either/or questions • Who …? • What …? • How many …?
III: Speech Emergence	ELLs: • Have good comprehen-sion • Can produce simple sentences • Still have grammar and pronunciation errors • Frequently misunder-stand jokes	1–3 years	• Why …? • How …? • Explain … • Questions requiring phrase or short-sentence answers
IV: Intermediate Fluency	ELLs: • Have comprehension skills • Still have some gram-matical errors	3–5 years	• What would happen …? • Why do you think …? • Questions requiring more than a sentence response
V: Advanced Fluency	ELLs: • Have a native-like speech	5–7 years	• Decide if … • Retell …

Source: Based on Hill and Björk (2008).

Statistics (NCES) indicates that the percentage of public school students in the United States who were ELLs was higher in school year 2011–2012 (10% or an estimated 5 million students) than in school year 2002–2003, which was 9%, or an estimated 4 million students (NCES, 2014).

NCES data indicates that, in 2011–2012, eight states with the highest percentages of ELL students in their public schools were in the West (NCES, 2014). These eight states were Alaska, California, Colorado, Hawaii, Nevada, New Mexico, Oregon, and Texas. ELLs consisted of 23.2% of public school enrollment in California. A total of 14 states and

Percentage of Growth of ELL Population since 1994-95 – 2004-05

% of Growth of ELL
Population since
1994-95

400–714%

200–400%

100–200%

Figure 8.2.   The states with the fastest growth of ELL population. Data source from U.S. Department of Education's Survey of the States' Limited English Proficient Students and Available Educational Programs and Services.

the District of Columbia had percentages of ELL public school enrollment between 6% and 9.9%. In addition to the District of Columbia, these states were Arizona, Arkansas, Florida, Illinois, Kansas, Maryland, Massachusetts, Minnesota, New York, Oklahoma, North Carolina, Rhode Island, Virginia, and Washington. The percentage of ELL students in public schools was between 3.0% and 5.9% in 15 states and was less than 3.0% in 13 states, with West Virginia having the lowest percentage during this period. This means that although ELLs reside throughout the United States, they are heavily concentrated in these six states as of school year 2004–2005: Arizona, California, Texas, New York, Florida, and Illinois. This means these states have the largest ELL population or 6% of the nation's ELL population.

Yet data from the Migration Policy Institute indicates that the states with the largest ELL population were not the same as those states with the fastest growth of the ELL population (Jeanne & McHugh, 2010). The six states that had the fastest growth of ELL population from 1994–1995 to 2004–2005 were in this rank: South Carolina, Kentucky, Indiana, North Carolina, Tennessee, and Alabama (see Table 8.4). However, there was a shift in terms of ELL growth. For example, the 12 states that had the fastest growth of the ELL population from 1997–1998 to 2007–2008 were South Carolina, Indiana, Nebraska, Arkansas, North Carolina, Virginia, Delaware, Georgia, Alabama, Kentucky, Tennessee, and Ohio. South Carolina remained the first in terms of fastest growth in the ELL population

**Table 8.4.   Six States With Greatest Growth
in ELL Population From 1994–1995 to 2004–2005**

State	Number of ELLs	Percentage of Growth
South Carolina	15,396	714
Kentucky	11,181	417
Indiana	31,956	408
North Carolina	70,288	372
Tennessee	19,355	370
Alabama	15,295	337

Sources: U.S. Department of Education's Survey of the States' Limited English Proficient Students and Available Educational Programs and Services, 1991–1992 through 2000–2001 summary reports; state publications (1998–1999 data); enrollment totals from the National Center for Educational Statistics Core of Common Data, 1998–1999.

**Table 8.5.   Six States With The Fastest Growth
of the ELL Population (1997–2008 to 2007–2008)**

State	Total Pre-K-12 Enrollment 2007–2008	ELL Enrollment 2007–2008'	% ELLs Among All Pre-K–12 Students	ELL Enrollment 1997–1998	% Change in ELL Enrollment From 1997–1998
United States	49,914,453	5,318,164	10.7	3,470,268	53.2
South Carolina	712,319	28,548	4.0	3,077	827.8
Indiana	1,046,766	46,417	4.4	9,144	409.3
Nevada	429,362	134,377	31.3	30,425	314.7
Arkansas	479,016	26,003	5.4	6,717	287.1
North Carolina	1,458,035	106,180	7.3	28,709	269.8
Virginia	1,230,857	89,968	7.3	24,876	261.7

Sources: Based on State Title III Directors and 2007/2008 State CSPR; NCELA, State Title III Information System. Retrieved from www.ncela.gwu.edu/t3sts/

from the data compared from 1994–1995 to 2004–2005 to that of 1998–1999 to 2008–2009 (see Figure 8.4). However, by 2008, the top six states that had the fastest growth in the ELL population were shifted to these six states: South Carolina, Indiana, Nebraska, Arkansas, North Carolina, Virginia (see Table 8.5). In other words, there were more states (e.g., Nebraska, Arkansas, and Virginia) that added ELLs and became the states with the fastest growth in ELL population.

As the ELL population continues growing, their academic progress becomes the concern of educators. The National Assessment of Educational Progress (NAEP), often referred to as a national agency, provides representative assessment data on what students know in core academic subjects. NAEP data is regarded as an official tool for comparing the academic performance of students with different ethnicity and socioeconomic status. Since the 1970s, the average score gaps between ELL and non-ELL students at the elementary, middle, and secondary levels have been consistent, that is, ELLs' scores were well below their peers on NAEP reading and math assessments (NAEP, 2011). For example, NAEP data reveals the achievement gaps between ELL and non-ELL students on the reading assessment data were 36 points at the 4th-grade level and 44 points at the 8th-grade level. In other words, as the grade level progresses, the gap become greater (i.e., from 36 points to 44 points). At the 4th-grade level, the achievement gap was not measurably different from that in any assessment year since 2002. At the 8th grade, the achievement gap between non-ELL and ELL students in reading scores was also not measurably different from the achievement gap in 2002.

In addition, 80% of the ELL population consists of Hispanic students. Hispanic students have the highest dropout rates of any other ethnic group, which is directly attributed to their poor academic performance (NCES, 2014; Williams, 2001). For example, one third of Latino students perform below grade level, which increases their chances of dropping out of school, with the number from 50% to 98%, depending on how far behind they are. There is also a wide gap between Latino college enrollment and attainment (NAEP, 2011). Latino students also tend to enroll in community colleges more than any other ethnic group, but more than half of them never complete a postsecondary degree and only 16% of Latino students graduate with a bachelor's degree, compared to 37% of Caucasian students and 21% of African Americans (NAEP, 2011; NCES, 2014).

Knowing the achievement gaps of ELL students, teachers should be more informed of the need to improve their academic work. Teachers and educators need to know that ELLs' academic progress is related to learning English as their L2 while they are also learning subject area content (NEA, 2013). Most ELLs face multiple barriers that prevent them from improving academic achievement, high school completion, and postsecondary attainment. Research by the National Center for Education Statistics (2014), the Migration Policy Institute (2011), and other agencies identifies the following key challenges facing ELLs, which prevent them from succeeding academically and even later in life:

- Disproportionate attendance at resource-poor schools;
- Lack of access to fully qualified teachers;

- Lack of participation in rigorous, college-preparatory coursework;
- Parents with low household incomes and low levels of formal education;
- Unmet instructional needs;
- High mobility of students whose families are migrant farmworkers; and
- Students who are undocumented and who cannot attend college or work legally even after attaining a college degree.

ELLs are the fastest growing population in schools. This population is also the most heterogeneous subgroup with multiracial, multinational, and diverse needs, and very diverse educational and socioeconomic backgrounds (Jeanne & McHugh, 2010; NCES, 2014; NEA, 2013). ELLs are often expected to master content in English before they have reached the level of English proficiency. Accommodations during the testing are often limited. On top of the math and reading tests, ELLs also must meet English proficiency benchmarks as required. Therefore, ELLs have many challenges to conquer. Meeting the learning needs of ELL students is a big task for schools and teachers. It requires coordination and collaboration throughout the educational system. This means every teacher and educator must support the learning of ELLs. Therefore, better preparing all teachers of ELLs become important.

Suggestions for Teacher Education Programs

The purpose of teacher education programs is in general to prepare prospective teachers with the knowledge, attitudes, and skills needed to perform the tasks in classrooms, schools, and the community (Darling-Hammond, 2006; McNergney & Herbert, 2001; Murillo & Smith, 2008). Teacher education is often divided into these three phases: *initial teacher training education* (i.e., preservice courses) before entering the classroom as a fully responsible teacher; *induction*, which is the procedure of acceptance into the program after the first few years of training or the first year in a particular school; and *teacher development* or *continuing professional development* for the in-service process for practicing teachers. The increase in the ELL population has created implications for teacher education related to what it means for teacher quality and effectiveness in improving educational outcomes. This means teachers need be able to teach different types of students. In fact, the nation's teachers are now and will increasingly encounter more diversity in classrooms, which requires that every teacher has sufficient knowledge and skills to meet the unique needs of all students, including ELLs (Perez & Holmes, 2010; Samson & Collins, 2012).

The increase in ELL school enrollment requires that teachers have appropriate training so that they are able to meet their students' language and learning needs and to facilitate academic growth. Yet data indicates most teachers lack this training and, although there are promising teaching methods for working with ELLs, the actual knowledge and skills that teacher candidates need to support effective instruction for ELLs does not always reach them (Darling-Hammond & Hammerness, 2005; Samson & Collins, 2012). For example, at the various stages of teacher preparation, certification, and evaluation, there is insufficient information on what teachers should know about teaching ELLs. Without specific required training, knowledge, and skills relating to the unique learning needs of ELLs, it is difficult for teachers to teach these students adequately. Also, although completion of the state approved teacher-preparation programs often requires a passing score on the state teacher exam, these examinations often do not specifically measure teacher knowledge or skills relevant to teaching ELLs.

Some states require specific coursework (Arizona, California, Florida, Pennsylvania, and New York), while other states make a general reference to the special needs of ELLs, and many states have no requirements (Ballantyne, Sanderman, & Levy, 2008; Samson & Collins, 2012). For instance, California has specific teacher-performance expectations that address the needs of English language learners, and teachers must meet a "Developing English Language Skills" requirement. In Florida, all K–12 teachers are required to take at least three semester hours of TESOL (Teaching English as a Second Language) courses. If the teachers will be providing primary literacy instruction, then they must take 15 semester hours in TESOL. In New York, all teachers are required take six semester hours in general language acquisition and literacy, applying both to native English speakers and ELLs. Pennsylvania also requires that all teachers complete three credits of coursework that addresses the needs of ELLs.

While these state requirements are a step forward toward meeting the needs of ELLs, no specific requirements are in place that inform what a teacher needs to know about how to serve ELLs. In addition, many states have no specific requirements for teacher preparation relevant to ELLs. Yet ELLs are required to take standardized tests and teachers are held accountable for their ELL students' progress. In addition, ELLs will continue to increase in number in classrooms, with the rate going from 1 in 10 students in 1990 to 1 in 8 in 2005; and is projected to rise to 1 in 4 students by 2020 (NCELA, 2011; NEA, 2013). With the adoption of Common Core Standards and the high stakes of teachers' evaluations, improving teaching practices to meet the needs of ELLs and all students must be adequately addressed.

Professional Development for In-Service Teachers

Professional development for in-service teachers in general refers to ongoing learning or training opportunities provided to teachers and other school personnel through their schools and districts with the purpose of upgrading teachers' content knowledge and pedagogical skills (Darling-Hammond, 2006; Kaufman, 2004; McNergney & Herbert, 2001; Samson & Collins, 2012). With the ELL population growing faster in public schools, the challenge for mainstream in-service teachers serving ELLs has become even greater. Based on the NEA Policy Brief (NEA, 2013), teachers themselves have reported that they feel unprepared to work with ELLs and lack the necessary knowledge. For example, in an NEA survey conducted in 2006, some 57% of over 1,200 teachers reported that they needed more information in order to work effectively with ELLs. To summarize the findings of this survey, K–12 teachers face the following challenges in working with ELLs in mainstream classrooms:

- Lack of skills to teach ELL students
- Lack of appropriate assessment tools to determine ELLs' linguistic and academic needs and to measure student learning,
- Wide range of English language skills and academic skills among ELLs
- Poor communication among ELL students, teachers, parents, and the community
- Lack of professional development opportunities.

An increasing body of research and literature has addressed the importance of professional development for improving ELL student learning. Ongoing professional development allows teachers to share their ideas and concerns, and support one another in finding ways to work effectively with ELLs (Ballantyne et al., 2008; Darling-Hammond, 2006; McNergney & Herbert, 2001; NEA, 2013; Samson & Collins, 2012). K–12 general education teachers need to become familiar with the areas in which ELL students may encounter challenges in a school's curriculum. K–12 general education teachers need practical, research-based information, resources, and strategies to teach, evaluate, and nurture ELL students. Therefore, appropriately prepare teachers become crucially important to meet the needs of ELL students. The NEA (2013) recommends providing ongoing professional development training for teachers that focuses on the following essential components as a comprehensive professional development program for general education teachers of ELLs:

- A process for establishing high standards for English language acquisition, English language development, and academic content in lesson planning and instruction.
- A process for integrating teachers' understanding of academic content and English-language proficiency standards with instruction in teaching methods and assessments.
- Knowledge and use of effective pedagogy.
- Methods for implementing instructional strategies that ensure that academic instruction in English is meaningful and comprehensible.
- Exposure to a demonstration showing how to implement strategies that simultaneously integrate language acquisition, language development, and academic achievement.
- Exposure to a demonstration showing why increasing academic achievement of ELLs is dependent upon multiple instructional approaches or methodologies.
- Providing a "strategies toolkit" for teachers, which offers ways to enhance and improve instruction for struggling students, based on assessment results.

Cultural awareness is also an important component of a professional development program. To maximize achievement opportunities for ELLs, educators must understand and appreciate students' different cultural backgrounds. (NEA, 2013)

In all, professional development training programs for in-service teachers should provide basic knowledge and skills relevant to ELLs as a beginning step in helping ELLs to realize greater academic gains (NEA, 2013). It is important to prepare all teachers who work with ELL students. This is not only because of ELL enrollment is on the increase but also because of the achievement gap between ELL students and their English-speaking peers. Providing professional development opportunities for general education teachers at every stage in their career is a key step toward ensuring great teachers in great public schools for all students.

Preservice Teacher Education Program

Darling-Hammond (2006) states that, within the preservice teacher education program, reform initiatives have brought much discussion about the structures of teacher education programs. For example, there has been discussion related to teacher education programs and the certification categories. Yet there has been little or no discussion about what goes on inside the courses and clinical experiences that teacher candidates encounter or about how the experiences programs design for teacher candidates cumulatively add up to a set of knowledge, skills, and dispositions that determine what teachers actually do in the classroom. Yet the teacher is the most important element in any educational program. It is the teacher who is mainly responsible for implementation of the educational process at any stage. It is imperative to invest in preparing teachers, which starts with preparing preservice teachers so that the future of the nation is secure through well-prepared teachers of all students.

Teacher education can also be defined as *initial teacher training education* through a degree program at a college or university. This process provides potential teachers the skills and knowledge necessary to teach effectively in a classroom environment (Darling-Hammond, 2006; Giambo & Szecsi, 2005; McNergney & Herbert, 2001). Specifically, teacher education is a program to train and prepare prospective teachers to teach, and it is a program to develop teacher proficiency and competence that will enable and empower teachers to meet the requirements of the profession and face the challenges. Teacher education programs must prepare potential teachers' readiness by providing them with the formal and nonformal activities and experiences that help to qualify them to assume responsibilities as members of the educational profession and take responsibility effectively (NEA, 2013).

Preservice teacher students are expected to obtain pedagogical knowledge, teaching skills, and professional skills through teacher education programs. They need to meet general as well as specific requirements in order to receive teacher education degrees. Yet, with the increase in the ELL population, there has been increased discussion on requirements for preservice teachers as to what knowledge and skills they need teaching ELLs. For example, the National Council for Accreditation of Teacher Education (NCATE) has standards that have included ELLs under its diversity strand for teacher candidates and that require of teacher candidates knowledge and skills to work with ELLs (Fenner, 2013; NCATE, 2008). TESOL International Association, a member organization of the NCATE since 1999, with over 200 institutions of higher education, uses the TESOL P-12 Professional Teaching Standards as the framework for ESL programs. WIDA standards developed by the World Class Instructional Design and Assessment Consortia is used by 27 states and also by TESOL International Association in 2006. It is thus important that teacher education programs, whether offered by universities, states or local systems, include effective ELL instructional strategies for teacher candidates. The responsibility for educating ELLs no longer lies solely with ESOL teachers or bilingual educators, but with all K–12 teachers who have or may have ELLs in their classrooms.

Yet, according to the report entitled *Educating English Language Learners: Building Teacher Capacity Roundtable Report (Vol. 3)* on state requirements for preservice teachers of ELLs, the current condition is not promising. The statements on requirements for preservice teachers related to teaching ELLs are divided into these five categories:

1. Only 4 States have specific coursework or certification 1 requirements and they are *Arizona, California, Florida,* and *New York.*

2. 17 states have reference relating to the special needs of ELLs: *Alabama, Colorado, Idaho, Illinois, Iowa, Louisiana, Maryland, Massachusetts, Michigan, Minnesota Nevada, New Jersey, North Dakota, Rhode Island, Tennessee, Vermont,* and *Virginia.*

3. 7 States are pending to use the NCATE standards related to teaching ELLs: *Alaska, Connecticut, Delaware, Georgia, Kansas, Mississippi,* and *South Carolina.*

4. 8 States have reference to "language" as an example of diversity: *Arkansas, Montana, New Mexico, North Carolina, Ohio, Oregon, West Virginia,* and *Wyoming.*

5. 15 States have no requirement at all on teachers' expertise or training to work with ELLs: *Hawaii, Indiana, Kentucky, Maine, Missouri, Nebraska, New Hampshire, Oklahoma, Pennsylvania, South Dakota, Texas, Utah Washington, Wisconsin,* and the *District of Columbia* (Ballantyne et al., 2008).

The information from this report is mainly referring to teacher candidates who seek initial licensure or certification. Also, this report includes the standards or requirements for formal teacher education programs. In order words, alternate routes to certification are not addressed, nor are requirements for transferred teachers and experienced teachers. Yet, regardless of the differences in each state's requirements, all prospective teachers need to have three areas of basic knowledge and skills when working with ELLs.

First, teacher candidates need knowledge and skills to support ELLs' *oral language development,* which should be required for all teacher candidates. This is because oral language proficiency allows ELLs to participate in academic discussions, understand instruction, and build literacy skills. For example, ELLs with more developed first language skills are better able to develop their second language skills (Cummins, 2000; Samson & Collins, 2012). Vocabulary knowledge plays an important role in oral language proficiency. ELLs need explicit instruction in new words along with opportunities to learn new words in context through hearing, seeing, and speaking as well as during indirect encounters with authentic and motivating texts. Building oral proficiency in an L2 can support their use of nonverbal cues, visual aids, gestures, and multisensory hands-on methods. Other strategies include establishing routines, extended talk on a single topic, providing students with immediate feedback, opportunities to converse with teachers, speaking slowly, using clear repetition, and paraphrasing. ELLs should receive explicit instruction and preparation techniques to aid in speaking with others by teaching them words and grammatical features used in academic settings.

Second, teacher candidates need knowledge and skills to *explicitly teach ELLs academic English*, which should be required for all prospective teachers. This is because academic language is decontextualized, abstract, technical, and literary (Giambo & Szecsi, 2005). It is even difficult for native English speakers and thus academic language become more difficult for ELLs. Also, academic language is not limited to one area of language but requires skills in multiple domains, including vocabulary, syntax, grammar, and phonology. Understanding the differences of informal language and academic language is important. Opportunities to learn and practice academic language are essential. Students must be exposed to sophisticated and varied vocabulary and grammatical structures and avoid slang and idioms. Opportunities and instruction on using academic language accurately in multiple contexts and texts is of critical importance for all English language learners. School-wide efforts and coordination of curriculum by content area teachers helps build on a foundation of prior knowledge.

Third, teacher candidates need knowledge and skills to *value cultural diversity*, which should be required for all prospective teachers. This is because ELLs generally face many challenges in the transition from their home language and culture to school culture and English. Yet most of these challenges are related to their culturally diverse backgrounds. Schooling experiences should reaffirm the social, cultural, and historical experiences of all students (Giambo & Szecsi, 2005; Samson & Collins, 2012). Teachers and students should be expected to accept, explore, and understand different perspectives and be prepared as citizens of a multicultural and global society. Opportunities for teachers and students to interact with diverse cultures can be created in multiple ways through inclusive teaching practices, reading and multimedia materials, school traditions and rituals, assembly programs, and cafeteria food that represent all backgrounds. Involving parents and community in a meaningful way with outreach and letters to homes, bulletin boards, and staff helps build appreciation of diversity.

SUMMARY

This chapter begins with the scenario to address the issue of who is responsible for teaching ELLs, Common Core Standards, trends in teaching ELLs, programs for ELLs, assessment and related issues, ELL population data and statistics, and suggestions for teacher education programs. With the implementation of the Common Core State Standards, the role of ESOL teachers is not limited to teaching English only to ELLs, but to advocating for ELLs and actively collaborating with the mainstream teachers to provide the academic language needed for ELLs to succeed. Trends in teaching ESOL were discussed. Cummins' (1999) research on BICS and CALPS provides a theoretical foundation for the critical need to develop ELLs' academic language in content areas. The shift from teaching the four language skills only to incorporating content knowledge, academic language, and assessment in ESOL into teaching ELLs has taken place. Different types of programs for ELLs are discussed as well. This chapter also discusses assessment issues, the purpose and types of assessments, the characteristics of each stage of ELLs' language development as well as strategies to assess ELLs. As the result of ELL school demographics, every teacher will have ELLs in his or her classroom. The ESOL teacher will not be the only person in a school district who will be involved in facilitating the language development of ELLs. Classroom teachers need to have training in working with students from diverse cultural and linguistic backgrounds so that they can better serve ELLs in mainstream classrooms. Thus, preparing both preservice and in-service teachers with effective instructional practices and knowledge as well as skills is critical, and these professionals play a critical role in bringing positive outcomes to ELLs' academic progress. Suggestions for effectively pre- and in-service teachers to work with ELLs are discussed.

REFERENCES

Antunez, B., DiCerbo, P. A., & Menken, K. (2000). *Framing effective practice: Topics and issues in educating English language learners.* Washington DC: U.S. Department of Education Office of Bilingual Education and Minority Languages Affairs.

Ballantyne, K. G., Sanderman, A. R., & Levy, J. (2008). *Educating English language learners: Building teacher capacity (Vol. 3): State requirements for pre-service teachers of ELLs.* Washington, DC: National Clearinghouse for English Language Acquisition. Retrieved from http://www.ncela.us/files/uploads/3/EducatingELLsBuildingTeacherCapacityVol3.pdf

Brown, C. L. (2004). Content based ESL curriculum and academic language proficiency. *The Internet TESL Journal, 10*(2).

Callahan, R. (2005). Tracking and high school English learners: Limiting opportunity to learn. *American Educational Research Journal*, *42*(2), 305–328.

Carasquillo, A. L., & Rodriguez, V. (2002). *Language minority students in the mainstream classroom* (2nd ed.). Philadelphia, PA: Multilingual Matters.

Clair, N. (1995). Mainstream classroom teachers and ESL students. *TESOL Quarterly, 29*(1), 189–196.

Coelho, E. (2004). Creating a supportive language learning environment. In D. Rivers (Ed.), *Adding English: A guide to teaching in multilingual classrooms* (pp. 183–199). Ontario, Canada: Pippin.

Colorín Colorado. (2007). *Identifying language proficiency for program placement.* Retrieved online from http://www.colorincolorado.org/educators/assessment/identification/

Common Core. (2012). State Standards Initiative: Preparing America's Students for College and Career. Retrieved from http://www.corestandards.org/about-the-standards/

Cook, H. G., & Zhao, Y. (2011, April). *How English language proficiency assessments manifest growth: An examination of language proficiency growth in a WIDA state.* Paper presented at the annual meeting of the AERA, New Orleans, LA.

Cummins, J. (1984). *Bilingualism and special education: Issues in assessment pedagogy.* San Francisco, CA: College-Hill.

Cummins, J. (2000) *Language, power and pedagogy: Bilingual children in the crossfire.* Clevedon, UK: Multilingual Matters

Darling-Hammond, L. (2006). Constructing 21st-century teacher education. *Journal of Teacher Education*, *57*(3), 300–314.

Darling-Hammond, L., & Hammerness, K. (2005). The design of teacher education programs. In L. Darling-Hammond & J. Bransford (Eds.), *Preparing teachers for a changing world: What teachers learn and be able to do* (pp. 390–441). San Francisco, CA: Jossey-Bass.

Echevarria, A., & Graves, A. (2007). Sheltered content instruction: Teaching English language learners with diverse abilities. Boston, MA. Allyn & Bacon.

Echevarria, J., Vogt, M. E., & Short, D. (2010). *Making content comprehensible for English language learners: The SIOP model.* Boston, MA: Allyn & Bacon.

Fenner, D. S. (2013, April). *Implementing the Common Core State Standards for English learners: The changing role of the ESOL teacher.* Retrieved from http://www.tesol.org/docs/default-source/advocacy/ccss_convening_final-5-7-13.pdf?sfvrsn=8

Gelzheiser, L. M., Meyers, J., & Robert, R. M. (2010). Effects of pull-in and pull-out approaches to reading instruction for special education and remedial reading students. *Journal of Educational and Psychological Consultation, 3*(2), 133–149.

Giambo D., & Szecsi, T. (2005). Opening up the issues: Preparing preservice teachers to work effectively with English language learners. *Childhood Education, 82*(2), 267–277.

Gottlieb, M. (2006). *Assessing English language learners: Bridges from language proficiency to academic achievement.* Thousand, CA: Sage.

Gottlieb, M. (2012). *Common language assessment for English learners.* Bloomington, IN: Solution Tree.

Harklau, L. (1994). ESL versus mainstreaming classes: Contrasting L2 learning environments. *TESOL Quarterly, 28*(2), 241–272.

Haynes, J. (2014). Stages of second language acquisition. *everything ESL.net.* Retrieved from http://www.everythingesl.net/inservices/language_stages.php

Hill, J. D., & Björk, C. L. (2010). *Classroom instruction that works with English language learners: Facilitator's guide.* Boston, MA: Allyn & Bacon.

Hill, J. D., & Flynn, K. M. (2006). *Classroom instruction that works with English language learners.* Alexandria, VA: Association for Supervision and Curriculum Development.

Hinkel, E. (2006). Current perspectives on teaching the four skills. *TESOL Quarterly, 40*(1), 109–131.

Honigsfeld, A., & Dove, M. (2010). *Collaboration and co-teaching: Strategies for English learners.* Thousand Oaks, CA: Corwin.

Huba, M. E., & Freed, J. E. (2000). *Learner-centered assessment on college campuses: Shifting the focus from teaching to learning.* Needham Heights, MA: Allyn & Bacon.

Jeanne, B., & McHugh, M (2010). Number and growth of students in U.S. schools in need of English instruction. Washington DC: Migration Policy Institute.

Kaufman, D. (2004). Issues in constructivist pedagogy for L2 learning and teaching. *Annual Review of Applied Linguistics, 24*(3), 303–319.

Krashen, S. D., & Terrell, T. D. (1983). *The natural approach: Language acquisition in the classroom.* London, UK: Prentice Hall Europe.

Mancilla-Martinez, J., & Lesaux, N. K. (2011). The gap between Spanish speakers' word reading and word knowledge: A longitudinal study. *Child Development, 82*(5), 1544–1560.

Marchand-Martella, N. E., Klingner, J. K., & Martella, R. C (2010). *Effective reading intervention practices for English language learners.* Boston, MA: McGraw-Hill.

McCormick-Lee, R. K., & Fenner, D. S. (2011). The road to the Common Core State Standards: Building a bridge for ELLs. Presentation at Learning Forward Conference in Anaheim, CA. *¡Colorin!colorado.* Retrieved from http://www.colorincolorado.org/common-core/ells/basics/road/

McNergney, R. F., & Herbert, J. M. (2001). *Foundations of education: The challenge of professional practice.* Boston, MA: Allyn & Bacon.

Migration Policy Institute. (2011). *Limited English proficient individuals in the United States: Number, growth, and linguistic diversity.* Washington DC: Migration Policy Institute.

Montgomery, P., Roberts, M., & Growe, R. (2003). *English language learners: An issue of educational equality.* Retrieved from http://files.eric.ed.gov/fulltext/ED482753.pdf

Murillo, L. A., & Smith, P. H. (2008). Cultural diversity: Why it matters in school and what teachers need to know. In Y. S. Freeman, D. E. Freeman, & R. Ramirez (Eds.), *Diverse learners in the mainstream classroom* (pp. 3–30). Portsmouth, NH: Heinemann.

National Assessment of Educational Progress (NAEP). (2011). *Achievement gaps: How Hispanic and White students in public schools perform in mathematics and reading—The NAEP 2011 highlights* (NCES 2011-485). Washington, DC: NAEP.

National Center for Education Statistics (NCES). (2014). *The condition of education 2014* (NCES 2014-083). Washington, DC: U.S. Department of Education.

National Council for Accreditation of Teacher Education (NCATE). (2008). *2008 NCATE unit standards: A summary of the NCATE unit standards rubrics at the acceptable level.* Retrieved from http://www.ncate.org/documents/boeMaterials/ncate_unit_stnds_%20summary2008.pdf

National Clearinghouse for English Language Acquisition (NCELA). (2011). The growing numbers of English learners students. Retrieved from http://www.ncela.us/files/uploads/9/growing_EL_0910.pdf

NEA. (2013). *Professional development for general education teachers of English language learners.* Retrieved from http://www.nea.org/assets/docs/PB32_ELL11.pdf

Norrid-Lacey, B., & Spencer, D. (2000). Experiences of Latino immigrant students at an urban high school. *NASSP Bulletin, 84*(619), 43–54.

Ovando, C. J., & Collier, V. P. (1998). *Bilingual and ESL classrooms: Teaching in multicultural contexts* (2nd ed.). Boston, MA: McGraw-Hill.

Ovando, C. J., Collier, V. P., & Combs, M. C. (2003). *Bilingual and ESL classrooms: Teaching in multicultural contexts.* New York, NY: McGraw-Hill.

Peregoy, S. F., & Boyle, O. F. (2008). *Reading, writing, and learning in ESL: A resource book for teaching K–12 English learners* (5th ed.). Boston, MA: Pearson Education.

Perez, D., & Holmes, M. (2010). Ensuring academic literacy for ELLs. *American Secondary Education, 38*(2), 32–43.

Pitoniak, M. P., Young, J. W., Martiniello, M., King, T. C., Buteux, A., & Ginsburgh, M. (2009). *The guidelines for the assessment of English language learners.* Princeton, NJ: Educational Test Service.

Platt, E. H., Harper, C., & Mendoza, M. B. (2003). Dueling philosophies: Inclusion or separation for Florida's English language learners? *TESOL Quarterly, 37*(1), 105–133.

Reed, B., & Railsback, J. (2003). *Strategies and resources for mainstream teachers of English language learners.* Portland, OR: Northwest Regional Education Laboratory. (ERIC Document Reproduction Service No. ED 478 291).

Reeves, J. (2004). "Like everybody else": Equalizing educational opportunity for English language learners. *TESOL Quarterly, 38*(1), 43–66.

Samson, J., & Collins, B. (2012, April). Preparing all teachers to meet the needs of English language learners: Applying research to policy and practice for teacher effectiveness. *Center for American Progress.* Retrieved from http://files.eric.ed.gov/fulltext/ED535608.pdf

Short, D. J. (1993). Assessing integrated Language and content instruction. *TESOL Quarterly, 27*(4), 627-656.

Stoller F. L. (2004). Content-based instruction: Perspectives on curriculum planning. *Annual Review of Applied Linguistics 24*, 261–283.

Thomas, W. P., & Collier, V. P. (2002). *A national study of school effectiveness for language minority students' long-term academic achievement.* Santa Cruz, CA/Washington, DC: Center for Research on Education, Diversity and Excellence.

Venn, J. J. (2000). *Assessing students with special needs* (2nd ed.). Upper Saddle River, NJ: Merrill.

Wikipedia. (2014). *Formative assessment.* Retrieved from http://en.wikipedia.org/wiki/Formative_assessment

Williams, J. (2001). Classroom conversations: Opportunities to learn for ESOL students in mainstream classrooms. *Reading Teacher, 54*(8), 750–757.

Wright, W. E. (2010). *Foundations for teaching English language learners: Research, policy, and practice.* Philadelphia, PA: Caslon.

Xanthou, M. (2010). Current trends in L2 vocabulary learning and instruction: Is CLIL the right approach? *Advances in Research on Language Acquisition and Teaching, 10*(1), 459–471.

APPENDIX

SUBJECT GLOSSARY

Addition: A mathematical term that represents the total amount of objects together in a collection. In other words, it is finding the total or sum by combining two or more numbers It is signified by the plus sign (+). (Chapter 5)

Advanced Fluency: An L2 development stage and it takes about from 5 to 7 years for ELLs to achieve cognitive academic language proficiency (CALP). ELLs at this stage will have the ability to perform in content area learning. At this stage, ELLs should have exited from L2 support programs and be able to function appropriately in classrooms. (Chapter 8)

Affective Filter Hypothesis: This explains how emotional factors can affect ELLs in learning English language skills. If ELLs are nervous, unmotivated, bored, frustrated, or stressed, they may not be receptive to language input and thus may filter the input. (Chapter 2)

Amphibians and Reptiles: *Amphibian* means living two lives (i.e., on land and in water). Amphibians have no scales and breathe by means of gills and lungs. They live in damp places where their skin won become dry. Examples of amphibians are frogs and toads. A *reptile* is an animal that has dry, scaly skin and breathes by means of lungs. Examples of reptiles are snakes, lizards, crocodiles, and turtles. (Chapter 5)

Angle: Mentioned in Academic English Words in Chapter 5. It is a term used in geometry. An angle is the figure formed by two rays, sharing a

A Book for Every Teacher: Teaching English Language Learners
pp. 227–240
Copyright © 2015 by Information Age Publishing
All rights of reproduction in any form reserved.

common endpoint, called the vertex of the angle. An acute angle is less than 90°; an obtuse angle is greater than 90° but less than 180°; a right angle is equal to 90°. (Chapter 5)

Assessment and Related Issues: The wide variety of methods that educators use to evaluate, measure, and document academic outcomes. Assessment provides useful feedback for improving teaching and learning. (Chapter 8)

Basic Color Words: Primary, secondary, and tertiary colors. The primary colors are red, yellow, and blue. The three secondary colors are green, orange, and purple, and are achieved by mixing two primary colors. A tertiary color is made by mixing either one primary color with one secondary color or two secondary colors. (Chapter 5)

Basic Interpersonal Communication Skills (BICS): The social language in everyday life or the oral English needed and used mostly in conversational contexts. BICS is gained through communication and interaction (Cummins, 1999). (Chapter 2)

Bilingual Program: It refers usually to the education program in an English-language school system in which students with little fluency in English are taught in both their native language and English. The purpose is to build a bridge that helps students become proficient in their native language and English. (Chapter 8)

Bloom's Taxonomy: A classification of the different objectives that teachers can set for students. Bloom (1956) set six levels of thinking skills with the purpose for educators to set learning objectives for students who can achieve their highest potentials. (Chapter 3)

Capacity: The maximum amount that something can contain. Usually it means volume, such as milliliters (ml) or liters (l) in metric, or pints or gallons. (Chapter 5)

Choral Responses: The technique that incorporates whole class speaking together, usually repeating after the teacher on a sentence or dialogue they have read. This is an easy way for a lower level of students to practice speaking, especially with a large class size. This can help beginner ELLs who are not comfortable speaking on their own. (Chapter 4)

Cognitive Academic Language Proficiency (CALP): The academic language that is specifically related to the subject content areas, in which cognitively demanding language skills are required (Cummins, 1999). (Chapter 2)

Common Core State Standards: A U.S. education initiative that seeks to bring diverse state curricula into alignment with each other by following the principles of standards-based education reform. For example, it details what K–12 students should know in English language arts and mathematics at the end of each grade. The initiative is sponsored and supported by the National Governors Association (NGA) and the Council of Chief State School Officers (CCSSO), which seek to establish consistent educational standards across the states and ensure that students graduating from high school are prepared to enter credit-bearing courses at 2- or 4-year college programs or to enter the workforce. (Chapter 8)

Community: The group of people with diverse characteristics who are linked by social ties, share common perspectives, and engage in joint action in geographical locations or settings; or people who live in the same area, such as a city, town, or neighborhood and people who have the same interests, religion, and race. (Chapter 5)

Comprehensible Input: Krashen (1982) believes that the best ways to learn a second language is to supply comprehensible input in low anxiety situations. In other words, the language message input conveyed to the ELLs must be comprehensible. (Chapter 2)

Content-Based ESOL Program: An L2 support program such as structured immersion, sheltered English, and Specially Designed Academic Instruction in English (Brown, 2004; Reed & Railsback, 2003; Hill & Flynn, 2006). They all share the same goal of teaching English language learners both English language and academic content. (Chapter 8)

Continents and Oceans: A *continent* refers to one of the seven main landmasses of the globe (Europe, Asia, Africa, North America, South America, Australia, and Antarctica). *Oceans* refers to the large expanse of sea and each of the main areas is divided geographically (the Atlantic, Pacific, Indian, Arctic, and Antarctic Oceans). (Chapter 5)

Directions: Words and expressions to tell about directions, positions, and locations relevant to a surrounding or space. (Chapter 6)

Division, Divide, Dividend, Divisor, Quotient, and **Remainder:** Mathematics terms. *Division* is an arithmetic operation and means splitting into equal parts. The *dividend* is the number that is being divided. The *divisor* is the number that the dividend will be divided by. *Quotient* refers to a result obtained by dividing one quantity by another. *Remainder* is the amount "left over" after performing some computation. (Chapter 5)

***Early Production*:** A stage of L2 development that may last up to 6 months in which ELLs may develop a receptive vocabulary of about 1,000 words. In this stage, ELLs can usually speak in one- or two-word phrases. They can use short language chunks memorized, although these chunks may not always be used correctly. (Chapter 8)

***Energy*:** Power derived from the utilization of physical or chemical resources, especially to provide light and heat or to work machines. (Chapter 5)

***English as a Foreign Language (EFL)*:** It refers to English that is taught by teachers whose native language is not English. An EFL program is for students who learn English as a foreign language in a country where English is not the L1. (Chapter 1)

***English as a Second Language (ESL)*:** It refers to the fact that English is taught by teachers whose native language is English. The term of an ESL student is now less common term than ELL and ESL is more often to refer to an educational approach to support ELLs to learn English. (Chapter 1)

***English for Speakers of Other Languages (ESOL)*:** A program in which English is taught by teachers whose native language is English. It is also referred to as ENL, *English as a New Language.* The ESOL program offered in public schools often pulls ELLs out of regular classes to learn English. (Chapter 1)

***English Language Learner (ELL)*:** A student who is in the process of acquiring English, whose primary language is not English. This term has been used more frequently in recent years to substitute for other terms, such as, LEP or ESL. (Chapter 1)

***English Learner (EL)*:** A student who is in the process of learning English. This term is interchangeable with the term *ELL.* In recent years, this term has been used by U.S. Department of Education as a substitute for the previous term *LEP.*

***Environment*:** The surroundings, conditions, or the natural world in which a person, animal, or plant lives or operates. (Chapter 5)

Families and Relatives: *Family* refers to a basic social unit that consists of parents and their children. Or it can refer to a bigger group of related people including grandparents, aunts, uncles, cousins, and such. A *relative* is a person connected by blood or marriage. (Chapter 6)

Family Support: This refers to building the relationships that strengthen the developmental journey with families. It helps the family construct a solid foundation from which to foster the growth of child learning. (Chapter 4)

Five Senses: The faculties of sight, smell, hearing, taste, and touch (Chapter 5).*Flip Book*: One of the earliest forms of interactive media, with a series of pictures that vary gradually from one page to the next. Making a flip book can arouse children's interest and can also connect writing with reading to motivate students to write (Chapter 3)

Flow Chart: A diagram of the sequence of movements or actions of people or things involved in a complex system or activity. It shows the steps as boxes of various kinds and their order by connecting them with arrows (Chapter 3).

Food and Cafeteria: *Food* refers *To* any nutritious substance that people or animals eat or drink, or that plants absorb, in order to maintain life and growth. *Cafeteria* refers to a restaurant or dining room in a school or a business in which customers serve themselves or are served from a counter and usually pay for before eating (Chapter 6).

Formative Assessment: A process used by teachers and students during instruction that provides feedback to adjust ongoing teaching and learning to improve students' achievement of intended instructional outcomes. They are generally low stakes because of low or no point value. Examples include asking students to *draw a concept map in class to represent their understanding of a topic, submit one or two sentences identifying the main point of a lecture*, or *turn in a research proposal for early feedback.* (Chapter 8)

Generation 1.5 Students: Those ELLs who are U.S. educated but who may not be proficient in academic language related to school achievement, yet they may have strong L2 oral stills. They are caught between generations, that is, they belong to neither Generation 1 nor Generation 2 of immigrants. Thus, they may also have limited L1 skills. (Chapter 1)

Geographic Features: The components of the Earth. Two types of geographical features are natural geographical features and artificial geographical features. Natural geographical features include but not limited to landforms and ecosystems. Artificial geographical features can include buildings and other man-made structures. (Chapter 5)

***Geometry*:** The branch of mathematics concerned with the properties and relations of points, lines, surfaces, solids, and higher dimensional analogs. (Chapter 5)

***Google Earth*:** An Internet tool to introduce cities and geographic features. It provides a virtual globe, map, and geographical information. It can take ELLs, virtually, to a place that they cannot go in reality and learn the plural form of nouns by counting the number of objects they saw in the place or new city. (Chapter 3)

***Government*:** The governing body of a nation, state, or community or the system by which a nation, state, or community is governed. (Chapter 5)

***Greetings*:** Words and expressions or signs of welcome or recognition. Greetings can also be a message that expresses good wishes to someone. (Chapter 6)

***Human Body Features*:** Words that are regularly used to describe physical human body features and body names, such as hair, eyes, nose, and legs. (Chapter 5)

***Inclusion Program*:** An inclusion program for ELLs is in-class ESOL instruction that is provided by mainstream classroom teachers (Wright, 2010). However, there is debate as to the benefits of the inclusion program for ELLs. ELLs typically need additional resources and support to adjust to the various linguistic complications of learning a new language. Although some schools and states have adopted mandatory full-inclusion programs, educators argue that ELLs immersed in a regular-paced English class with students who are fluent in English do not benefit, although inclusion programs for ELLs saves costs, such as the cost of hiring ESL specialists for ELL students in an ESOL atmosphere for learning. (Chapter 8)

***Insects and Arachnids*:** An *insect* refers to a small arthropod animal that has six legs and generally one or two pairs of wings, such as flies, mosquitos, and bees. An *arachnid* is an arthropod of the class of joint-legged invertebrate animals, such as a spiders or scorpions. (Chapter 5)

***In-service Teacher*:** *In-service* means something that happens while someone is a full-time employee. Therefore, in-service teachers are ones who have a teaching license and are teaching in their own classrooms. (Chapter 8)

Initial Assessment: An assessment that is usually carried out at the beginning of a program to identify learners' strengths and weaknesses but can also take place at any stage, even before the program has begun. The assessment may be a specific check on a particular skill, understanding, or aptitude, or it may be a broad indicator of general areas that need attention to identify a learner's needs and strengths. (Chapter 8)

Interactive Writing: A teaching method in which children and teacher negotiate what they are going to write and then literally share the pen to construct writing and create a joint sentence or message. It helps children learn to view literacy in a more meaningful way through teacher-student interaction. (Chapter 3)

Intermediate Fluency: An L2 development stage. ELLs at this stage (Years 3–5) should have a vocabulary of 6,000 active words. They begin to use more complex sentences when speaking and writing and are willing to express opinions and share their thoughts. (Chapter 8)

Johnson-Reed Act: An immigration law created in 1924 with a quota system that discriminated against non-European immigrants. In 1968, this law was eliminated. Since then, the immigrant population has evidenced an increase in the United States, with a noticeable change in country sources. In other words, the immigrant population represents more diversity in its country source.

K-W-L Chart: A graphical organizer designed to help in learning. The letters KWL usually stand for what students already *know*, what they *want* to know, and what they ultimately *learn*. A KWL table is typically three columns. (Chapter 3)

Language Development: The process of ELLs developing L2 proficiency used in this book, which includes these stages of in the process of L2 development: preproduction, early production, speech emergence, intermediate fluency, and fluency. (Chapter 8)

Limited English Proficiency (LEP): ELLs who have a lower level of the English language skills. Many educators believe that this term has a connotation that focuses on limitation. In recent years, it is thus substituted with other terms, such as ELs or ELLs. (Chapter 1)

Language Learning Center (LLC): A strategy to welcome ELLs who do not speak English on the first of school by organizing space in the classroom with learning materials, pairing ELLs with buddies, and making ELLs feel comfortable. (Chapter 4)

Line Segment: A part of a line that is bounded by two distinct end points and contains every point on the line between its end points. Examples of line segments include the sides of a triangle or square. (Chapter 5)

Metric System: The decimal measuring system based on the meter, liter, and gram as units of length, capacity, and weight or mass. The system was first proposed by the French astronomer and mathematician Gabriel Mouton (1618–1694) in 1670 and was standardized in France under the Republican government in the 1790s. (Chapter 5)

Multiplication: A mathematical term referring to the process of multiplying or of combining matrices, vectors, or other quantities under specific rules to obtain their product. (Chapter 5)

Natural Disaster: An adverse natural event such as a flood, earthquake, hurricane, or volcanic eruption that causes great damage or loss of life. (Chapter 5)

Neutral Color Words: *Neutral color* refers to a color that does not attract attention or appear to be without color; yet, in many applications they often have undertones of color, such as beige, ivory, taupe, black, and gray. (Chapter 5)

Parallel Lines: The lines in a plane that do not meet and are always the same distance apart. (Chapter 5)

Performance-Based Assessment: This type of assessment is based on classroom instruction and everyday tasks. Teachers can use performance-based assessments to assess ELLs' language proficiency and academic achievement through oral reports, presentations, demonstrations, written assignments, and portfolios (Cook & Zhao, 2011). (Chapter 8)

Perpendicular: A mathematic term referring to a straight line at an angle of 90° to another given line, plane, or surface. (Chapter 5)

Plane Figures: Any two-dimensional (2-D) shapes or flat shapes such as lines, circles, squares, triangles or other shapes that can be drawn on a surface. (Chapter 5)

***Plants*:** Living organism, typically growing in a permanent site, absorbing water and inorganic substances through their roots and synthesizing nutrients in leaves by photosynthesis using the green pigment chlorophyll. (Chapter 5)

***Portfolios*:** Another way of assessing student work throughout the entire year. With this method, teachers can systematically collect descriptive records of student work over time that reflects growth toward the achievement of specific curricular objectives. (Chapter 8)

***Preproduction Stage*:** The silent period in language development, which is usually during the first s6 months. ELLs may build up to 500 words in their receptive vocabulary but they are not yet able to speak. Some ELL students may repeat what the teacher says. Yet they are mainly listening, that is, not really producing language. (Chapter 8)

***Preservice Teacher*:** A term that generally refers to a college student in a teacher education program who is in the process of being prepared to teach through education and training provided before they undertake teaching. (Chapter 8)

***Preteaching*:** S method of teaching English language learners before an activity. For example, ELLs are going to hear a short discussion on environmental issues. Before listening, the teacher can help the students match key environment words to definitions. This helps ELLs develop confidence. (Chapter 3)

***Professional Development*:** A term that generally refers to ongoing learning and training opportunities available to teachers and other education personnel through their schools and districts. The purpose of such formal in-service training is for teachers to upgrade their content knowledge and pedagogical skills. (Chapter 8)

***Professions*:** An occupation that involves prolonged, specialized training and a formal qualification with the purpose of providing objective counsel and service to others. (Chapter 5)

***Pull-out Program*:** This refers to ELLs who are taken out of the mainstream classroom for a part of the day and receive language support from an ESL teacher and assistance during the portion of the day through the pull-out component. When pulling out, they go to the ESOL classroom for intensive instruction in English and also receive language support within each content area while they students spend the majority of their day in classrooms with English-speaking peers. This allows them to be a part of the student body within their school. (Chapter 8)

Rays: A mathematical term referring to a portion of a line that starts at a point and goes in a particular direction to infinity. (Chapter 5)

School Materials and Supplies: Items and small equipment commonly used by students in the course of their studies. The term may include not only stationery but such items as pocket calculators, display boards, or compasses. (Chapter 5)

Self-Contained ESOL Program: In the self-contained program model, ELLs are placed with other ELLs for the entire day, where they receive sheltered instruction from teachers trained in sheltering techniques. ELL students in such a program are grouped together in one classroom to receive instruction at their language proficiency level. Usually, only a district with a large population of ELL students offer a self-contained ESOL program. (Chapter 8)

Semantic Mapping: An important visual aid strategy that helps students expand vocabulary based on their prior knowledge by displaying in word categories that are related to one another and by showing the relationships among the components. (Chapter 3)

Sheltered Instruction: An approach to teaching English language learners that integrates language and content instruction. It consists of a set of teaching strategies designed for teachers of academic content, which lowers the linguistic demand of the lesson without compromising the integrity or rigor of the subject matter. It was originally designed for content and classroom teachers who teach in English. See more on SIOP model. (Chapter 8)

SIOP Lesson Model: The term SIOP stands for *Sheltered Instruction Observation Protocol*. It is an empirically tested approach that helps teachers prepare all students, especially English language learners, to become college and career ready (Person, 2013). In a SIOP lesson, teachers adjust the language demands of the lesson in many ways, such as modifying speech rate and tone, using context clues and models extensively, relating instruction to student experience, adapting the language of texts or tasks, and using certain methods familiar to language teachers (e.g., demonstrations, visuals, graphic organizers, or cooperative work) to make academic instruction more accessible to students of different English proficiency levels. (Chapter 3)

Solid Figures: Three-dimensional (3-D) shapes that have width, depth, and height. Examples of solid figures are cylinder, sphere, cone, cube, and rectangular. (Chapter 5)

Speech Emergence: A language development stage (Years 1–3). ELLs may have developed a vocabulary of 3,000 words and may be able to communicate with simple phrases and sentences. They may ask simple questions that are not grammatically correct. (Chapter 8)

Subtraction: A mathematical term that refers to the process, act, or instance of taking one number or amount away from another or an action of subtracting. (Chapter 5)

Summative Assessment: The assessments used to evaluate student learning, skill acquisition, and academic achievement at the conclusion of a defined instructional period and summarizes achievement at a particular time. It is different from the initial or ongoing assessment because the summative assessment provides an evaluation of the final quality with an overall grade or score. (Chapter 8)

Teacher Education: The procedures of preparing prospective teachers with the knowledge, attitudes, and skills needed to perform their tasks in the classroom, school, and community. Teacher education is often divided into these stages: *initial teacher training education* (i.e., preservice courses) before entering the classroom as a fully responsible teacher; *induction*, the procedure of acceptance into the program after the first few years of training or the first year in a particular school; *teacher development* or *continuing professional development* for an in-service process for practicing teachers. (Chapter 8)

Teacher-Student Relationships: The foundation of a successful classroom and particularly one that includes English language learners. Research indicates that a positive teacher-student relation is the most powerful weapon for teachers in fostering a favorable learning climate with positive learning outcomes (Boynton & Boynton, 2005; Thompson, 1998). (Chapter 4)

Teaching English to Speakers of Other Languages (TESOL): Teaching English to speakers whose L1 is not English. TESOL is also an international association with the mission of advancing professional expertise in English language teaching and learning for students of languages other than English. (Chapter 1)

Think Aloud: A teaching strategy that requires students to say out loud what they are thinking about when reading an assigned text. This strategy helps students learn to monitor their thinking while reading the passage and to become skilled readers. (Chapter 3)

Thumb Up/Thumb Down: A strategy that is commonly known as TUTD. It is especially helpful for ELLs who cannot express orally. It is also a fun way to test the student's knowledge. (Chapter 3)

Total Physical Response (TPR): The teaching method, developed by James Asher in the 1960s, based on the theory that memory is enhanced through association with physical movement (Byram, 2000). It incorporates physical movement to react on verbal input and allows students to react to language without thinking too much and thus reduces stress, lowers affective filter, and facilitates long-term retention. (Chapter 3)

Traditions and Holidays: The transmission of customs or beliefs from generation to generation, or the fact of being passed on in this way. (Chapter 7)

Transportation: The action of transporting someone or something from one place to another place or the process of being transported. (Chapter 5)

Trends in L2 Teaching: The development and continuation of language (L2) teaching debates that began in the 1990s on how and what L2 teaching and learning is. In the past 15 years, several crucial factors have combined to affect current perspectives on the teaching of English worldwide: (a) the decline of methods, (b) a growing emphasis on both bottom-up and top-down skills, (c) the creation of new knowledge about English, and (d) integrated and contextualized teaching of multiple language skills (Hinkel, 2006). (Chapter 8)

Venn Diagram: A graphic organizer with a set of diagrams that shows all possible logical relations, such as the similarities and differences between concepts. Venn diagrams were created around 1880 by John Venn, an English logician and philosopher. (Chapter 3)

Weather and Sports: *Weather* refers to the state of the atmosphere at a place and time with regard to heat, dryness, sunshine, wind, rain, and so on. *Sports* is a term that refers to an activity that involves physical exertion and skill in which an individual or team competes against another or others for entertainment. (Chapter 6)

Word Walls: An organized collection of words prominently displayed in a classroom. This display is used as an interactive tool for teaching reading and spelling to children. There are many different types of word walls, including high frequency words, word families, and names. (Chapter 3)

Writer's Workshop: A method of teaching writing, also known as a Writing Workshop (Calkins, 2006). It focuses on fostering lifelong writers with four basic principles, such as students will write about their own lives, they will be engaged in a consistent writing process, they will work in authentic ways, and it will foster independence. (Chapter 3)

ABOUT THE AUTHOR

Dr. Nan Li is a professor, writer, and researcher with over 20 publications, which include books, book chapters, co-authored chapters, and journal articles. Dr. Li was the recipient of South Carolina Governor's Distinguished Professor Award, along with several other distinguished awards, including Exemplary Service to the Teaching Profession awarded by SCATE. Dr. Li received multiple grant awards, totaling $3.2 million in external funding for professional development and training of the K–12 teachers and preservice teachers to prepare them for teaching and working with the ELL students in classrooms. Her grant programs also received several prestigious awards, including 2014 Rose Duhon Sells Multicultural Education Program Award and The 2014 Teacher Education Innovation Program Award.

Graduating from Indiana University of Pennsylvania with a 4.0 GPA, her dissertation research was on the learning experiences of English language learners. Since graduation, her research, teaching, and service have focused on L2 education and teaching diversity. Dr. Li has presented her research at over 40 national and international conferences. Currently, she is Associate Professor and Project Director of the ELL Center, a project co-funded by the U.S. Department of Education and South Carolina Commission on Higher Education. Dr. Li plays a key role in training teachers and prepares preservice and K–12 inservice teachers who work with ELLs for their academic success. This book is dedicated to the continued professional training and use by teachers and is the result of her knowledge and many years of experience working with teachers through professional development opportunities. This book weaves together her research, experiences, and hard work. Dr. Li wants to share this much needed information and teaching strategies with teachers who work with ELLs.

CPSIA information can be obtained
at www.ICGtesting.com
Printed in the USA
LVOW01s0251300116

472674LV00001B/1/P

9 781681 230504